PENITENTIAL PRAYER
IN SECOND TEMPLE JUDAISM

SOCIETY OF BIBLICAL LITERATURE

EARLY JUDAISM AND ITS LITERATURE

Series Editor
John C. Reeves

Editorial Board

Shaye J. D. Cohen, Brown University
Betsy Halpern-Amaru, Vassar College
Carl R. Holladay, Candler School of Theology, Emory University
James C. VanderKam, University of Notre Dame

Number 13

PENITENTIAL PRAYER
IN SECOND TEMPLE JUDAISM
The Development of a Religious Institution

by
Rodney Alan Werline

PENITENTIAL PRAYER
IN SECOND TEMPLE JUDAISM
The Development of a Religious Institution

by
Rodney Alan Werline

Scholars Press
Atlanta, Georgia

PENITENTIAL PRAYER IN SECOND TEMPLE JUDAISM
The Development of a Religious Institution

by
Rodney Alan Werline

Copyright © 1998 by the Society of Biblical Literature

All rights reserved. No part of this work may be reproduced or transmitted in any form or by any means, electronic or mechanical, including photocopying and recording, or by means of any information storage or retrieval system, except as may be expressly permitted by the 1976 Copyright Act or in writing from the publisher. Requests for permission should be addressed in writing to the Rights and Permissions Office, Scholars Press, P.O. Box 15399, Atlanta, GA 30333-0399, USA.

Library of Congress Cataloging-in-Publication Data
Werline, Rodney Alan, 1961–
    Penitential prayer in Second Temple Judaism : the development of a religious institution / by Rodney Alan Werline.
      p. cm. — (Early Judaism and its literature ; no. 13)
    Includes bibliographical references and indexes.
    ISBN 0-7885-0325-1 (cloth : alk. paper). —ISBN 0-7885-0326-X (pbk. : alk. paper)
    1. Worship in the Bible. 2. Seliḥot. 3. Bible. O.T.—Prayers—History and criticism. 4. Apocryphal books (Old Testament)—Prayers—History and criticism. 5. Judaism—History—Post-exilic period, 586 B.C.–210 A.D. I. Title. II. Series.
BS1199.P68W47 1997
221'.6—dc21   97–41090
                                                                       CIP

Printed in the United States of America
on acid-free paper

To Kathy, Madison, and Baylee

CONTENTS

LIST OF TABLES ix

PREFACE xi

INTRODUCTION 1
    The State of Prayer Study 1
    The Historical Limits of this Study 2
    The Focus of this Study 2
    Previous Critical Methodology 4
    The Approach of this Study 6
    Plan of Study 7

CHAPTER ONE
THE DEVELOPMENT OF PENITENTIAL PRAYER IN BIBLICAL LITERATURE FROM THE EXILIC AND PERSIAN PERIODS 11
    Introduction 11
    Deuteronomy 4 and 30 12
    Solomon's Dedicatory Prayer in 1 Kgs 8:22-61 18
    Excursus I : The Date of the Deuteronomic History 27
    Jeremiah 29:10-14 29
    Penitential Prayer during the Restoration: Third Isaiah 30
    Penitential Prayer in the Late Persian Period: Ezra-Nehemiah
        and 2 Chronicles 45
    Excursus II: Confession in Leviticus 48
    Conclusion 62

CHAPTER TWO
THE PRAYERS IN DANIEL 9:1-27 AND BARUCH 1:15-3:8 65
    Introduction 65
    The Literary Relationship between the Two Prayers 66
    Interpretation of Daniel 9 67
    Interpretation of Baruch 1:1-3:8 87

Conclusion 106

CHAPTER THREE
PENITENTIAL PRAYER AND BIBLICAL INTERPRETATION AMONG THE QUMRAN SECTARIANS AND SIMILAR GROUPS 109
Introduction.. 109
Jubilees 1 110
Jubilees 23 113
1 Enoch.. 115
The Testament of Moses... 120
Testaments of the Twelve Patriarchs.. 124
The Qumran Community 126
Conclusion... 157

CHAPTER FOUR
PENITENTIAL PRAYERS OF PIOUS SUFFERERS AND THOSE OPPRESSED BY ARROGANT RULERS 161
Introduction.. 161
Tobit 3:1-6.. 162
The Prayer of Azariah.. 168
3 Maccabees 2:1-20... 179
Esther's Prayer in the Greek Additions to the LXX....................... 183
The Psalms of Solomon... 185
Conclusion... 188

CONCLUSION 191

BIBLIOGRAPHY 197

INDEXES 215

LIST OF TABLES

Table 1. A Comparison of Covenantal Curses in 1 Kings and Deuteronomy.21

Table 2. A Comparison of Lists of Religious Leaders 76

Table 3. Appearance of the Ideas Human as Sinner, God as Righteous, and the Knowledge in the *Hodayot* 140

PREFACE

This book is a revision of my doctoral dissertation written under the supervision of George W. E. Nickelsburg at the University of Iowa. I am indebted to him for suggesting the topic to me and also for his countless suggestions, ideas, and insights. I have greatly benefited from his scholarship. Helen Goldstein also read the manuscript several times and made many helpful comments. Her work went beyond duty. I thank J. Kenneth Kuntz who read chapter one especially carefully and offered several helpful criticisms and bibliographical additions. I was also fortunate to have Jonathan Goldstein on the thesis committee before his retirement. I and other students of Second Temple Judaism at the University are grateful for the many times he served as the outside reader for dissertation defenses. Also, I thank James McCue for always reminding me that I should not say more than the facts allow.

The Urbana Christian Church (Disciples of Christ), Urbana, IA, allowed me the time to finish this project while serving as its minister. I am deeply thankful for their graciousness.

Several other individuals contributed to the work. I thank Larry Fett for reading much of the manuscript and for offering helpful suggestions about writing style and strategies. My graduate assistant at Wartburg Theological Seminary, Dubuque, IA, Kelli Schacht, carried out the tedious task of checking the Biblical references and also proof read the work in its various stages. Once I arrived at Emmanuel School of Religion, my assistant, Brad Dewing, checked the text and did the bulk of the work on the indexes.

In Iowa, I received computer support from Richard Beals and Dennis Fox. I am also deeply grateful John Mark Wade, our computer specialist at Emmanuel School of Religion, who gave significant time to solving my software problems, and on one occasion saved me from a minor disaster.

I worked with two editors at Scholars Press, William Adler and John Reeves. Both worked quickly. The task of checking the final document, though, fell to John Reeves, who helped me clean up several errors and gave constant encouragement during my struggles to get the book to press. I thank him for his kindness, patience, and for the genuine humanness he contributed to the process. Of course, I am responsible for any shortcomings that this book might have.

My deepest thanks, however, go to my wife Kathy, and my two daughters, Madison and Baylee, for their love, sacrifice and patience. The book is dedicated to them.

INTRODUCTION

The State of the Study of Prayer

In 1987 Lawrence Schiffman observed that "[t]he study of Qumran liturgy is in its infancy. The liturgical texts are only now beginning to appear and definitive results are still forthcoming."[1] Significant advancements have come in this area as a result of the publication of Bilhah Nitzan's book, *Qumran Prayer and Religious Poetry*.[2] Still, the analysis of the Qumran liturgical texts remains in its initial stages. If one adds to the large number of Qumran prayer and liturgical texts all the prayers and hymns that appear in the post-exilic biblical literature, the apocrypha, and the pseudepigrapha, the collection of liturgical texts from Second Temple Judaism increases exponentially.[3] While commentaries and articles have examined some of these texts, scholars have yet to offer a systematic analysis of this material.[4]

This book seeks to fill in a portion of this gap in scholarship with a systematic analysis of penitential prayers from the period of the exile through the Second Temple period. Scholarship has frequently noted the familial relationship of several penitential prayers: 1 Kgs 8:22-53; Ezra 9:5-15; Neh 1:4-11; 9:6-37; Dan 9:3-19; Bar 1:15-3:8; the Prayer of Azariah; Tob 3:1-6; 3 Macc 2:1-10; and "The Words of the Heavenly Lights" (4Q504). The prayers in these texts contain confessions of sin that are heavily influenced by deuteronomic language and ideology, especially Deuteronomy 4, 28-30, and 1

---

[1] L. Schiffman, "The Dead Sea Scrolls and the Early History of Jewish Liturgy," *The Synagogue in Late Antiquity* (ed. L. I. Levine; Philadelphia: American Schools of Oriental Research, 1987) 44.

[2] B. Nitzan, *Qumran Prayer and Relígous Poetry*, Studies on the Texts of the Desert of Judah 12 (trans. J. Chipman; Leiden: Brill, 1994).

[3] For a quick sampling of these texts, see E. Glickler Chazon, "Prayers from Qumran," *SBLSP* 32 (1993) 758-772. Cf. also her discussion in "Prayers from Qumran and their Historical Implications," *DSD* 1 (1994) 265-284. See also Kiley, M., ed. *Prayer from Alexander to Constantine: A Critical Anthology* (New York: Routledge, 1997).

[4] The same cannot be said of prayer in Rabbinic literature. For a bibliography, see J. H. Charlesworth, ed., *The Lord's Prayer and Other Prayer Texts from the Greco-Roman Era* (Valley Forge: Trinity, 1994) 140-151. See also, J. Heinemann, *Prayer in the Talmud— Forms and Patterns*, StJud 9 (Berlin: De Gruyter, 1977).

Kings 8.[5] Because of these shared features, modern critics generally treat these prayers as a group, but have seldom discussed their individual characteristics and the development of this penitential tradition.

The Historical Limits of this Study

For several reasons, 586 BCE - 70 CE serves as an appropriate historical era for this study. First, the prayers seem to originate from deuteronomic traditions. Since these traditions date to the exile, this provides the starting point for the investigation. Second, if one goes beyond the end of the Qumran community, rabbinic literature becomes the primary source material. This literature is distinct from the writings of Second Temple Judaism in its literary forms, world view, idea of authority, and historical and social milieus. Besides these differences, interpretation of rabbinic literature is fraught with complicated methodological problems, especially the difficulty of dating rabbinical sayings. Thus, the destruction of the Second Temple provides the obvious historical limit to this discussion.

The Focus of this Study

This book examines the development of penitential prayer as a religious institution for dealing with sin. Thus, it does not offer an overarching study of prayer, but only an examination of a particular subcategory of prayer—penitential prayer in the Second Temple Period. A penitential prayer is a direct address to God in which an individual or group confesses sins and petitions for forgiveness. Frequently, the petitioner hopes that the prayer will also be the first step toward removing the problems facing the community or the petitioner. Because most of the prayers are on behalf of the community or communal prayers, penitential prayers of individuals, like the prayers in Psalm 51 and the Prayer of Mannasseh, are not of primary interest. Also, the deuteronomic traditions are not as influential in these prayers of individuals as

---

[5]This observation is obviously not new. See e.g., K. Baltzer, *The Covenant Formulary* (trans. D. E. Green; Philadelphia: Fortress, 1971); O. H. Steck, *Israel und das gewaltsame Geschick der Propheten: Untersuchungen zur Überlieferung des deuteronomistischen Geschichtsbildes im Alten Testament, Spätjudentum und Urchistentum*, WMANT 23 (Neukirchen: Neukirchen-Vluyn, 1967); J. M. Scott, "Paul's Use of the Deuteronomic Tradition," *JBL* 112 (1993) 645-665; cf. also G. W. E. Nickelsburg, *Jewish Literature between the Bible and the Mishnah* (Philadelphia: Fortress, 1981) e.g., 28-30, 77, 80-82, 86-87, 109-111, and 135; H. G. Reventlow, *Gebet im Alten Testament* (Kohlhammer: Stuttgart, 1986) 274.

Introduction

the communal prayers listed above. The above definition stands in contrast to those offered by Corvin and Reventlow.[6] They define prayer more broadly so that everything from liturgy to hymns becomes prayer. While devotees perform all these acts with the same pious fervor and attitude, for the purpose of this study, a narrow definition is more helpful because it allows for more precise literary analyses and systematic comparisons of the variety of pious expressions.

As stated above, this book also seeks to understand penitential prayer as a religious institution. An action becomes a religious institution when a religious community generally accepts it, practices it, and prescribes a basic function for it. In the case of penitential prayer, then, observations about how the practice becomes accepted in Israel and determinations about the prayers' functions assist in understanding the prayers a religious institution.

The development of formulaic expressions in Second Temple Jewish prayers testifies to their frequent use and suggests that they have developed into an institution. For example, several prayers employ a similar threefold or fourfold confession of sin. Further, they frequently and similarly declare God's righteousness: "You are righteous, O Lord." With this declaration, the suppliant hopes to demonstrate that he recognizes that God has rightfully punished the people for their sins. Therefore, the prayers follow the basic deuteronomic ideology of sin—punishment. They also usually contain a petitionary section that begins with the rhetorical marker ועתה, "And now..."

Second, establishing specific times for prayers also indicates movement toward their institutionalization.[7] These times, however, may have not been "normative" or "officially" prescribed for all Jews. Nevertheless, the prayers in Daniel 9, Nehemiah 9, Bar 1:15-3:8, and 4Q504 are connected to specific prayer times, either festivals or daily times of prayer.

Third, the existing penitential texts agree that penitential prayer removes sin. This, then, is one of penitential prayer's primary functions and it dates to at least 1 Kings 8, an exilic text, and continues through the Second Temple period. However, prayer is not the only religious institution in this period that removes sins. Sacrifice, giving alms, suffering oppression, and obedience also atone for sin.

Fourth, several texts from this era which are not prayers according to literary genre either refer to penitential prayer or include penitential

---

[6] J. Corvin, "Stylistic and Functional Study of the Prose Prayers in the Historical Narratives of the Old Testament" (diss., Emory University, Atlanta, Georgia, 1972) 23; Reventlow, *Gebet*, 89.

[7] For a detailed investigation into fixed prayer and its development, see B. Nitzan, *Qumran Prayer*, 35-116.

vocabulary. Examples of these phenomena occur in *Jubilees* 1 and 23, the Animal Apocalypse and Apocalypse of Weeks in *1 Enoch*, and the *Testament of Moses*. These texts also testify to penitential reform movements in the Second Temple era that call fellow Jews to repentance.

Despite penitential prayers' formulaic speech and similarities in their basic form, their precise wording and time of performance is not fixed, an issue about which the rabbis argue in a later period.[8] Second Temple authors freely alter the wording in the prayers and employ them in a variety of settings. These changes in wording are important for they reflect the authors' own agendas, tendencies, and ideology. Further, whenever the author infuses the prayer with his own ideas, even traditional, formulaic language achieves new meaning. For example, when an author confesses the people's sins, he may well have his own unique opinion about what constitutes sin. Similarly, to speak of a national crisis as God's rightful punishment of a sinful people is to interpret history through one's own ideology. While the prayers seem to express the petitioners' contrition, they are also an indictment of the nation. The author is sending a message to the reader that the people are disobedient and that their actions have caused the nation's disastrous situation. Therefore, while the prayers may contain several formulaic expressions, the authors of the prayers are consciously reinterpreting the penitential traditions for their own purposes and in light of their respective historical situations. In this way, prayer traditions and traditional phrases acquire new meanings.

Previous Critical Methodology

Previous studies on penitential prayer in Second Temple Jewish literature have relied on the methodology and conclusions of Hebrew Bible form critics. For form critics, the value of biblical texts for the study of prayer primarily lies in what they reveal about ancient religious festivals. The interpreter's goal, therefore, does not specifically rest in the explanation of the text, but in reconstructing the cultic setting that stands behind the text and influences it. Using the form critical method and information from other Ancient Near Eastern texts, scholars like Gunkel and Mowinckel produce theoretical constructions of

---

[8]E.g., see S. Talmon ("The Emergence of Institutionalized Prayer in Israel in the Light of the Qumran Literature," *Qumrân: Sa piété, sa théologie son milieu* [ed. M. Delcor; Paris: Leuven University, 1978] 265-284, esp. 271-273) who cites *mBer* 4.4 as evidence that not all rabbis approved of fixed prayer. See also, B. Nitzan, *Qumran Prayer*, 35-45.

Introduction

hypothetical cultic ceremonies.[9] This school becomes interested in penitential prayer as it relates to the school's theoretical reconstructions of an annual covenant renewal ceremony. Following Mowinckel's[10] theory of an annual fall new year's festival to renew the covenant, von Rad,[11] Alt,[12] Mendenhall,[13] and Baltzer[14] work to develop the idea of covenantal religion—its structure, ratification, and renewal. According to this circle of interpreters, penitential prayer originates in the covenant renewal ceremony as an attempt to repair a covenant that the people's sins had broken. For example, both von Rad and Noth agree that Ezra 9, which contains a penitential prayer, is an example of a covenant renewal. As von Rad states: "... We have to understand (Ezra 9) as a kind of renewal of the covenant."[15] Baltzer asserts the same when he examines Ezra 9-10.[16]

Two other works that attempt to locate the origins of Second Temple penitential prayer within this notion of covenant renewal ceremony are O. H. Steck's *Israel und das gewaltsame Geschick der Propheten*, and E. Lipinski's *La liturgie pénitentielle dans la Bible*. Steck sorts out the various traditions that have merged in the texts that speak of Israel's rejection of the prophetic message. Since penitential prayers include references to Israel refusing to obey the prophets, the prayers figure into his investigation. After his detailed work, and recognition of lively interpretive activity in the period from the exile through the Second Temple, he identifies the *Sitz im Leben* of these prayers as the covenant renewal ceremony.[17] Lipinski examines the Psalms, prophetic texts, and the penitential prayers from the Hebrew Bible in order to reconstruct

---

[9]For the importance of distinguishing between literary form and *Sitz im Leben* see R. R. Wilson, *Prophecy and Society in Ancient Israel* (Philadelphia: Fortress, 1980) 11. Form criticism did not sufficiently recognize that a literary form could borrow from some *Sitz im Leben* and yet never intend that form of speech to be used in the *Sitz im Leben* from which it was borrowed. Further, the term *Sitz im Leben* could refer either to the setting in which the passage was used or the one from which it was borrowed.

[10]See, e.g., S. Mowinckel, *The Psalms in Israel's Worship*, vol. 1 (trans., D. R. AP-Thomas; Nashville: Abingdon, 1962) 154-157.

[11]G. von Rad, "The Form of the Hexateuch," *The Problem of the Hexateuch and other Essays* (trans. E. W. T. Dicken; Edinburgh: Oliver and Boyd, 1963) 1-78; *Old Testament Theology*, vol. 1, 18-19, 88-89, 192.

[12]R. Alt, "The Origins of Israelite Law," *Essays on the Old Testament and Religion* (trans. R. A. Wilson; Oxford: Blackwell, 1966) 79-132.

[13]G. E. Mendenhall, "Law and Covenant in Israel and the Ancient Near East," *BA* 17 (1954) 26-76.

[14]K. Baltzer, *Covenant Formulary*, 60-62.

[15]G. von Rad, *Theology*, I, 89.

[16]K. Baltzer, *Covenant Formulary*, 47.

[17]O. H. Steck, *Israel und das gewaltsame Geschick der Propheten*, 134-135.

Israel's great penitential ceremonies. While he occasionally disagrees with Gunkel on particular points, Lipinski places himself neatly in line with Gunkel.[18] Consequently, when he turns to consider the prayers of Ezra 9, Nehemiah 9, Daniel 9, the Prayer of Azariah, Baruch 1:15-3:8, The Words of the Heavenly Lights (4Q504), and the Community Rule, he connects them to the covenantal renewal ceremony.[19] For Lipinski, these prayers assist Israel in mending the break in its covenant with God.[20] Lipinski's assertion that Israel held special convocations expressly for the purpose of repentance enjoys stronger evidence than the notion of a covenant renewal ceremony. In general, however, in Lipinski's work, the text becomes a window through which one can view Israel's cultic worship if one peers long and hard enough.

In writing penitential prayers, authors undeniably draw from Deuteronomy. However, the notion that penitential prayer belongs to the covenant renewal ceremony suffers from a problem. The evidence that Israel or the Jews of the Second Temple period held an annual covenant renewal ceremony is meager. The only example of a rite resembling a covenant renewal ceremony is 1QS 1.16-2.18. Furthermore, these form critical studies generally do not focus on the way in which authors reinterpret traditions so that they serve new purposes. Consequently, a reexamination of penitential prayer from the exilic period to the Second Temple is justified.

The Approach of this Study

This work will examine and compare texts related to the penitential prayer tradition in order to show that the authors of penitential prayers reinterpret penitential traditions for their respective purposes. Linguistic analysis of the penitential traditions will assist in accomplishing this. This involves examining individual words and phrases in the texts, comparing the words to previous traditions, and determining the new meaning that the author has assigned to the traditional language. Along with this analysis, an examination of material that is unique to each prayer will begin to reveal the author's own interests.

Second, this study will compare the literary forms of the prayers, as well as the elements from other literary forms that authors incorporate into the prayers. Occasionally, as in the covenant ceremony in the *Community Rule* and in the conversation between Israel and Judah in the *Testament of Moses*, an author might use the basic components of penitential prayer in a completely different literary form. Therefore, the study of the literary structures of the

---

[18]E. Lipinski, *La Liturgie Pénitentielle dans la Bible*, LD 52 (Paris: Cerf, 1969) 7.
[19]Ibid., 37-38. Lipinski footnotes K. Baltzer's *Covenant Formulary* at this point.
[20]Ibid., 38.

penitential texts intends to discover if the forms of the texts influence their meanings.

Third, the use of redaction criticism will show that the literary context in which a prayer appears influences a prayer's content and the meaning of its traditional expressions. Authors incorporate some statements in their prayers because they fit their respective literary contexts. Further, a prayer's literary context is especially valuable in determining the prayer's function. Identifying the reason that the person prays and analyzing the results of the prayer help in determining these possible functions for the prayer.

Finally, as it traces the developments and transformations in the uses and meanings of the prayers, this book will also become a history of the penitential tradition and religious ideas related to it. In this regard questions about why an author might change a traditional idea, or why an idea disappears from the literature will be essential.

Plan of Study

The work proceeds in the following manner. Chapter one traces the development of penitential prayer from the discussion on sin—punishment—repentance—deliverance in Deuteronomy 4 and 30 to the penitential prayers in Ezra-Nehemiah. In this development, 1 Kings 8 reflects a crucial transitional moment in deuteronomic thought because it recasts Deuteronomy's idea of repentance into a theory for penitential prayer. According to 1 Kings 8, the nation can bring an end to the ultimate covenantal curse—foreign domination and exile—by confessing its sins in prayer. An examination of Third Isaiah will show that penitential prayer grew strong roots in the exilic community. Third Isaiah attributes the failure of Second Isaiah's prophecies to the people's sins and he again calls them to repentance. The prayer in Ezra 9 broadens the category of sins to which penitential prayer is the proper response. In Deuteronomy and the deuteronomic traditions, Israel's cardinal sin is idolatry. This sin brings the nation's ultimate destruction, and for this it must repent through prayer. Ezra, however, offers a penitential prayer in response to the sin of intermarriage. He may oppose intermarriage because it may lead to a Jew accepting the gods of the foreign spouse. If this is his thought, Ezra has built a fence around the Torah. Even so, his prayer yields a vivid example of an author who adapts the penitential traditions to his own interests or agenda.

Chapter two investigates two prayers that extensively resemble one another, Dan 9:3-19 and Bar 1:15-3:8. In fact, they are so similar that one must be literarily dependent on the other, or both dependent on a common source. Despite the similarities in language, these prayers appear in different literary genres, express different notions of Israel's primary sin, and have different functions. Therefore, a comparison of these two prayers will especially help in substantiating the thesis that the authors of penitential prayers are intentionally reinterpreting penitential traditions and giving them new functions. Besides this, these two prayers also testify to the close relationship between penitential prayer and biblical interpretation. Both prayers are related to the proper interpretation of a specific biblical text.

Chapter three has several emphases. First, it shows how texts that are not prayers refer to penitential prayer or draw on language or ideology of penitential prayers. These texts include *Jubilees* 1 and 23, the Animal Apocalypse and the Apocalypse of Weeks in *1 Enoch*, the *Testament of Moses*, and several texts from the Qumran Scrolls. Second, these texts testify to penitential reform movements in this era. Because the authors of these texts believe that the majority of Jews live in apostasy, they call their contemporaries to repent. Their message, however, meets resistance. Disappointed by the response to their message, these movements distinguish themselves from fellow Jews and imagine themselves as the faithful recipients of biblical promises. Some of these movements, especially those represented in *Jubilees* 1 and 23 and the Qumran Scrolls, justify their existence through a reinterpretation of the deuteronomic historical scheme. The repentance about which Deuteronomy speaks no longer applies to Israel as a whole, but to the author's penitential movement. Occasionally, this Chapter refers to those who believe a particular author's message as a "group." The use of this term does not imply any kind of social organization for these people. Simply, some word must designate those who believe an author's message. "Group" functions in this way. Finally, Chapter three explores the role of penitence in the Qumran community's memory of its origins, in a person's entrance into the sect, and in its daily life.

Finally, Chapter four explores the tensions between penitential prayer and the problem of theodicy. While Deuteronomy teaches that God punishes the wicked and rewards the righteous, the events of history sometimes conflict with this belief. This is a crucial problem in the penitential traditions since the righteous occasionally suffer especially because of their righteousness. Tobit 3, the Prayer of Azariah, 2 Maccabees 7, and *Testament of Moses* wrestle with this tension. A second problem occasionally arises in the deuteronomic idea of punishment because God gives the task of punishing Israel to a foreign ruler. In their vanity and arrogance, these rulers take the glory of their victory for themselves and fail to acknowledge that God has given them their success. Further, they may also punish the nation to excess. The prayers in the Prayer of Azariah, 3 Macc 2:1-20, the Greek additions to Esther, and several hymns in the *Psalms of Solomon* attempt to adjust deuteronomic ideology so that it accounts for the arrogant foreign ruler.

Introduction

All English translations of the Hebrew Bible, Apocrypha, Pseudepigrapha, and the Qumran Scrolls are my own except for the English text of the *Testament of Moses*. For this I quote J. Priest's translation in *The Old Testament Pseudepigrapha*, vol. 1. All quotations of the MT are from *Biblia Hebraica Stuttgartensia*. The Greek texts of Tobit, 2 Maccabees, and Sirach are taken from *Septuaginta: Vetus Testamentum Graecum, Auctoritate Academiae Scientiarum Gottingensis editum*. The rest of the quotations from the LXX are from Alfred Rahlfs' *Septuaginta*. Citations for critical editions of the other texts appear in the book wherever necessary.

CHAPTER ONE

The Development of Penitential Prayer in Biblical Literature from the Exilic and Persian Periods

Introduction

The first example of a penitential prayer in biblical literature appears without any explanation about the act or justification for it. It occurs in Ezra 9 when Ezra prays upon learning that the people have intermarried with the people of the land, i.e., non-Jews. In Ezra's estimation, the practice of mixed marriage results in a grave religious crisis, and the prayer, along with other acts of contrition and a pledge of renewed obedience, functions as a key component in the situation's resolution. Two other examples of penitential prayer also occur in Nehemiah 1 and 9. As in Ezra 9, the author neither justifies their inclusion in the narrative nor explains their functions.

The lack of any explanations or justifications for the prayers means that Ezra-Nehemiah's audience already knows about and understands the practice of penitential prayer. The narrative scenes seem completely natural to the original readers. Thus, the practice of penitential prayer exists before the writing of Ezra-Nehemiah.

Despite the original author's and readers' familiarity with such prayers, they are actually a new literary phenomenon in the literature of the Hebrew Bible; there is no instance of penitential prayer in the biblical literature prior to Ezra-Nehemiah. This new literary phenomenon evokes several important questions. How and why did such prayers emerge? What traditions have been reinterpreted and incorporated into the prayers? Do traditions acquire new meanings and functions? This chapter answers these questions by explaining the origin of these penitential prayers and the developments in the subsequent tradition.

Because modern scholars have already noticed the deuteronomic themes and language in Ezra-Nehemiah's prayers, this investigation of the penitential prayer tradition begins with an examination of Deuteronomy's instructions about repentance. However, we immediately encounter a problem in the research. While Deuteronomy explicitly states that the people must repent, it contains no penitential prayer, nor does it direct the people to offer a penitential prayer in order to enact repentance. Its only other instruction about repentance lies in the ambiguous phrase "you shall *seek* (בקש ,דרש) God." How does one properly repent? Thus, an understanding of the movement from Deuteronomy's idea of repentance to the prayers in Ezra-Nehemiah requires an hypothesis that explains how Israel comes to believe that penitential prayer properly enacts the nation's repentance as Deuteronomy envisioned it.

The material needed to construct such a hypothesis about the transition from Deuteronomy to Ezra-Nehemiah lies within several texts other than Deuteronomy and Ezra-Nehemiah, namely, the deuteronomic history (especially 1 Kings 8), Jeremiah, Third Isaiah, and 2 Chronicles. These texts are pertinent for our investigation because they either develop Deuteronomy's idea of repentance or contain comparable ideas about repentance and penitential prayer.

Besides tracing the development of penitential traditions, this chapter also argues that penitential prayer in its deuteronomic form is an established religious institution in the exilic period and a widely accepted religious practice for dealing with sin. The presence or influence of the practice in another tradition, namely Third Isaiah, substantiates this claim. While it does not stand within the deuteronomic tradition, Third Isaiah contains penitential ideas that correspond to deuteronomic traditions. Further, two of its poems are basically penitential prayers. Therefore, data from Third Isaiah along with information from the deuteronomic traditions suggest that penitential prayer is a well established religious institution in the exilic period and at the beginning of the Second Temple period.

This chapter, then, embarks on two basic quests. First, it traces the origins of the penitential prayers extant in biblical literature to Deuteronomy and the deuteronomic traditions, and describes how these traditions develop into the prayers in Ezra-Nehemiah. Second, it shows that penitential prayer in its deuteronomic form is an established religious institution in the exilic and post-exilic periods.

Deuteronomy 4 and 30

As I state in the introduction to this chapter, Deuteronomy provides the starting point for explaining the penitential prayer tradition even though it does not itself contain a penitential prayer. Since repentance is a basic theme in penitential prayers, the task of explaining the prayers begins with an analysis of Deuteronomy's idea of repentance, and continues to use this as the foundation for investigating all the texts and penitential prayers that follow in this work. Deuteronomy's notion of repentance appears in chapters 4 and 30. Both these chapters relate repentance to Israel's sin, exile and restoration. Consequently, the following analysis examines Deuteronomy's idea of repentance within this set of topics, and determines its function within the nation's religion.

Deuteronomy 4

The discussion of repentance in Deuteronomy 4 follows closely upon Moses' prediction that the people will eventually disregard what YHWH requires of them. Set within the context of the Exodus and giving of the land, Israel's disobedience stands in striking contrast to YHWH's gracious saving activity. Recognizing the people's propensity for idolatry,[21] Moses strictly prohibits graven images of both YHWH (v. 15) and foreign gods (v. 19). Recalling its encounter with YHWH at Horeb, Moses reminds the nation that it saw only smoke and fire, not God's form. To be sure, then, any image of God remains impossible because Israel has never seen his form. Moreover, YHWH prohibits making idols that represent other gods because Israel must give total allegiance to him. Despite these warnings, Moses knows that Israel will violate this latter ordinance (v. 25).

According to deuteronomic ideology, disobeying YHWH on this most crucial commandment means that he will send severe punishment. Here, Moses informs the people that their punishment will be in the form of exile; i.e., YHWH will "scatter" (פוץ) them among the nations (v. 27). He hopes that the exile will teach the people first hand that idols cannot deliver them (v. 28).[22]

Despite the catastrophic dimensions of the punishment, Moses leaves room for hope.[23] Although exile is inevitable, God will deliver the people if they repent. Given their status as exiles, their repentance must take place in a foreign territory instead of in Israel. Moses describes the moment of repentance as follows:

---

[21]Cf. Deut 8:19.

[22]The idea that God delivers Israel over to idols that cannot answer is prevalent in prophetic writings. See, e.g., Jer 2:26-29.

[23] H. G. Reventlow, *Gebet*, 274; H. W. Wolff, "Das Kerygma des Deuteronomistischen Geschichtswerks," *ZAW* 73 (1961) 183-186. See M. Weinfeld (*Deuteronomy 1-11*, AB 5 [Garden City: Doubleday, 1991] 216-217) on the optimism of Deuteronomy and 1 Kings 8. In contrast, M. Noth (*The Deuteronomistic History*, JSOTSupp [trans. J. Dull; Sheffield: University of Sheffield, 1981] 197) claims that the message of the deuteronomistic historian was ultimately one of judgment: "Clearly he saw that the divine judgment was acted out in his account of the external collapse of Israel as a nation as something final and definitive and he expressed no hope for the future, not even in the modest and simple form of an expectation that the deported and dispersed people would be gathered together."

And from there you will seek YHWH your God, *and you will find* [him] if *you seek* him with all your heart and with all your soul. And *in your distress*, when all these things have found you, in the latter days, *you will turn* to YHWH your God, and obey his voice (Deut 4:29-30).

ובקשתם משם את־יהוה אלהיך ומצאת כי תדרשנו בכל־לבבך ובכל־נפשך:
בצר לך ומצאוך כל הדברים האלה באחרית הימים ושבת עד־יהוה אלהיך ושמעת בקלו:

The terms שוב, דרש and בקש metaphorically denote repentance. The other phrases are vintage deuteronomic phrases and ideas. An examination of Hos 5:15-6:1, though, indicates that some of Deuteronomy's language existed prior to Deuteronomy. Like Deuteronomy, Hos 5:15-6:1 depicts God waiting for the people's repentance once they have encountered distress:[24]

I will go and return to my place
until they recognize their guilt, and *seek* my face.
In their *distress* they will seek my favor.
"Come, *let us return* to the Lord ..."

אלך אשובה אל־מקומי
עד אשר־יאשמו ובקשו פני
בצר להם ישחרנני
לכו ונשובה אל־יהוה

As the underlined words indicate, both Hosea and Deuteronomy share the image of Israel "turning" (שוב) and "seeking" (בקש) God in the midst of "distress" (צר).[25] Yet, Deuteronomy does not simply reproduce the tradition. Instead, the author of Deuteronomy 4 combines this tradition with the typical deuteronomic expressions "with all your heart and soul" and "obey his voice" and also places the tradition within the deuteronomic scheme of history. The tradition as it now exists in Deuteronomy no longer applies to eighth century BCE Israel, but explains how the nation can recover from the catastrophe of 586 BCE. Therefore, Deuteronomy 4 does not mindlessly reproduce the tradition, but reworks it through a different ideology for a different set of circumstances; Deuteronomy itself is the product of an interpretive enterprise.

---

[24]M. Weinfeld, *Deuteronomy and the Deuteronomistic School* (Oxford: Oxford, 1972) 218; and *Deuteronomy 1-11*, 48-49; cf. J. Unterman, *From Restoration to Repentance: Jeremiah's Thought in Transition*, JSOTSupp 54 (Sheffield: University of Sheffield, 1987) 74.

[25]Cf. Jer 2:27.

Deuteronomy 28-30

The themes in Deuteronomy 28-30 extensively resemble those in chapter 4. Like chapter 4, Moses warns the people that if they commit the cardinal sin, idolatry (29:17-26), YHWH will unleash his wrath in the form of the covenantal curses (v. 27). Further, in their description of the covenantal curses, chapters 28-29 connect idolatry and punishment when the author creates an imaginative scene where Israel's children and the nations ponder the land's destruction. They ask: "Why has YHWH done thus to this land? What caused this great display of anger?" (29:24). The answer immediately follows: Israel abandoned the covenant it made with YHWH and served idols (vv. 25-26).

In its explanation about how Israel's situation can change, chapter 30 again resembles chapter 4. Repentance is the pivotal action.

> When all these things have come upon you, the blessings and the curses ... you will search your heart among the nations.[26] And *you will turn* (ושבת עד־יהוה אלהיך) to YHWH your God, and both you and your children will obey his voice with all your heart and with all your soul according to all that I am commanding you today (Deut 30:1-2).

Besides having the same profound contempt for idolatry and the opinion that the deity punishes those who practice it, the two texts share several key phrases.[27] The following parallel columns highlight the common phrases in the two texts:

4:29	30:2
... with all your heart and with all your soul.	... with all your heart and with all your soul.
בכל־לבבך ובכל־נפשך	בכל־לבבך ובכל־נפשך
4:27	30:3
YHWH will scatter you among the people...	Among whom YHWH your God has scattered you...
והפיץ יהוה אתכם בעמים	אשר הפיצך יהוה אלהיך שמה
	30:2
	... with all your heart and with all your soul.

---

[26]The LXX translates שוב with δεχόμαι in Deut 30:1. It uses ἐπιστρέφω in 30:2 and in 1 Kgs 8:47, a phrase similar to Deut 30:1.

[27]Cf. M. Weinfeld, *Deuteronomy 1-11*, 216.

בכל־לבבך ובכל־נפשך

30:3
Among whom YHWH your God has scattered you...

אשר הפיצך יהוה אלהיך שמה

This consistency in rhetoric suggests that in the deuteronomic circles the language that describes God's punishment and the nation's repentance has become formulaic.

Deut 30:1 uses a figure of speech rarely found in the Hebrew Bible: השבת אל־לבבך, rendered literally, "you will turn to your heart." Later penitential prayers in the deuteronomic traditions also occasionally reproduce this phrase. Since this wooden translation of the phrase means nothing in English, it requires further consideration. Similar expressions surface in Isa 44:19; 46:8; and Lam 3:21. In each instance, the phrase denotes mental recognition or reflection, for example:

> They do not know. They do not understand. Their eyes have become besmeared so that they do not see, their hearts from understanding. *No one searches his heart* (ולא־ישיב אל־לבו). He does not know and does not understand...

In this quote from Isa 44:18-19, language for "understanding" and "knowing" surround the phrase. Within in this context the phrase connotes the process of self examination. Its appearance in Deuteronomy probably has the same force. After experiencing the devastating force of the covenantal curses, the people reflect upon their situation—"turn to their hearts"—in order to ascertain their own responsibility for their distress. In this instance, their reflection must follow Deuteronomy's ideology. Deuteronomy teaches that a correlation exists between the nation's moral behavior and its prosperity or struggles: sin brings punishment, while obedience leads to blessing. Consequently, this leads to the conclusion that the nation suffers because of its sins, and only repentance can break the curses' hold on the nation.[28] Since "self examination" (שוב) leads to "repentance" (שוב), the author's unusual figure of speech also serves as a play on the word שוב.

Following the moment of repentance, Deuteronomy 4 and 30 also agree that the people must recommit themselves to obedience. In Deuteronomy 30, the author uses the phrase "with all your heart and all your soul" in order to

---

[28]Cf. also P. D. Miller, *They Cried to the Lord: The Form and Theology of Biblical Prayer* (Minneapolis: Fortress, 1994) 246-247.

emphasize the importance of complete obedience. The pledge of obedience later acquires a place in penitential prayer contexts. For example, after Ezra intercedes for the people's sins, they pledge obedience (Ezra 10). In deuteronomic ideology, only renewed obedience verifies the sincerity of repentance and completes it. When YHWH sees that obedience accompanies repentance, he will restore the people's fortunes (30:3),[29] and will reverse the curses listed in chapter 28.[30] He will "gather" (קבץ) the people from where he "scattered" (פוץ) them so that they may regain possession of the land that he gave to their ancestors (30:3-5).

Historical Setting of Deuteronomy 4 and 28-30

Determining the meaning and purpose of a text requires taking into account its historical setting. While Deuteronomy's literary development is complicated, scholars generally agree that the book achieved its final form during the exile.[31] Both Deuteronomy 4 and 30 bear the markings of an exilic text. First, because repentance is their focal point, both texts read as if YHWH is still waiting for the people to repent before restoration can take place. Second, the present literary context of Deuteronomy 30 suggests an exilic setting for the passage. Chapter 30 directly follows an explicit reference to the exile in 29:28. According to 29:28, Judah is now "uprooted from its land."

With its exilic setting, concern for repentance, and hope for restoration, the author of Deuteronomy presents a special message for exilic Israel, explaining why the world is like it is and how the people can change their future. Though punishment has come, there is reason for hope, a hope resting on the historical precedent of YHWH's mercy and his faithfulness to the promises to the ancestors (4:31; cf. 30:5). Further confirmation for hope resides in the prophecy—fulfillment pattern of these texts. Functioning as a faithful prophet, Moses has correctly foretold that God would scatter Israel for its disobedience. Just as he has predicted judgment, he also has offered the possibility of restoration to the land. The fulfillment of the first warning assures the realization of the restoration once the people have repented and pledged their obedience. As a trustworthy, reliable voice from the past, Moses

---

[29]Cf. Hos 6:1-2.

[30]J. M. Bracke, "*šûb šᵉbût*: A Reappraisal," *ZAW* 97 (1985) 241.

[31]See P. Ackroyd, *Exile and Restoration* (Philadelphia: Westminster, 1968) 62-63; M. Noth, *Deuteronomistic History*, 12-17; G. von Rad, *Deuteronomy*, 23-30; M. Weinfeld, *Deuteronomy 1-11*, 13-17. For the complicated relationship between Deuteronomy and Jeremiah, see W. L. Holladay, *Jeremiah 2: A Commentary on the Book of the Prophet Jeremiah Chapters 26-52*, Hermeneia (Minneapolis: Fortress, 1989) 53-63.

engenders confidence in the exilic reader.[32] The people's hope, then, consists of a careful blending of YHWH's mercy and the people's repentance and obedience.

Summary

Deuteronomy 4 and 30 contain a similar pattern. Israel's great sin, idolatry, brings punishment as YHWH disperses Israel among the nations. Exiled in a foreign land, Israel needs to "turn," that is, it must repent and pledge obedience. If the people perform these acts, YHWH will restore them to the land. This, Israel's promised future, Deuteronomy describes with consistent rhetoric. Especially as it focuses on the crucial turning point for Israel, this language has become formulaic.

Solomon's Dedicatory Prayer in 1 Kgs 8:22-61

Introduction

Having described Deuteronomy's pattern of sin—punishment—repentance and its formulaic language within this pattern, the task of proposing an explanation for the development of penitential prayer from these two features of Deuteronomy begins. As stated, Deuteronomy calls for repentance but does not specify how the nation should enact repentance. This ambiguity in Deuteronomy's message forces the exiles to consider how to repent and atone for the grave sins that have caused YHWH to drive them into exile. Moreover, the Temple's destruction and the discontinuation of the cult intensify the people's problems. Prior to the exile, these religious institutions play an important part in removing sin. Because Babylon brought an end to these institutions, Israel must search for a way to demonstrate its repentance and a means for atonement. How would Israel display its repentance in such an historical and religious crisis?

The exilic author of Solomon's prayer in 1 Kings 8 turns his attention to these problems and the ambiguities in Deuteronomy's message. Building upon the ideology of the deuteronomic traditions and borrowing their language, the author instructs his readers about proper repentance.[33] Placing a reference to the exile in the prayer's climax indicates that these problems are foremost in the author's mind. When the people find themselves left without Temple and

---

[32]Cf. M. Weinfeld, *Deuteronomy 1-11*, 216-217.
[33]H. G. Reventlow, *Gebet*, 274.

cult, Solomon indirectly instructs them to confess their sins in a penitential prayer. Solomon's prayer, therefore, provides crucial information for explaining the transition from Deuteronomy's teaching about repentance to penitential prayer as the enactment of repentance.

Solomon offers his prayer at the Temple's dedication. Of the prayer's seven petitions, all except two refer to national or individual sin (vv. 41-43 and 44-45). The author may be playing with the number seven since the prayer cult, Solomon indirectly instructs them to confess their sins in a penitential prayer. Solomon's prayer, therefore, provides crucial information for explaining the transition from Deuteronomy's teaching about repentance to penitential prayer as the enactment of repentance.

Solomon offers his prayer at the Temple's dedication. Of the prayer's seven petitions, all except two refer to national or individual sin (vv. 41-43 and 44-45). The author may be playing with the number seven since the prayer also has seven shifts in a word play on שוב, Solomon prays in the seventh month, and the celebration lasts seven days.[34]

Phrases from the Traditions in Deuteronomy 4 and 28-30

Several verbal similarities exist between 1 Kings 8 and Deuteronomy 4 and 28-30. The author of 1 Kings, then, has Deuteronomy in mind as he writes and intentionally develops these traditions. The following examples illustrate the numerous similarities between the texts:[35]

1 Kgs 8:47 and 48	Deut 30:1
And if they search their heart in the land to which they have been taken captive and they repent,	*If you search your heart*[36] among all the nations where YHWH your God has driven you...[37]
והשיבו אל־לבם בארץ אשר נשבו־שם ושבו	והשבת אל־לבבך בכל־הגוים אשר הדיחך יהוה אלהיך שמה

---

[34]See B. O. Long, *1 Kings with an Introduction to Historical Literature*, FOTL (Grand Rapids: Eerdmans, 1984) 104.

[35]While the comparisons are my own, see also J. Levenson, "From Temple to Synagogue: 1 Kings 8," *Traditions in Transformation: Turning Points in Biblical Faith* (eds., B. Halpren and L. D. Levenson; Winona Lake: Eisenbrauns, 1986) 160-162.

[36]The difference in spelling for לב in Deut 30:1 and 1 Kgs 8:47 excludes the possibility of common authorship. The form לבב appears in the parallel passage 2 Chr 6:37. See G. Braulik, "Spüren einer Neuarbeitung des deuteronomistischen Geschichtswerkes," *Bib* 52 (1971) 29-30.

[37]Cf. Deut 4:39; J. D. Levenson, "From Temple to Synagogue," 161.

and they plead to you in the land of their captors...

והתחננו אליך בארץ שביהם...

And if they turn to you with all their heart and all their soul in the land of their enemies who captured them...

ושבו אליך בכל־לבבם ובכל־נפשם בארץ איביהם אשר־שבו אתם...

Deut 30:2
If you turn to YHWH your God, and obey his voice *with all your heart and all your soul*

ושבת עד־יהוה אלהיך ושמעת בקלו ...בכל־לבבך ובכל־נפשך

Deut 30:10
... when *you turn to YHWH your God with all your heart and all your soul*...

כי תשוב אל־יהוה אלהיך בכל־לבבך ובכל־נפשך...

Deut 4:29
From there you will seek YHWH your God and you will find him if you seek him *with all your heart and with all your soul*.

ובקשתם משם את־יהוה אלהיך ומצאת כי תדרשנו בכל־לבבך ובכל־נפשך

1 Kgs 8:23
There is no God like you in heaven above or earth beneath.

Deut 4:39
For YHWH is God in heaven above and in the earth beneath. There is no other.

1 Kgs 8:41
And indeed the foreigner ... comes from a distant land.

Deut 29:22
And the foreigner who comes from a distant land.

1 Kgs 8:52
... When they call to you.

Deut 4:7
... When we call to him.

1 Kgs 8:51
For they are your people and your possession (ונחלתך)...

Deut 4:20
YHWH took you and brought you from the iron furnace, from Egypt,

1 Kgs 8:53[38]
For you separated them for yourself for a possession (לנחלה) from all the peoples of the earth as you said through Moses your servant when you brought our fathers from Egypt, O YHWH God.

to be his people and his possession (נחלה).

The rare reference to Egypt as the "iron smelter" in 1 Kgs 8:51 further confirms that the author of 1 Kings 8 knows the traditions in Deuteronomy 4. This designation for Egypt occurs elsewhere in the Hebrew Bible only in Deut 4:20 and Jer 11:4:

Deut 4:20   ויוצא אתכם מכור הברזל ממצרים

Jer 11:4   הוציאי־אותם מארץ־מצרים מכור הברזל

1 Kgs 8:51 אשר הוצאת ממצרים מתוק כור הברזל

Even though, as Braulik notes, Deut 4:20 more closely resembles the wording of Jer 11:4 than 1 Kgs 8:51, Deuteronomy and 1 Kings are so similar that one must infer that 1 Kings is dependent upon Deuteronomy. However, slight differences in phraseology and spelling in the two texts dispel the notion the texts originate from a common author.[39] The curses listed in Deuteronomy 28 also influence 1 Kgs 8:37 where the author mentions several curses. The chart on the following page compares the curses in the two texts.[40]

The reproduction of these curses and the numerous verbal similarities between 1 Kings 8 and Deuteronomy 4 and 30 indicate that the author of 1 Kings 8 has either a direct knowledge of Deuteronomy 4 and 28-30, or knows the same traditions as the author of Deuteronomy. Still, establishing a relationship between the passages does not explain their meanings and functions. Authors typically adapt traditions for their own purposes and agendas. How and why does 1 Kings 8 reshape Deuteronomy?

---

[38] J. Levenson (Ibid., 160-162) does not list v. 53.

[39] For G. Braulik ("Spüren einer Neubearbeitung des deuteronomistichen Geschichtswerkes," 30), the slight difference between the texts means that the author of Deuteronomy 4 is not the author of 1 Kings 8.

[40] Cf. also Amos 4 and Joel 2. Cf. J. Unterman, *From Repentance to Redemption*, 74.

Table 1. A Comparison of Covenantal Curses in 1 Kings and Deuteronomy

1 Kgs 8:37	Deuteronomy 28
famine	vv. 23-24, 48
blight	v. 22
mildew	v. 22
locust	v. 42 (uses צלצל)
caterpillar	-
enemy	vv. 25, 31, 48, 53, 55, 57, 68
plague	-
sickness	-

Casuistic Forms and Confession of Sin

A basic difference between Deuteronomy and 1 Kings lies in their literary forms. Solomon's prayer recasts Deuteronomy's wording into conditional sentences, the prayer's most prominent formal feature. The basic patterns follow casuistic legal formulations, i.e., circumstantial law.[41] The text contains several different conditional constructions. The first example employs אשר ... ו (vv. 31 and 32, 33 and 34). In v. 35, a second form occurs in which the protasis begins with ב and in v. 36 the apodosis commences with ו. Vv. 37-39 and 41-44 employ the form: "A famine, if there be in the land, a plague, if there be, ... (...רעב כי־יהיה בארץ דבר) then hear (ואתה תשמע)..."[42]Finally, the construction changes again in v. 44, where the final two conditions use כי ... ו (vv. 44 and 45, 46 and 49).[43]

Several diverse literary contexts attest to these conditional phrases prior to 1 Kings 8. Expectedly, the construction in v. 44 and v. 46 has precedents in Deuteronomy.[44] However, the conditional expressions in vv. 37-40 resemble

---

[41]B. O. Long (*1 Kings*, 103) and S. J. De Vries (*1 and 2 Chronicles*, FOTL 11 [Grand Rapids: Eerdmans, 1989] 260 make this same observation.

[42]This way of translating the text is from B. O. Long, *1 Kings*, 103.

[43]The NRSV does not reflect the different constructions.

[44] E.g., see Deut 15:12 ff.; 17:2 ff; 17:8 ff; 18:6-8; 21:15-17, 18-22; 22:13-19, 22-24, 28-29; 24:1-4; 25:1-3, 5-10. Cf. G. von Rad, *Deuteronomy*, 17.

those in Lev 13:2, 18, 24, 29, 38, and 47. For example, Lev 13:47 reads: "A garment, if there is a leprous disease in it, ... then..."[45] Long expresses surprise in discovering that the author of 1 Kings 8 follows a priestly legal model to formulate some of the conditions.[46] However, such borrowing seems strange only if one differentiates too sharply between "the circles" in ancient Israel.

The deuteronomic circles, then, have taken up the program for restoration and recast it into casuistic legal formulations. Solomon within the context of 1 Kings 8, is assuming the role of a deuteronomic exegete, recasting traditions from Deuteronomy, especially chapters 4 and 28-30, into a casuistic structure to explain to the people how they should respond to "future" crises. The real author, of course, has his contemporary exilic readers in mind as he writes.

The confession of sin stands within the protasis of the casuistic construction in v. 47. The text describes the confession as a prayer that the people make while in the land of their captors. The confession is brief: "We have sinned, and we have acted in iniquity, and have acted wickedly" (חטאנו והעוינו ורשענו). Confessions of offenses in the Hebrew Bible are usually formulated חטאנו ליהוה. Greenberg has shown that such confessions imitate inter-human speech and borrow their language from various sociological relationships.[47] The threefold expansion of the confession in 1 Kings 8 may reflect the increased discussion of sin in the prophetic literature. The first example of a triple confession occurs in Jer 14:7 where Judah complains to YHWH about the difficulties it faces. The people poetically appeal to YHWH to overlook their faults and bring salvation:

Although our iniquities testify against us,
　　act, O YHWH, for your name's sake;
our apostasies indeed are many,
　　and we have sinned against you.

אם־עונינו ענו בנו   יהוה עשה למען שמך
כי־רבו משובתינו   לך חטאנו

The confession for the Day of Atonement in Leviticus 16:21 contains another example of a threefold confession of sin.[48] According to the directions, the

---

[45] Again, this way of translating the text is from B. O. Long, *1 Kings*, 103.
[46] Ibid.
[47] M. Greenberg, *Biblical Prose Prayer: As a Window to the Popular Religion of Ancient Israel* (Berkeley: University of California, 1983). P. Miller (*They Cried to the Lord*, 250) also agrees with Greenberg's conclusions.
[48] For more on confession in Leviticus, see below.

high priest must offer a threefold confession of the nation's trespasses. Thus, the evidence indicates that ancient Israel typically makes threefold confessions.

The multiple confession, clearly pleonastic, conveys the contrition of the confessor and has a superlative effect; the suppliant admits that Israel is "most" sinful.[49] Moreover, the multiple confession most likely has a rhetorical strategy. By admitting what God already knows, i.e., that Israel has become extremely sinful, the petitioner believes that he might win God's favor. Further, the multiple confession displays the petitioner's complete surrender to God's mercy.

The casuistic constructions in 1 Kings 8 are also a rhetorical ploy for securing YHWH's response. While humans are the subject of apodoses in other conditional constructions, in 1 Kings 8 God is the subject of each apodosis. Consequently, the casuistic constructions encourage God to act when the people properly repent and pray. The result is almost an attempt to manipulate God into action. At least, Solomon assumes that God is sufficiently faithful and righteous to forgive a sincere penitent and answer the penitent's request. As God brought punishment because of sin, he will restore the people when they repent.

Solomon's Petitionary Language

Although Solomon does not complain, his prayer employs passionate petitionary language in vv. 27-30. A comparison of Solomon's petitions to those found in several psalms demonstrates his passion.

1 Kings 8:28	
Turn to the prayer of your servant and to his supplication...	Cf. (Heb) Pss 25:16; 69:17; 86:16; 102:18; 119:32
ופנית אל־תפלת עבדך ואל־תחנתו	
... to hearken to the cry and prayer...	Cf. Jer 7:16; 11:14; 14:12; (Heb); Pss 17:1; 61:2; 88:3; 142:7
לשמע אל־הרנה ואל־התפלה	
1 Kings 8:29	
Let your eyes be open to this house...	Cf. (Heb) Pss 9:14; 25:18; 31:7
להיות עינך פתחות אל־הבית הזה	

---

[49]Cf. P. D. Miller, *They Cried to the Lord*, 246, 250-251.

1 Kings 8:30	
Hear... (שְׁמַעְתָּ) (and at the beginning of each apodosis in vv. 32, 34, 36, 39, 43, 45, and 49)	Cf. (Heb) Pss 4:2; 6:10; 17:1; 99:4; 119:84; 140:13; 146:7

Despite Solomon's passionate language, his petitions stop short of lament. In order to assume the tone of lament, the author would need to insert "why" or "how long" questions: e.g., "Why do you not hear and maintain their cause?" Solomon does not ask "why." Penitential prayers generally do not include the language of lament for good cause.[50] In lament, the suppliant believes that he suffers unjustly, and expresses this opinion through complaining and questioning God. The casuistic deuteronomic ideology of 1 Kings 8 makes lament impossible. Deuteronomic ideology always maintains a correlation between obedience and reward, between disobedience and retribution.[51] These correlations necessarily depend on the idea that God is just. Accordingly, Solomon's prayer appeals to YHWH to act with justice: "Do justice" (וְעָשִׂיתָ מִשְׁפָּטָם) (vv. 45 and 49). Operating within the sphere of deuteronomic thought, Solomon assumes that YHWH also responds justly to repentance with deliverance.

A comparable hesitancy in using complaint stands behind the crafting of Deut 29:24-28.[52] In an imaginative scene in which Israel's children and the nations ask "why" such disaster has come, they do not ask their question in regard to the nation, but the land: "Why has the land suffered like this?" The answer comes: the people have sinned and God has justly punished them. There is no place in Deuteronomy for the language of the innocent sufferer.

Temple Theology

Besides reinterpreting Deuteronomy 4 and 30, the author of 1 Kings 8 also redefines the function of the Jerusalem Temple. In the religious life of ancient Israel, the Temple functions primarily as a place of sacrifice. Israel may offer

---

[50]C. Westermann ("Struktur und Geschichte der Klage im Alten Testament," *ZAW* 66 (1954) 72-73) claims that lament has two key parts: the prayer for God to turn to the suppliant (hear), and the request for intervention (help). He argues that penitential prayer springs from lament, but by the Second Temple period gives way to deuteronomic ideology. He reaches this conclusion because he traces the origins of penitential prayer to the Psalms. However, the penitential prayers in the surviving literature clearly spring from deuteronomic traditions. P. D. Miller (*They Cried to the Lord*, 256) recognizes that confession is opposite of lament.

[51]Cf. P. Ackroyd, *Exile and Restoration*, 78; Cf. G. von Rad (*Old Testament Theology*, vol. 1, 343, 357-8) and his notion of *Gerichtsdoxologie*.

[52]See also above.

prayers there, but the people go to the Temple to sacrifice.⁵³ However, the author of 1 Kings 8 develops a different role for the Temple; it serves as a place of prayer. Whether it historically functioned in this manner is a different issue. What traditions and ideas, then, does the author reshape in order to present the Temple as a place of prayer? Why would he propose this change in the Temple's function?

On several occasions 1 Kings 8 connects "prayer" (תפלה) and "supplication" (תחנה) to the Temple.⁵⁴ According to Solomon, the people should direct their prayers toward the Temple. However, to guard against the notion that YHWH is confined to the Temple, Solomon consistently locates God's dwelling place in heaven (vv. 30, 34, 36, 39, 43, 45, 49). Only YHWH's *name* is in the Temple, not YHWH himself: "that your eyes be open to this house night and day to the place which you said, '*My name shall be there...*'" (1 Kgs 8:29).⁵⁵ 1 Kgs 8:27 insists that YHWH cannot dwell in the Temple: "But will God indeed dwell on the earth? Even heaven and the highest heaven cannot contain you, much less this house that I have built!" (v. 27). Thus, when crises come, the people pray to the place where YHWH's *name* dwells.

The author of 1 Kings 8 draws several of these ideas from Deuteronomy 12, a text that explains the importance and the proper use of the central sanctuary.⁵⁶ According to Deuteronomy, the people must bring their sacrifices to the place that God chooses "to place his *name* there for its dwelling place" (Deut 12:5).⁵⁷ Deuteronomy's interests lie in the centralization of the cult and

---

⁵³See E. Bickerman, "The Civic Prayer for Jerusalem," *Studies in Jewish and Christian History*, vol. 2 (Leiden: Brill, 1980) 304-307; I. Knohl, "Between Voice and Silence: The Relationship between Prayer and Cult" *JBL* 115 (1996) 17-30.

⁵⁴Vv. 28, 29, 30, 33, 35, 38, 42, 44, 45, 47, 48, 49, 52; cf. J. D. Levenson, "From Temple to Synagogue," 158.

⁵⁵This is an example of the use of Yahweh's name as a theologoumenon. Occasionally in the Hebrew Bible, authors use "glory," "name," "face," and "messenger" in order to speak of Yahweh's presence and avoid the idea that Yahweh is confined to a place or solely identified with one group of people.

⁵⁶G. Braulik, "Spüren einer Neubearbeitung des deuteronomistischen Geschichtswerkes," 24-25. See M. Weinfeld (*Deuteronomy 1-11*, 37-44) for the discussion on the transformations in the centralization of the cult. His theory proposes dates for these transformations.

⁵⁷*Pace* NRSV which understands the pronominal suffix on לשכנו as a reference to God. In the other verses the central sanctuary is clearly a dwelling place for the "name." Cf. vv. 11, 14, 21.

sacrificing at a central shrine. In sum, the temple is the *locus* of sacrifice in Deuteronomy.[58]

Both Deuteronomy 12 and 1 Kings 8 employ the image of "placing" YHWH's "name" in the central shrine in order to protect his transcendence and sovereignty.[59] However, the Temple functions in significantly different ways in these two passages. While Deuteronomy concerns itself with sacrifices, Solomon never mentions sacrifice in connection with prayer or repentance. Admittedly, the king offers sacrifices at the conclusion of the prayer (vv. 62-64), and he makes the prayer before the altar (v. 22), but he never connects sacrifice with penitential prayers. Consequently, in Deuteronomy 12, the Temple is a place of sacrifice, but in 1 Kings 8 it is a place of prayer.

Why would the author of 1 Kings 8 shift the Temple's function from a place of sacrifice to a place of prayer? The answer relates to the historical setting at the time in which the author of 1 Kings 8 writes.

Excursus I: The Date of the Deuteronomic History

The deuteronomic history most likely achieved its final form during the exile. Jehoiachin's release from prison at the end of 2 Kings establishes a *terminus a quo* of 561 BCE.[60] The work's silence concerning Persia's defeat of Babylon, Judah's return, and work on rebuilding the temple in Jerusalem suggest a *terminus ad quem* predating Cyrus' victory in 539 BCE.[61] Debates continue on which layers of the texts appear first, and where the historians' pens refashion the sources.[62] This is a problem in 1 Kings 8, an important text in the history of deuteronomic studies, and

---

[58]M. Weinfeld, *Deuteronomy 1-11*, 40; J. Milgrom, *Leviticus 1-16*, *AB* 3 (Garden City: Doubleday, 1991) 28-29; J. D. Levenson, "From Temple to Synagogue," 158-159. Again, E. Bickerman ("The Civic Prayer of Jerusalem," 304-307) warns against primarily understanding the Temple as a place of prayer. The Jews undoubtedly offered prayers in the Temple, but it primarily functioned as a place of sacrifice.

[59]In contrast to 1 Kings 8, however, Deuteronomy 12 never mentions that God's dwelling place is in the heaven. See G. Braulik, "Spüren einer Neubearbeitung des deuteronomistischen Geschichtswerkes," 24.

[60]562 BCE in M. Noth, *The Deuteronomic History*, 12; Cf. P. R. Ackroyd, *Exile and Restoration*, 64.

[61]P. R. Ackroyd, *Exile and Restoration*, 64-65.

[62]This problem has been taken up especially by Cross and his students. See F. M. Cross, *Canaanite Myth and Hebrew Epic: Essays in the History of the Religion of Israel* (Cambridge: Harvard, 1973) 274-289. For a review of the scholarly work in this area, see P. Ackroyd, "The Historical Literature," *HBMI*, 300-305.

this present study.⁶³ However, the final form of Solomon's prayer suggests an exilic date since it climaxes with an appeal for God to hear the people when they are in the "land of their enemy" (vv. 46 and 48).

Writing during the exile, the author of 1 Kings 8 establishes an ideology of prayer especially suited for his nation's situation.⁶⁴ He does this by creating a scene that depicts the Temple as originally dedicated as a place of prayer, especially penitential prayer in response to punishment for sin. Moreover, the author maintains that even without the Temple the people can continue to practice the activity for which Solomon dedicated it—prayer. Thus, Israel gains a way to expiate sin without Temple sacrifice: repentance and penitential prayer toward the temple.⁶⁵ For 1 Kings 8, penitential prayer will restore exiled Israel.

Summary

Solomon's prayer is incongruous to the occasion. The Temple's dedication ought to be a joyous celebration because it demonstrates God's faithfulness to his covenant with David in 2 Samuel 7. Although, its completion is a tremendous historical, political, and personal accomplishment for Solomon, his prayer focuses on what Israel should do when devastated by the covenantal curses. According to Solomon, national struggles and defeats are punishments for Israel's sins. For the deuteronomic historians, idolatry represents the climax of Israel's sin, and consequently God sends the ultimate punishment—exile. However, even if Israel's behavior results in exile, there is hope. 1 Kings 8 instructs the exilic readers how to write the next chapter in their own history, the chapter beyond the formal ending of 2 Kings.⁶⁶ If they repent and confess through prayer, God will deliver them. I Kings 8 marks a transition from Deuteronomy's ambiguous teaching about repentance to penitential prayer as the enactment of repentance. Thus, the author has explicated the meaning of repentance in Deuteronomy 4 and 30, and has given Israel a specific practice to enact that repentance.

---

⁶³See M. Noth, *Deuteronomistic History*, 89-95; H. G. Reventlow, *Gebet*, 270; G. Braulik, "Spüren einer Neubearbeitung des deuteronomistischen Geschichtswerkes," 20-33; J. Unterman, *From Repentance to Redemption*, 68-74.

⁶⁴P. R. Ackroyd, *Exile and Restoration*, 27.

⁶⁵M. Weinfeld, *Deuteronomy 1-11*, 40.

⁶⁶P. R. Ackroyd (*Exile and Restoration*, 80-81) argues that Jehoachin's release from prison and his putting "aside his prison clothes" makes 2 Kings end on a hopeful note.

Jeremiah 29:10-14

Deuteronomic language and ideology also influence the text of Jeremiah. In fact, like 1 Kings 8, Jer 29:10-14 interprets traditions associated with Deut 4:29-30 and 30:1-4 while showing no detectable influence from 1 Kings 8. While scholars dispute the authorship of this passage,[67] Jeremiah 29 attests that an author besides the deuteronomic historians believes that repentance and prayer are the solution to exile.[68]

Jeremiah's text is a letter that he writes from Jerusalem to the Babylonian exiles. In it, he predicts that the exile will last seventy years. The number seventy is simply a round number to indicate that the exile will be lengthy. Therefore, the people should not live as if they will soon return to Israel.

At the end of the seventy years, Jeremiah prophesies that the people will repent. This would initiate the restoration. His idea of repentance resembles the description of repentance in Deuteronomy 4.

Deut 4:29	Jer 29:13
From there *you will seek* YHWH your God, *and you will find* him *if you seek* [him] *with all your heart* and with all your soul.	And *you will seek* me *and you will find* me *if you seek me with all your heart*.
ובקשתם משם את־יהוה אלהיך ומצאת כי תדרשנו בכל־לבבך ובכל־נפשך	ובקשתם אתי ומצאתם כי תדרשני בכל־לבבכם

The comparison discloses that Jer 29:12 and Deut 4:29 share important terms. Both refer to Israel "seeking" (both the terms בקש and דרש appear) and "finding" (מצא) YHWH. Except for the change in person and the absence of the phrases "YHWH your God" and "with all your soul" in Jer 29:12, the texts are basically identical. Even the spelling of "heart" in Jeremiah 29 is the same as Deuteronomy 4. Since Jeremiah prefers לב,[69] literary dependency on Deuteronomy 4 may be possible.

---

[67]See W. L. Holladay, *Jeremiah 2*, 53-63. J. Unterman, *From Repentance to Redemption*, 63.

[68]G. von Rad (*Deuteronomy*, 50-51) and M. Weinfeld (*Deuteronomy 1-11*, 217) reach the same conclusion.

[69]W. L. Holladay, *Jeremiah 2*, 133.

Further, the prophet describes the restoration with key deuteronomic terms and ideas:

Deut 30:3-4	Jer 29:14
And YHWH your God *will restore your fortunes* and have mercy on you and turn, *and gather you from all the peoples among whom YHWH your God scattered you, even if you are scattered...*	And *I shall restore your fortunes* and *I shall gather you from all the nations and from all the places where I drove you,* says the Lord.

ושב יהוה אלהיך את־שבותך
ורחמך ושב
וקבצך מכל־העמים אשר הפיצך יהוה
אלהיך שמה: אם־יהוה נדחך...

ושבתי את־שביתכם
וקבצתי אתכם מכל־הגוים
ומכל־הקומות אשר הדחתי אתכם שם
נאם־יהוה...

Like 1 Kgs 8:48-49, Jer 29:12 refers to the people praying to God: "And you will call (קרא) on me and come, and pray (פלל) to me, and I will hear (שמע) you."

Summary

The author of Jeremiah 29 believes that repentance and prayer are the solution to exile. The author's language and ideas so closely resemble Deuteronomy that the author must have drawn on traditions closely associated with Deuteronomy 4 and 30. The uniqueness of Jeremiah's interpretation of these traditions is his prophecy that the exile would last seventy years. While the author must not have recognized the result of combining a temporal prediction with the condition of repentance, he has nevertheless created an ideological tension within the text. He has mixed prophetic determinism with deuteronomic ideology, a problem that arises again in Daniel 9.[70]

Penitential Prayer during the Restoration: Third Isaiah

Introduction

The people most closely associated with the authors responsible for Deuteronomy and the deuteronomic history undoubtedly believed that YHWH

---

[70]See Chapter Two.

had called Israel to repent and perform repentance through penitential prayer. They must have practiced these as well. But had repentance and prayer become a generally accepted religious institution in exilic Israel and the restored community? Third Isaiah attests to the importance of penitential prayer in the life of Israelites who are not associated with Deuteronomy and the deuteronomic history. Whereas the text's expressions about repentance and prayer parallel those in the deuteronomic tradition, they show no indication of direct dependence on that tradition.

Reinterpreting Second Isaiah

Isaiah 56-66 probably represents the work of several authors who wrote in Jerusalem around 520 BCE, during the rebuilding of Jerusalem's temple. The authors' opposition to the temple's reconstruction in Isa 66:1 supports this date.[71] In part, Third Isaiah reinterprets Isaianic traditions in order to understand the limited success of the restoration.[72] Anticipating Cyrus' triumph over Babylon, Second Isaiah had predicated that Cyrus would decree that Israel could return to the land. After a glorious return, the people would reconstruct a magnificent Temple. However, at the time of Third Isaiah, Second Isaiah's prophecies remain unfulfilled. In fact, the return in no way resembled the glory he depicted. The failure of these prophecies needed explanation. Thus, Third Isaiah wrestles with two basic questions: Why did the prophecies of Second Isaiah fail? What will change the nation's situation?

Although Second Isaiah begins with the declaration that Israel's exile has paid for its sins (Isa 40:1-2), his message concludes with a call to repentance:

---

[71]For issues related to dating and examples of those who date Third Isaiah to this time period, the problem of authorship, and the integrity of Isaiah 56-66, see P. D. Hanson, *The Dawn of Apocalyptic: The Historical and Sociological Roots of Jewish Apocalyptic Eschatology* (Philadelphia: Fortress, 1979) 32-46; K. Koch, *The Prophets*, vol. 2, 153-3; D. L. Petersen, *Late Israelite Prophecies: Studies in Deutero-Prophetic Literature and in Chronicles*, SBLMS (Missoula: Scholars Press, 1977) 23; C. Westermann, *Isaiah 40-66: A Commentary*, OTL (trans. D. M. G. Stalker; Philadelphia: Westminster, 1969) 295-308; E. Achtemeier, *The Community and Message of Isaiah 56-66: A Theological Commentary* (Minneapolis: Augsburg, 1982) 11-18.

[72]W. Zimmerli, "Zur Sprache Tritojesajas," in *Gottes Offenbarung* (München: Kaiser, 1963) 217-233; K. Koch, *The Prophets*, vol. 2, 152; D. L. Petersen, *Late Israelite Prophecy*, 23-27.

Isa 55:6-7

> *Seek* the Lord while he *may be found*,
>   *Call* on him in the day he is near.
> Let the wicked forsake his *way*,
>   And the evil man his *devices*
> Turn to the Lord and he will have mercy,
>   To our God for he abundantly forgives.

דרשו יהוה בהמצאו קראהו בהיותו קרוב:
יעזב רשע דרכו ואיש און מחשבתיו
ישב אל־יהוה וירחמהו ואל־אלהינו כי־ירבה
לסלוח:

Third Isaiah reworks this call to repentance in order to explain the failure of Second Isaiah's prophecies. Isa 65:1-2 pictures God complaining that he was ready for the people's repentance, but they refuse the offer:

> I *was ready to be sought* by those who did not ask for me,[73]
> I *was ready to be found* by those who did not *seek me*.
> I said, "Behold! Here I am!"
>   to a nation that did not *call* on my name,
> I held out my hands all day long
>   to a rebellious people,
> Who walk in *the way* that is not good,
>   after *their own devices*.

נדרשתי ללוא שאלו נמצאתי ללא בקשני
אמרתי הנני הנני אל־גוי לא־קרא בשמי
פרשתי ידי כל־היום אל־עם סורר
ההלכים הדרך לא־טוב אחר מחשבתיהם:

As the underlined words indicate, the author of Isaiah 65 draws his language from Isa 55:6-7. While, the metaphors "seek" (בקש and דרש) and "call" (קרא) are elastic in meaning, in these passages they have penitential overtones. Isaiah 55 uses these terms in conjunction with שוב, which leaves no doubt that they function as terms for repentance. Deuteronomy 4:29 and Jer 29:12-14 assemble a similar collection of metaphors in order to discuss repentance (see above). Thus, through this group of metaphors, Third Isaiah connects the dis-

---

[73]Reading with LXX, Syr, Targum.

appointing nature of the return to the people's refusal to accept Second Isaiah's call to repentance.

The "Servants"

While Third Isaiah thinks that Israel as a whole has rejected God's offer of forgiveness, Isaiah 65 claims that some in Israel have accepted it. The text designates these people as "servants." YHWH also addresses them as follows: "My people, who seek me" (לעמי אשר דרשוני)(65:10b). This designation itself suggests the "servants'" repentance. According to the author, the rest of the nation has forsaken YHWH and forgotten God's holy mountain (v. 11). In contrast, Deuteronomy maintains that the nation as a whole would repent. Third Isaiah distinguishes between groups in the restored community. This text has given up on the idea that the entire nation would repent and teaches that only the "servants" within Israel constitute the penitent. Consequently, YHWH limits his salvation to them. This explains vv. 8-9 and 13-15, which sharply contrast the futures of YHWH's "servants" and the wicked.[74] These "seekers" experience God's deliverance and blessings (cf. v. 10a). According to vv. 8-9, his "servants," here designated as a "cluster" within Israel, will find satisfaction and rejoice, while the opponents will suffer. The opponents will have their name used for a curse, while the "servants" receive a new name (v. 15). The author's description of the new era in vv. 17-25 borrows from Isaiah of Jerusalem (especially chap. 11) and Second Isaiah (Isa 42:9; 43:18-19; 48:6),[75] and may also intentionally reverse the curses in Deuteronomy 28.

Isaiah 57 also distinguishes between the righteous and the wicked and their corresponding rewards. In this passage, the penitents enjoy "healing" (v. 18) and "reviving" (v. 15). In other texts, the terms "to heal" (לרפא) and "to revive" (להחיות) are metaphors for salvation, and are also anticipated rewards for repentance. For example, in Hos 6:1-2, the people claim to be "turning" (שוב) to YHWH, i.e., "repenting", with the expectation that he will "heal" (ירפאנו) and "revive" (יחינו) them. In Jeremiah 14, because YHWH withholds healing because of the people's sins, the people mourn and pine away in distress. In their passionate plea, they question why there is no "healing" (רפא, twice in v. 19). Also reminiscent of Isaiah 57, where the wicked experience no peace, the people in Jeremiah hope for peace (v. 19). So, in Isaiah 57 the poet has employed traditional terms for salvation that frequently appear in peniten-

---

[74]G. W. E. Nickelsburg, "Eschatology (Early Jewish)" *ABD* vol. 2 (New York: Doubleday, 1994) 581.
[75]C. Westermann, *Isaiah*, 408.

tial contexts. He gives the traditional language his own twist when he makes the "servants" the beneficiaries of future divine blessings and the unrepentant Israelites the recipients of punishment. The wicked receive none of these blessings of salvation: "There is no peace, says my God, for the wicked" (Isa 57:21).

Perhaps Isa 59:20 best summarizes Third Isaiah's understanding of repentance and the "servants" that perform it: "He (i.e., God) comes to Zion as Redeemer, and for those who turn from transgression in Jacob, says the Lord" (cf. Isa 66:6-16). Those who believe the prophet's message claim a unique relationship with God that the rest of Israel did not enjoy. Penitence, then, in part separates the "servants" from the rest of Israel. Again, deliverance does not come to *all* of Israel, but to a defined *group within* Israel.

Temple Ideology

The "servants'" apparent opposition to the Temple's reconstruction may relate to their understanding of repentance. Unfortunately, the text is not clear about the reasons for this protest, and its occasional polemical language even further obscures the problem. The "servants" did not wholly despise the cult or formal religion.[76] For example, when the new era comes, the Gentiles come to Zion, which remains one of the text's primary interests, to offer sacrifices on the "holy mountain" (56:7). The sabbath is crucial in Third Isaiah (56:2-8). Still, in protest, the text appears to criticize those rebuilding the Temple:

> Heaven is my throne
>   and the earth is the footstool for my feet;
> What is this house that you are building for me,
>   and what is this resting place? (Isa 66:1).

The language and ideas recall 1 Kgs 8:27:

> But will God indeed dwell on the earth? Even heaven and the highest heaven cannot contain you, much less this house that I have built!

Clearly, both Third Isaiah and 1 Kings 8 are warning their readers against the vulgar notion that God literally lives in the Temple. However, Third Isaiah has something more in mind than this basic theological tenet. God's earthly dwelling place is not in a building, but with a group of people. As Isa 66:2 testifies:

---

[76]*Contra* P. D. Hanson, *The Dawn of Apocalyptic*, e.g., 161-186.

But this is the one to whom I will look,
To the poor and broken in spirit,
The one who trembles at my word (Isa 66:2b).

ואל־זה אביט אל־עני ונכה־רוח וחרד על־דברי

Isaiah 57:15 contains a similar assertion. God dwells in heaven *and* with a group of people:

Isa 57:15
For thus says the one high and lifted up,
    who dwells in eternity, and whose name is Holy,
I dwell in the high and holy place,
    and also with the crushed and humble in spirit;
to revive the spirit of the humble,
    and to revive the heart of the crushed (57:15).

כי כה אמר רם ונשא   שכן עד וקדוש שמו
מרום וקדוש אשכון   ואת־דכא ושפל־רוח
להחיות רוח שפלים   ולהחיות לב נדכאים

It is tempting to spiritualize the designations "poor" (עני) and "crushed" or "broken in spirit" (ואת־דכא ושפל־רוח in 57:15, and נכה־רוח[77] 66:2) in order to oppose inward spirituality to external rituals. The NRSV yields to this temptation, and, thus, adheres to the old Protestant tradition of lauding inward religion (faith) while dismissing any trace of the cult (works). However, the terms in this text have a sociological connotation and probably describe the "servants." Simply, the group experiences oppression and disenfranchisement (cf. Prov 34:18 [19]).[78] Isaiah 63:16 confirms this marginalizing of the "servants" as the author complains that the rest of Israel does not recognize them.

While the words "poor" and "broken spirit" do not depict a spiritual attitude, the phrase "those who tremble at his word" (החרדים אל־דברו), may have a penitential flavor. It shows up again in 66:5:

---

[77]The Qumran text reads ונכאי. *BHS* suggests ונכאה.

[78]I thank Professor Helen Goldstein for her observations about this problem in interpretation and in the NRSV. J. L. McKenzie (*Second Isaiah*, 161) calls them the "pious poor."

> Hear the word of the Lord,
> *those who tremble at his word.*
> Your people who hate you,
> and reject you because of my name's sake...

Ezra twice employs the same phrase in the penitential context of chapters 9-10 (Ezra 9:4 and 10:3). Those who "tremble" join Ezra in mourning, fasting, and confessing sin.[79] In Third Isaiah, the designation "those who tremble" (חרד) at least signifies those who hear the prophetic word and heed it. It probably implies penitence since an important component of this prophetic word is repentance.

Such statements about the temple and the importance of repentance lead to the conclusion that Third Isaiah teaches that the first step toward restoration is not rebuilding "the house," but penitence. For some groups in Israel, the rebuilding of the Temple is key to the restoration program. As noted, Second Isaiah predicted that Israel would return to the land and worship in a magnificent Temple. After the time of Third Isaiah, the prophet Haggai pushes for the Temple's speedy reconstruction. According to his ideology, the delay in the Temple's reconstruction has caused the post-exilic community's miserable state (Hag 1:9-11). The building's completion would mark the commencement of a splendid new era.[80] Third Isaiah's message may simply be one of hope in the midst of Israel's disappointment that the glorious Temple has not yet been built. If this is the case, Third Isaiah would be telling the people that they can make do without a Temple.[81] They simply need to repent. This repentance, in fact, will lead to the fulfillment of Second Isaiah's promises. Nevertheless, the author(s) of Isa 57:15 and 66:1 and 2b unambiguously insists that God favors "servants," not temple builders.

Penitential Poems in Third Isaiah

While it does not reject the cult or various legal requirements, Third Isaiah thrusts prayer into the foreground of Temple activities. In fact, in its future glory, the Temple will function as "a house of prayer" for all the nations

---

[79]J. Blenkinsopp, *A History of Prophecy in Ancient Israel* (Philadelphia: Westminster, 1983) 248-251. He argues that the group Ezra refers to is the prophetic group of Third Isaiah. While his hypothesis is attractive, more work must be done to determine if these groups are the same or if common penitential vocabulary and actions have developed in Israel.

[80]See P. D. Hanson, *The Dawn of Apocalyptic*, 175-176 and 240-262.

[81]Professor Jonathan Goldstein suggested this interpretation of Third Isaiah to me.

(56:7).[82] With Third Isaiah's emphasis on repentance and the Temple as a place of prayer, the presence of two texts that resemble penitential prayers is no surprise. These penitential poems reveal Third Isaiah's understanding of repentance, the function of confession, and display how the "servants'" particular ideas and world view influence the poems.

Isaiah 59:1-20

In regard to its logical, rhetorical, and literary consistency, this poetic text is a single literary unit.[83] The passage combines the forms of lament, prophetic pronouncement of judgment, and a salvation oracle.[84] Some scholars discern liturgical features in the text.[85] It divides into four sections according to content and shifts in personal pronouns. Vv. 1-3 answer an implied question: Why has God's salvation not come? Second person plural pronouns dominate the verses. Vv. 4-8 indict the people for their sin. The pronouns change to third person plural. Vv. 10-15b contain lament and confession. The pronouns switch to first person plural, which make the words originate from some group in Israel. The Divine Warrior brings retribution and recompense in vv. 15c-20.[86]

The passage opens with a prophetic response to an implied criticism that YHWH lacks the power to save:

---

[82]G. J. Polan's (*In the Ways of Justice Toward Salvation: A Rhetorical Analysis of Isaiah 56-66* [New York: Peter Lang, 1986] 73-74) rhetorical analysis has shown that the structure of this verse places the emphasis on the phrase "house of prayer" rather than the sacrifices. See also G. W. E. Nickelsburg (*Resurrection, Immortality*, 20-21) for a comparison of this idea with 1 Macc 7:37.

[83]G. J. Polan, *In the Ways of Justice*, 245-251; P. D. Hanson, *The Dawn of Apocalyptic*, 119-120; C. Westerman, *Isaiah*, 344; E. Achtemeier, *The Community and Message of Isaiah 56-66*, 63-64; J. Muilenburg, *Isaiah*, 686; J. Blenkinsopp, *A History of Prophecy in Israel*, 248; J. L. McKenzie, *Isaiah*, 171.

[84]P. D. Hanson, *The Dawn of Apocalyptic*, 119-120; C. Westerman, *Isaiah*, 344-345. Hanson asserts that Third Isaiah contains mixed genres. This, he claims, is a characteristic feature of post-exilic literature. See also P. D. Hanson, "Apocalyptic Literature," *HBMI*, 473.

[85]E.g., C. Westermann, *Isaiah 40-66*, 344; E. Achtemeier, *The Community and Message of Isaiah 56-66*, 64; J. Blenkinsopp, *A History of Prophecy in Israel*, 248.

[86]This division differs from G. J. Polan (*In the Ways of Justice Toward Salvation*, 252-257) and J. Muilenburg (*Isaiah*, 686-687), who also differ from one another. They divide the passage by poetic structure. My divisions are related more to person(s) speaking or addressed and the content. My outline more closely resembles P. D. Hanson, *The Dawn of Apocalyptic*, 119-120.

> Behold! The hand of YHWH is not too short to deliver,
> his ear is not too dull too hear (Isa 59:1).

הן לא־קצרה יד־יהוה מהושיע ולא־כבדה אזנו משמוע:

The text echoes a passage from Second Isaiah.

> When I came, why was there no one present?
> When I called, why did no one answer?
> Is my hand too short that it cannot redeem?
> Or do I have no power to deliver? (Isa 50:2)

מדוע באתי ואין איש   קראתי ואין עונה
הקצור קצרה ידי מפדות   ואם־אין־בי כח
להציל

Consistent with Isa 65:1-2, the poem has recast a tradition from Second Isaiah in order to address Israel's new problems. Still, Third Isaiah contains some basic differences. YHWH speaks in Second Isaiah. He asks his questions in amazement that no one has responded to his offer of deliverance. The prophet himself speaks in Third Isaiah. Third Isaiah employs the tradition to set up his criticism of Israel's behavior. That is, YHWH's apparent inactivity is the result of the people's sin. This "separates" (בדל) them from YHWH, and has caused him to "hide his face" (הסתירו פנים) (Isa 59:2).[87] The latter phrase in the Hebrew Bible depicts YHWH's apparent absence, especially when someone experiences a delay in deliverance.[88] While an innocent sufferer might use this metaphor, in this instance the metaphor signifies YHWH's punishment for the people's sins.

The author begins a long litany of the people's sins with another allusion to an Isaianic tradition:

Isa 59:3   Your hands are defiled with blood.
            כי כפיכם נגאלו בדם

Isa 1:15   Your hands are full of blood.
            ידיכם דמים מלאו

---

[87]This reading follows the LXX. This is the form in 63:9; 64:2; 64:6.

[88]See S. A. Balentine, *The Hidden God: The Hiding of the Face of God in the Old Testament* (Oxford: Oxford, 1983) for a full discussion of the metaphor in the Hebrew Bible and ancient Near Eastern texts. For more about Yahweh's absence, see S. Terrien, *The Elusive Presence: Toward a New Biblical Theology* (New York: Harper, 1978).

The description of the people's actions continues in vv. 4-8. Their crimes resemble the accusations against the wicked in laments. Like Third Isaiah, laments also constantly refer to the wicked with an ambiguous "they."[89] The verses are, therefore, stereotypical polemical descriptions of the wicked. Using such verses to identify and characterize the "servants'" opponents requires tremendous caution.

In vv. 9-15b, the people speak. The "therefore" in v. 9 shows that they have made an immediate connection between the vices catalogued in vv. 4-8 and the absence of YHWH's deliverance. Their initial statements use the language of lament. Vv. 9-10 play with the metaphors of light and darkness. Light represents salvation while darkness depicts their deplorable present state. Third Isaiah frequently uses light as a metaphor for salvation (58:8, 10; 60:1, 19-20; cf. 42:16). Second Isaiah also uses light in order to represent salvation. For example, Isa 51:4-5 closely relates God's justice (משפט), deliverance (צדק), salvation (ישע), and light (אור).

The image of groping about like those who are blind resembles one of Deuteronomy's curses: "You shall grope about at noon as blind people grope in the darkness, but you shall be unable to find your way..." (Deut 28:29). Since Third Isaiah contains curses that closely parallel Deuteronomy (Isa 62:8-9 and 65:21-23; cf. Deut 7:19; 28:30-33), perhaps the author takes this image from deuteronomic traditions.

The rhetoric in v. 11 remains true to lament. Laments often use the verb קוה, "to await," "to expect," or "to look for," followed by a desired status. Then the sufferer contrasts this hope to the actual, desperate, and persistent situation. The formula is as follows: "we wait for X, but..."

As the plural pronouns indicate, a group confesses its sins in vv. 12-13. While the voices are anonymous, the members of the "servants" are most likely the speakers (cf. v. 20):

---

[89]See P. D. Miller ("Trouble and Woe: Interpreting the Biblical Laments," *Int* 37 [1983] 32-45) for an insightful discussion about polemical complaints in laments and stereotypical language about the wicked. Cf. Pss 5:9; 7:14-16; 10:5-11; 14:4; 17:8-12; 35:11-12, 20-21; 36:1-4; 53:1-4; Jer 9:3-9; 14:10. The Song of Moses in Deuteronomy 32 speaks of Israel's sinful practices in a similar manner. Cf. also L. Johnson ("The New Testament's Anti-Jewish Slander and the Conventions of Ancient Polemic" *JBL* 108 [1989] 419-441) on how to read polemical texts.

For our transgressions are many before you,[90]
    and our iniquities we know,
Transgressing and acting deceptively against the Lord,
    turning away from our God.
Speaking oppression and apostasy[91]
        conceiving[92] and uttering lying words from the heart.

כי־רבו פשעינו נגדך וחטאותינו ענתה בנו
כי־פשעינו אתנו ועונתינו ידענום
פשע וכחש ביהוה ונסוג מאחר אלהינו
דבר־עשק וסרה הרו והגו מלב דברי־שקר:

Like Jer 14:7 and 1 Kgs 8:47, these verses contain multiple admissions of sin in order to produce an overall impression of the confessor's sincere contrition.[93] The confession in v. 13 in the form of an infinitive absolute conforms to the form of the indictment in v. 4.[94]

Immediately following the "servants'" confession of sin and plea of helplessness, the Divine Warrior rises to fight (vv. 15c-20).[95] Thus, the prophet directly links confession to the arrival of deliverance. YHWH himself brings the deliverance since there is no human to do it—neither a Davidic king (as in Isaiah of Jerusalem) nor Cyrus (as in Second Isaiah). This also contrasts to the notion that speedy reconstruction of the Temple will inaugurate a glorious era. According to Third Isaiah, salvation does not come through human efforts, but only by an act of God. Penitence serves as the program for the realization of divine promises.

Who is the Divine Warrior's enemy and whom is he redeeming? The Warrior himself declares whom he has come to redeem: "those who turn from transgression in Jacob" (ולשבי פשע ביעקב) (v. 20), i.e., the penitent. They

---

[90]Cf. W. L. Holladay (*Jeremiah* 1. 126 and 432), who argues that the particle כי has the force of "how." He translates a similar confession in Jer 14:7 as follows: "How great are our transgressions."

[91]J. Muilenburg (*Isaiah*, 693) suggests a metathesis here which changes עשק, "oppression," to עקש, "deceit."

[92]Missing in Isaiah Scroll from Qumran. J. Muilenburg (*Isaiah*, 693) proposes a dittography. However, one can better understand the Qumran Isaiah scroll as an example of haplography. Keeping הרו continues the double verb pattern in the text.

[93]*Contra* J. A. Thompson (*The Book of Jeremiah* [Grand Rapids: Eerdmans, 1980] 370-380) on Jer 14:7 who presses the meaning of each term.

[94]J. Muilenburg, *Isaiah*, 693.

[95]Cf. the Divine Warrior character with Exod 15:1-18; Deut 33:26-29; Jud 5:4-5; Ps 24:8; 68. For a discussion of the Divine Warrior myth, see F. M. Cross, *Canaanite Myth*, 91-111; P. D. Hanson, *The Dawn of Apocalyptic*, 124-130.

were those speaking in vv. 9-13. They heard the message of judgment from the anonymous prophetic voice and heeded it. Unlike some earlier texts in which the Divine Warrior rises to do battle, in Third Isaiah he comes not only to fight the nations that oppose Israel, but also to punish those *within* Israel who oppress the faithful penitents.[96] According to v. 15, those who are a part of this penitential group that "turn from evil" (סר מרע) are oppressed ("despoiled," משתולל), apparently by fellow Israelites. Their need for deliverance is obvious. Thus, the author has worked the division into his poem so that God punishes the oppressors.

Isaiah 63:7-64:12

Isa 63:7-64:12, another penitential piece, has several features similar to Isa 59:1-20: lament rhetoric,[97] the connection of the present predicament to the nation's sins, a confession, a division between the penitents and the rest of the nation, a request for God's direct intervention, and the arrival of the Divine Warrior. However, the two texts differ. Lament, although present in Isaiah 59, is more dominant in Isa 63:7-64:12. Further, Isa 63:7-64:12 imitates psalms that recount Israel's history, especially Psalms 44, 74, 78, 79, 105, 106, and 136.

The text is a unity and easily divides into units according to form and content: the history of Israel's salvation and rebellion (63:7-14); petition for God to see and request for a theophany (63:15-64:5b); confession of sin (64:4c-7); a final petition on behalf of the temple (64:8-12).[98]

The author creates a tension between past and present. He begins by directing the reader to the past: "I will recount the gracious deeds of YHWH" (חסדי יהוה אזכיר) (Isa 63:7; cf. Ps 71:16). Formerly, God was a savior and present with the people (vv. 8-9). Through his servant, Moses, he led the people from Egypt (v. 11),[99] and through the "divided waters" (v. 12). Divine security and peace dominated their existence (vv. 13b-14). These past gracious deeds, though, contrast to the nation's present dismal situation. The nation in

---

[96] P. D. Hanson, *The Dawn of Apocalyptic*, 125 and 130; E. Achtemeier, *The Community and Message of Isaiah 56-66*, 70.

[97] Cf. C. Westermann, "Struktur und Geschichte der Klage," 50.

[98] This outline follows J. Muilenburg, *Isaiah*, 729.

[99] The reference to Moses is missing in LXX mss. The MT should be emended to read עבדו as the NRSV does. Hanson argues for "(and) his people" by saying that this is the subject of what follows. However, the participle המעלם immediately follows and needs Moses as the antecedent. Emending עמו to עבדו would make משה appositional, thus making "Moses" the closest antecedent, and, therefore, grammatically smoother.

its rebellion (63:10) and sin has driven away God's presence. Or, in the metaphor of the text, God has "hidden his face" (64:7 [6]). Formerly, his presence, "face," had saved them (63:9).

The author structures his poem in this manner in order to instruct his audience that the nation's dismal situation results from sin. The author employs vivid literary pictures to depict the results of sin. The people are all unclean (64:6 [5]) and they fade like leaves that are then carried away by the wind of their iniquity (64:6 [5]).

As is the case in Isa 63:7-64:12, several psalms also recount God's past saving deeds: Pss 44:1-8 (especially vv. 1-3); 78:1-55; 105:12-42; 106:7-12; 136:10-22. While the primary event in these psalms is the Exodus, they also mention events from the wilderness wandering, the conquest, the period of the judges, and the early monarchy. Psalms 78 and 106, however, contrast God's faithfulness and saving acts to Israel's unfaithfulness. As it depicts this unfaithfulness, Psalm 78 uses deuteronomic language and themes in a manner reminiscent of the Song of Moses in Deuteronomy 32.[100] After some introductory lines, Psalm 106 begins its recollection of Israel's past with a confession of sin that resembles 1 Kgs 8:37:[101]

> Both we and our ancestors have sinned; we have committed iniquity; we have done wickedly (v. 6).

Situating it early in the psalm transforms the retelling of the nation's past into a confession of sin. Instead of retelling all God's saving deeds, the psalm focuses on the Exodus as the event that should have evoked Israel's faithfulness. Yet, the nation quickly forgets that event and perpetually disobeys.

The coupling of lament with confession of sin in Isa 63:7-64:12 generates a tension. Third Isaiah admits the sinfulness of the people (Isa 63:10; 64:5c-7 [4c-6]), yet questions why God does not intervene immediately:

> Where are your zeal and might?
> Where are your compassion and mercy (63:15c)?
>
> Do not be exceedingly angry, O YHWH,
> and do not remember iniquity forever (64:9 [8]).

---

[100] E.g., vv. 17-20, 30-31, 32, 40, 42, 56-57. R. J. Clifford, "In Zion and David A New Beginning: An Interpretation," *Traditions in Transformation: Turning Points in Biblical Faith* (eds. B. Halpren and J. D. Levenson; Winona Lake, IN: Eisenbrauns, 1981) 121-141.

[101] Cf. Jer 14:20.

> After all this, will you restrain yourself, O YHWH?
> Will you remain silent, and punish us so severely (64:12 [11])?

The author continues the plea for God's deliverance with the questions: "Where is the one who ..." Psalm 136 extensively employs this formula while describing God's past saving deeds and his work in creation. Such questions reveal an author's longing for God's deliverance as in the "good ole days."[102] This tension was impossible in Deuteronomy and 1 Kings 8.

Several other features of the text hope to coax God into action, thus bringing an end to the delay of salvation. Comparable to Ps 74:4-8 (especially v. 7), the author of Isa 63:7-64:12 reminds God of Zion's desolation and the violated, burned sanctuary (64:10-11; cf 63:18).[103] Further, he is their father (63:16), and they are his servants and the tribes of his heritage (63:7), and the petitioners are the work of God's hand (64:8 [7]). God's tardy response to the admission of sin has in part contributed to the anguish of the speaker and led him to introduce these other themes, which the author hopes will end Israel's problems.

The tension between admitting sins and questioning God about his delay in bringing forgiveness and salvation also surfaces in Psalm 79, Jeremiah 14, and Lamentations. In Psalm 79:8-9, the poet confesses both the sins of the ancestors and the present generation's sins. Yet, the author complains about the tardiness of God's deliverance and persistent anger: "How Long, O Lord? Will you be angry forever?" (v. 5). Lamentations yields the same tension. When Lam 3:40-43 calls the people to examine their ways, they respond by

---

[102]Psalm 44 speaks of God's past deliverances and pleads for God to rise up and defend Israel (vv. 23, 26). Unlike Isa 63:7-64:12, this psalmist petitions God to act because of the nation's innocence (vv. 17-19). He inquires how long this will continue until God acts:

> Arouse! Why do you sleep, O Lord?
> Awake, do not reject us forever!
> Why do you hide your face?
> Why do you forget our affliction and oppression (44:23-24 [24-25])?

Psalm 74 mourns the destruction of the Temple. The entrances and carvings were hacked with axes (vv. 5-6) and the sanctuary burned (v. 7). The poet asks:

> Why do you turn back your hand?
> Why do you restrain your hand in your bosom (v. 11)?

Like Psalm 44, Psalm 74 calls for God to "rise up" and bring salvation (v. 22). This psalm, as well, makes no reference to the people's sins.

[103] In contrast to Third Isaiah, Psalm 74 never mentions the people's sins.

confessing their transgressions and rebellion. Yet, the author of Lamentations still complains about the continuation of the nation's horrible condition. The themes of confession and complaint unite again to close the final chapter. This time the people recognize that they have incurred punishment because of the sins of the ancestors (v. 7).[104] The work concludes by inquiring of God why their problems continue:

> Why have you forgotten us completely?
> Why have you forsaken us for so many days?
> Return us to yourself, O YHWH, that we may be returned.
> Renew our days as of old,
> Unless you have completely rejected us,
> And are exceedingly angry with us (5:20-22).

The lament and confession in Jer 14:1-22 demonstrate the same kind of tensions as the people confess their sins and then question God's delay.

These examples illustrate that Third Isaiah is not alone in creating such a tension. While a modern reader may think that the authors are inconsistent, obviously ancient writers had no problem expressing both complaint and confession within the same text. The phenomenon may be analogous to the shifting between praise and complaint in several of the canonical psalms. Apparently, in ancient Israel nothing requires an author to stick with one mood throughout a poetic composition.

As in Isaiah 59, Isa 63:7-64:12 assumes that if the people repent and confess their sinful history, YHWH will come as Divine Warrior. In 63:10-14, the author alludes to the Divine Warrior's past appearances with the reference to YHWH's "glorious arm" marching with Moses. Another allusion arises in 63:15 when the author appeals for God to recover his "zeal" and "might." Of course, not every reference to "God's arm," "zeal," and "might" alludes to the Divine Warrior motif. The terms sometimes simply refer to YHWH's work in the Exodus. The Divine Warrior motif, though, certainly stands within Third Isaiah's literary repertoire, as the penitential poem in Isaiah 57 reveals. Further, the Divine Warrior's vengeance against Edom and Bozrah in 63:1-6 mentions the Warrior's arm that brings the victory (63:5). The author's unambiguous reference to the Divine Warrior in 64:1-3 confirms the allusions in 63:5 and 10-14. The deity's arrival means retribution on the prophetic group's adversaries. The author's images of quaking mountains and fire typically accompany the Divine Warrior theophanies and recall past moments of

---

[104]Cf. Jer 14:20.

deliverance.[105] The author hopes that God will come again in this way. However, most important for this investigation is the relationship between the advent of the Divine Warrior and confession of sin; confession, in part, leads to the arrival of the Divine Warrior and salvation.

Summary

Third Isaiah's reinterpretation of Second Isaiah places it squarely within the Isaianic traditions. The authors of Third Isaiah believe that Israel's historical circumstances demand such a reinterpretation because, although the people have returned to the land, they remain in a miserable condition. According to the authors, Israel's sin is the cause of the nation's troubles and explains the failure of Second Isaiah's prophecies.

For the "servants," penitence, and the confessional statements that are a part of this, not only function as a way to remove problems, but also stand as a line of social demarcation. Those who are penitent receive YHWH's salvation. Those who oppose them, stand outside the circle of YHWH's favor and, therefore, will incur his wrath. Penitence is also the key to Israel's destiny as it, not the Temple's rebuilding or the reinstitution of the cult (66:3), brings the arrival of the new era; penitence was *the program* for full restoration. That God responds to contrition receives further confirmation in the penitential confessions in Isa 59:1-20 and 63:7-64:12 as the Divine Warrior responds to confession, "to those in Jacob who turn from transgression" (59:20).

Penitential Prayers in the Later Persian Period:
Ezra-Nehemiah and 2 Chronicles

Introduction

The deuteronomic traditions and Third Isaiah reflect the importance of penitential prayer in the religion of exilic and early post-exilic Israel. Even so, the literature of this period contains no example of a penitential prayer. In 1 Kings 8, Solomon instructs the people to pray, but his prayer is not a penitential prayer; it supplies an ideology for penitential prayer. Jeremiah 29 predicts the people's future repentance and prayer; it is not itself a prayer. After reflecting upon the failure of Second Isaiah's prophesies, the authors of Third Isaiah direct their readers to repent. Furthermore, for these authors, penitents engage

---

[105]See Jud 5:4-5 and Ps 18:7-8; J. K. Kuntz, *The Self-Revelation of God*, 179-185.

in prayer. The poems in Third Isaiah include confessions of sin, yet the authors do not consciously cast the poems into the form of prayer.

Consequently, the first literary examples of penitential prayers within the deuteronomic tradition occur in Ezra-Nehemiah. However, situated within an already existent penitential prayer tradition, Ezra-Nehemiah displays a new literary form for the expression of penitence.

Ezra 9

Ezra's penitential prayer responds to his discovery of the Jews' perceived moral failure—they have intermarried.[106] According to Ezra, this is a sin that threatens the survival of the community and its reestablishment in the land; God's wrath will surely descend upon the community. This sin, then, becomes an obstacle for the community in its quest to restore normal life in Palestine. This obstacle fits well into Ezra-Nehemiah's plot, which turns on the community's struggles in overcoming continuous obstacles to rebuilding the temple, Jerusalem's walls, and generally reestablishing itself in the land. However, while the other threats originate from sources external to the Jewish community, this threat in chapter 9 is internal.

In the prayer itself, Ezra explains why such marriages are an offense to YHWH (vv. 10-12).[107] They violate a specific commandment. However, the Torah attests no such commandment. Instead, the author has woven together commands from Exod 34:11-17, Deut 7:1-3 and 23:4-9, and has combined them with the warnings in Leviticus 18 about the Canaanites' evil practices.[108] Even though the prophetic texts contain no such regulation about marriage, Ezra attributes this commandment about marriage to the prophets: "Because we have forsaken your commandments which you commanded by the hand of your servants the prophets..." (vv. 10-11).[109] The author would have no problem attributing a statute of Moses as a prophetic command because the Hebrew Bible considers Moses a prophet. However, "prophet" is plural in this instance. While it might include Moses, it does not refer exclusively to him. The author may also credit the prophets with this statement because the indictment of disobeying the prophetic voice has become a formulaic expression to

---

[106]See T. Eskenazi (*In an Age of Prose: A Literary Approach to Ezra-Nehemiah*, SBLMS 36 [Atlanta: Scholars, 1988] 62-70) for a discussion of the role of the peoples in Ezra.

[107]For the list of the people of the land, see Ezra 9:1.

[108]M. Fishbane (*Biblical Interpretation in Ancient Israel* [Oxford: Clarendon, 1985] 115-121) accounts for all the author's exegetical moves and principles at work in the interpretation. Cf. also Blenkinsopp, *A History of Prophecy in Israel*, 185.

[109]For a discussion of this formula, see my treatment of 2 Chronicles below.

summarize Israel's disobedience.[110] Whether done consciously or unconsciously, the prayer also elevates the prophetic voice to a level of authority similar to Torah.[111]

The prayer, then, testifies to a change in the kinds of sin that threaten the nation's survival and require penitential prayer. In Deuteronomy 4 and 30, the "quintessential sin" is idolatry, which Moses warns, if practiced, will lead to exile. Solomon's prayer in 1 Kings 8 is ambiguous when it refers to sin.[112] It does not distinguish any particular sin as more reprehensible than another. Apparently, any sin might bring punishment. Elsewhere in the deuteronomic history, however, the text warns that idolatry will bring both Israel's and Judah's ultimate destruction. Therefore, in 1 Kgs 9:6-9, when God instructs Solomon that forsaking the commandments and statutes brings punishment, idolatry probably remains the "quintessential sin." Further, the text identifies idolatry and refusal to listen to the prophetic call to repentance as the cause of Israel's fall to Assyria (2 Kgs 17:7-18). Judah never fully overcomes the damage that results from Manasseh's idolatry. In fact, the deuteronomic history attributes Judah's fall to Babylon to Manasseh's idolatry (2 Kgs 23:26-27).

At the time of the text of Ezra-Nehemiah, however, the category of sins that might lead to severe punishment from God seems to encompass more than idolatry; it now includes intermarriage. In fact, the category of dangerous sins may have been broadened to include any sin that violates the prophetic word, or, in the case of Ezra, any commandment that an author attributes to the prophets. The applications for penitential prayer are increasing. This kind of growth also suggests that penitential prayer among the Jews is growing in acceptance and practice.

Ezra's prayer and its context include a collection of words that appear in preistly literature. According to Ezra, the sin of intermarriage is a מעל (Ezra 9:2, 4; 10:6; 10:2 and 10 employ the verb form), and the verb to describe Ezra's prayer is "confess" (ידה). Later in the prayer, Ezra declares: "From the days of our ancestors to this day we have been in great *guilt* (אשמה)" (Ezr 9:7). In 10:10, he again announces the people's "guilt" (אשמה) and instructs them to "confess" (ידה) in v. 11. In Ezr 10:19, the guilty offer a "guilt

---

[110]See O. H. Steck (*Israel und das gewaltsame Geschick der Propheten*) for a thorough discussion of this theme in the Hebrew Bible, Second Temple Judaism, and the New Testament.

[111]H. G. M. Williamson, *Ezra, Nehemiah*, WBC (Waco: Word, 1985) 137.

[112]Cf. P. Miller, *They Cried to the Lord*, 246.

offering" (ויאשמם).¹¹³ Adding to all these priestly technical terms, the author has Ezra assume the role of *priest* while handling the problem. These priestly terms first occur together in the *'asham* offering in Leviticus 5, a tradition that has influenced Ezra 9.¹¹⁴

Excursus II: Confession in Leviticus

The most important Levitical texts for an investigation of penitential prayer and Ezra-Nehemiah are those that employ the term "to confess" (ידה) and discuss the procedures for the *'asham* offering. Milgrom's *Cult and Conscience* and commentary on Leviticus offer the most comprehensive and authoritative modern investigation of these texts. Because I find his interpretation of confession in priestly legal theory convincing, the discussion that follows heavily depends upon his logic and conclusions.

Milgrom consistently dates the origin of several priestly traditions, even the Day of Atonement, to pre-exilic Israel.¹¹⁵ He establishes the time of Hezekiah as a *terminus a quo*, and the exile as the *terminus ad quem*.¹¹⁶ Leviticus, then, contains the earliest use of the word "confess," ידה usually in the hithp. While it usually means "to thank" or "to praise" in the hiph., it can mean "confess" in that form as well.¹¹⁷ Conversely, one can translate it "praise" in the hithp.¹¹⁸ The noun from the same root is rendered "thanksgiving" or "praise."¹¹⁹ The LXX translates the verb with a form of ἐξαγορεύω, which means "to declare." The term ידה occurs in three contexts in Leviticus: in the discussion of the *'asham* offering in Leviticus 5; in the Day of Atonement ceremony (Leviticus 16); and, finally, in Leviticus' version of the reason for the exile and method for restoration (Leviticus 26).

Leviticus 5

The *'asham* sacrifice is for a deliberate sin, a מעל.¹²⁰ According to the text, the Law requires confession for deliberate, not unintentional, sin.¹²¹ When a person "feels guilt" (אשם), the person should "confess" (ידה) the guilt (Lev 5:5).¹²² As v. 6

---

¹¹³This reading requires emending the text from ואשמים, "the guilty ones," to "their guilt offering," ואשמם.

¹¹⁴For more discussion, see J. Milgrom, *Cult and Conscience: The Asham and the Priestly Doctrine of Repentance* (Leiden: Brill, 1976) 71-73.

¹¹⁵J. Milgrom, *Leviticus 1-16, AB* 3, (New York: Doubleday, 1991) 13-35, 1070-1071.

¹¹⁶Ibid., 27.

¹¹⁷Ibid., 301; cf. Ps 32:5; Prov 28:13.

¹¹⁸Cf. 2 Chr 30:22. J. Milgrom, *Leviticus 1-16*, 301.

¹¹⁹F. Brown, S. R. Driver, and C. A. Briggs, *A Hebrew English Lexicon of the Old Testament* (Oxford: Clarendon, 1979) 392-393.

¹²⁰J. Milgrom, *Leviticus*, 50, 301.

¹²¹Ibid., 301, 1042.

¹²²For a discussion of the meaning of the verb אשם, see Milgrom, *Cult and Conscience*, 1-12; *Leviticus 1-16*, 5, 339-345.

clearly states, the penitent confesses *before* going to the sanctuary,[123] and then travels to the sanctuary to present an offering to the priest.[124] From his analysis, Milgrom concludes the following about the function of confession in Leviticus 5: "Confession is the legal device fashioned by the Priestly legislators to convert deliberate sin into inadvertencies, thereby qualifying them for sacrificial expiation."[125]

Leviticus 16

Milgrom persuasively argues for the same interpretation of the confession over the scapegoat on the Day of Atonement in Leviticus 16. The Priestly legislator means nothing magical in the use of the confession. Rather, confession in the rite functions judicially "to reduce the gravity of a nonexpiable wanton sin to an inadvertency expiable by sacrifice."[126] The high priest's confession with his hands on the goat transfers the sins of the people to the goat.[127] Leviticus 16 does not record the confession, but it does instruct the priest to confess the people's "iniquities" (עונת), "transgressions" (פשעים), and "sins" (חטאת)(v. 21).

Leviticus 26

Leviticus 26 parallels Deuteronomy 28-30. Both teach that obedience results in blessings, while disobedience brings curses, even though they differ in the nature of the curses, literary refrains, and typological numbers.[128] Leviticus 26 also pays special attention to the land enjoying its sabbaths while Israel is in exile. Once the people's sins have activated the curses and God has scattered them among the nations, they must "confess" (ידה) their "iniquity" (בעינת) (vv. 39-40) and demonstrate that their "uncircumcised heart is humbled" (יכנע לבבם הערל) (v. 41).[129] Their confession and humility cause God to remember the covenant with Abraham, Isaac, and Jacob, and the land. Then restoration comes. Thus, without the Temple and its sacrificial cult for removing sin, confession must serve a double function.[130] It now provides both the legal means to reduce the nation's prolonged intentional sins to inadvertencies and a method to *remove* them!

Whatever theological, ideological, and linguistic differences exist between the priestly legislation and the deuteronomic traditions, the two still share a few important ideas. One way to deal with the sin that caused the exile is to repent, (שוב

---

[123]J. Milgrom, *Leviticus*, 302.
[124]Ibid. Milgrom maintains that Num 5:7 prescribes the same actions.
[125]Ibid., 301-302.
[126]Ibid., 1042.
[127]Ibid.
[128]M. Weinfeld, *Deuteronomy 1-11*, 35.
[129]Cf. the discussion below on 2 Chronicles' penchant for the term "to humble" (כנע). Cf. Neh 1:5 below.
[130]Cf. J. Milgrom, *Leviticus*, 301.

in Deuteronomy and אשם in Leviticus), and pray or confess sin, (פלל in 1 Kings 8 and ידה in Leviticus).[131]

Although "confession" arose as a technical term in the priestly literature in connection with the *'asham* offering to reduce a deliberate sin, a מעל, to an inadvertency, it eventually separated from those practices. This separation began even in the priestly literature itself, as Leviticus 26 shows. Now, Israel must confess in order to remove the sin that precipitates the exile and to prompt the people's return. Thus, penitential prayers can be called "confessions" apart from the *'asham*.

Several acts of contrition precede Ezra's prayer. He tears his clothes, pulls out his hair and beard, fasts, and sits "appalled" until the evening sacrifice (Ezra 9:3-5). Elsewhere these actions accompany mourning over a death or anticipate impending doom. The acts here may portray Ezra's feeling that either God's certain judgment makes the people as good as dead, or that their moral failure is a death of sorts. The actions at least display Ezra's shock, contrition, and consternation. Similar deeds occur in other penitential contexts: Neh 1:4; 9:2; 2 Chron 34:27; Jon 3:5-8; and Joel 2:12-13. In Joel, for example, the prophet calls the people to respond to the locust plague with repentance, which they should manifest outwardly through fasting, weeping, and mourning. However, he transforms the practice of rending clothes into an internal act of tearing one's heart (Joel 2:13).[132] Joel's internalization of part of this act assumes the reader's familiarity with penitential practices. The connection of rituals to penitential prayer in Ezra points to the institutionalization of the prayers.

Ezra falls on his knees and stretches out his hands when he prays (cf. 1 Kgs 8:22). The prayer begins with a reference to the people's shame: "And I said, 'I am ashamed (בשתי), O my God, and I am humiliated (ונכלמתי)'" (v. 6). "Shame" (בש) in Hebrew can connote more than just the idea of embarrassment. It occurs in judgment contexts in order to indicate the humiliation related to being caught in a crime.[133] For example, Jer 2:26 depicts a thief's "shame" when caught, and then claims that this is analogous to Israel being caught in its sins. Jer 3:25 also combines terms like those in Ezr 9:6-7:

> Let us lie down in our *shame* (בבשתנו)! May our *humiliation* (כלמתנו) cover us! For we have sinned against YHWH our God, we and our ancestors *from our youth to this day* (מנעורינו ועד־היום הזה), and we did not obey the voice of the Lord our God (Jer 3:25).[134]

---

[131]Ibid., 375-376.
[132]For more discussion on this, see E. Lipinski, *La liturgie pénitentielle*, 11-25.
[133]G. W. E. Nickelsburg, *Resurrection, Immortality*, 12-13.
[134]W. L. Holladay (*Jeremiah* 1, 125-126) suggests that the text in Jeremiah contains a subtle condemnation of the Baal cult.

Like Jer 3:25, Ezra claims that the people's sins have persisted from the days of the ancestors until the present moment (Ezra 9:7). In Jeremiah's intercessory confession in chapter 14, the people also announce their shame (Jer 14:3). Ezr 9:6-7, then, has incorporated this judgment material. The people feel shame because God has caught them in their deeds.

Ezra's primary concern is that the intermarriage will jeopardize the nation's already precarious existence. Similar to Third Isaiah, the prayer maintains that Israel has experienced only a partial restoration, not the restoration that the prophets promised. For this reason, Ezra refers to the people as a "remnant," an idea that several prophets employ.[135] The term generally possesses a negative connotation since it implies a punishment so severe that only few survive. Here, however, the remnant has a double meaning. First, it ironically demonstrates YHWH's graciousness (v. 8), for he could have utterly destroyed the people (v. 13).[136] Thus, it is a reason for hope. Conversely, the self-designation as remnant generates a tone of despair in the prayer because it also pictures the people as close to complete annihilation. A sin like the one of which they are now guilty threatens to wipe out what remains of them. The remnant image also reminds the people that God continues to punish them for their sinfulness. This new sin of intermarriage will certainly not improve their situation; it can only make life worse.

Besides the partial optimism in the remnant image, Ezra employs other ideas to communicate his optimism. He considers the partial restoration as a demonstration of God's favor (v. 8). As the metaphors in vv. 8-9 picture, they have started regaining their hold on the homeland and Jerusalem. They have a "tent peg" in the land, a metaphor which probably means "to have a hold."[137] The reference to the "wall" (גדר) in v. 9 is another image for the partial restoration, and does not refer to Nehemiah's wall.[138] Their eyes are brighter (להאיר עינינו) (v. 8), a phrase that the Hebrew Bible uses to speak of recovery from weakness caused by lack of nourishment (1 Sam 14:27), illness (Ps 38:10), or escaping death (Ps 13:4).[139] God has given them a "reviving"

---

[135]For an engaging study of the idea of remnant as the resolution of the dialectic between catastrophic disaster and possible salvation, see R. P. Carroll, *When Prophecy Failed: Cognitive Dissonance in the Prophetic Traditions of the Old Testament* (New York: Seabury, 1979) 24-29.

[136]Cf. H. G. M. Williamson, *Ezra, Nehemiah*, 135.

[137]Ibid.; J. Blenkinsopp, *A History of Prophecy*, 183.

[138]H. G. M. Williamson, *Ezra and Nehemiah* (Sheffield: JSOT, 1987) 60; *Ezra, Nehemiah*, 136; J. Blenkinsopp, *A History of Prophecy*, 184. The usual word for a city wall is חומה.

[139]H. G. M. Williamson, *Ezra, Nehemiah*, 136.

(לתת־לנו מחיה) (v. 9). This language resembles God's expected response in prior penitential settings like Hos 6:2 ("He will revive us") (יחינו) and his promises in Third Isaiah that he "revives" (להחית) the oppressed, who are also the penitent.[140] In Ezra, however, the people have experienced only a partial (מעט) (v. 8) reviving since they remain "slaves" (עבדים) to a foreign ruler (v. 9). So, the tension between hope and despair influences this metaphor as well.

Combining this reviving language with Ezra's mourning practices produces rich life/death images. These nicely correspond to the blessings/curses of the covenant.[141] According to Deuteronomy, if Israel obeys the law, it will experience "blessing and life." However, if it disobeys God's commandments, then it will encounter "curses and death." Moses summarizes this either/or as follows: "See, today I set before you life (החיים) and good, death (המות) and evil" (Deut 30:15).

The punishments in Ezra 9:7 recall several curses from Deuteronomy. Ezra's notion that the people are slaves alludes to Deut 28:48 where service to a foreign ruler is part of the covenantal curses. With more allusions to Deuteronomy 28, Ezra states that the people and their leaders experience sword (cf. Deut 28:22), captivity (cf. Deut 28:41), and plundering (cf. Deut 28:47-52). With the author's knowledge of the deuteronomic traditions, he must have believed that the curses were still in effect and were the punishment for the nation's sins. These ideas also lie behind the declaration of God's righteousness: "O YHWH, God of Israel, you are righteous" (צדיק אתה)(v. 15). This pronouncement, which von Rad calls a *Gerichtsdoxologie*, comes from the deuteronomic idea that punishment justly came because of sin.[142] With the acknowledgment, Ezra submits to God's judgment with hope that such deference will secure and protect Israel's modest restoration. Only implicitly does the prayer hope for complete restoration. This tension between hope and despair is perhaps the prayer's most dominant feature.[143]

Summary

The prayer in Ezra 9 borrows from many traditions: the *'asham* in Leviticus 5, the rejected prophetic message in the deuteronomic histories and other circles,

---

[140]Cf. also Pss 71:20 and 85:6; M. Weinfeld, *Deuteronomy 1-11*, 220.

[141]I am indebted to Professor G. W. E. Nickelsburg for suggesting this correspondence between Ezra 9 and the covenantal blessings and curses.

[142]See also P. Miller, *They Cried to the Lord*, 252-253.

[143]For this tension in post-exilic literature, see O. H. Steck, "Das Problem theologischer Strömungen in nachexilischer Zeit," *Ev Th* 28 (1968), 445-458, esp. 454-455.

legal material from Deuteronomy 7, 23, and Leviticus 18, the curses in Deuteronomy 28, and Jeremiah's language of shame and remnant. Joining the prayer to a commandment requiring endogamy, which is an entirely new commandment that results from the combined interpretation of several traditions, the prayer in its context teaches the people the word of the prophet and challenges them to obey it. Thus, the prayer has a didactic or hortative function.

All those who recognize the correctness and seriousness of Ezra's interpretation are in the group of "those who tremble" (חרד) at God's commandments (9:4, 10:3; cf. 10:9). These people hold to Ezra's interpretation of the Law, and believe that the correct response to the situation is penitence and dissolution of the marriages.[144]

Nehemiah 1:4-11

Nehemiah's penitential prayer is his repsonse to news from Jerusalem about the city's condition. Like Ezra's reaction to the news of mixed marriages, Nehemiah sits down, weeps, mourns, fasts, and prays (v. 4). However, perhaps as part of his ostentatious character, Nehemiah continues this activity for days.[145]

The scene has the following outline: Nehemiah's initial response to the news (v. 4); appeal to YHWH to hear the prayer (vv. 5-6); confession of sins (v. 7); reference to Deuteronomy's promises (vv. 8-9); and a final request for national and personal success (vv. 10-11).

---

[144]Cf. Isa 66:2: "Those who tremble (חרד) at my word." J. Blenkinsopp (*A History of Prophecy*, 248-251) holds that the "quakers" (his designation) in Third Isaiah are the same people as those mentioned in Ezra; Ezra found his support among the prophetic eschatological group of Third Isaiah. Although Blenkinsopp's hypothesis is suggestive, it suffers from a lack of evidence and from some serious tensions between the two texts. First, Third Isaiah has a more universalistic perspective in regard to other nations. It is difficult to think that the group would support Ezra's hard line about intermarriage. Second, Third Isaiah clearly argues that the new era will come at God's initiative. Would such a group have approved of Persian sponsorship in the temple's reconstruction? Thus, the text's shared designation, "those who tremble," only indicates that in post-exilic Israel this word described groups that one could, in part, identify by their penitence.

[145]For further characterization of Nehemiah see T. Eskenazi, *In an Age of Prose*, 144-152. She contends that although Nehemiah might initially appear pious like Ezra, the comparison ends there. Nehemiah is a foil. She argues that he consistently "exaggerates his own importance" (145) and proposes that the prayer in 1:4-11, especially v. 11, reveals this tendency in his character.

The prayer's opening words immediately root the prayer in deuteronomic traditions. YHWH is the one "who keeps the covenant and shows steadfast love[146] to those who love him and keep his commandments" (שמר הברית וחסד לאהביו ולשמרי מצותיו). With these words, the author has Deut 7:9 in mind: "... The one who keeps the covenant and shows steadfast love to those who love him and who keep his commandments..." (שמר הברית והחסד לאהביו ולשמרי מצותו). His description of YHWH as the "great and awesome God" (האל הגדול והנורא) derives from Deut 7:21: "... great and awesome God" (אל גדול ונורא)(cf. Neh 9:32).

Nehemiah's pleas for God to hear his prayer in vv. 6 and 11 resemble Solomon's prayer in 1 Kings 8:

Neh 1:6	1 Kgs 8:28
Let your ear be attentive and your eyes[147] be opened to hearken to the prayer of your servant that I am praying before you day and night...	Turn to the prayer of your servant and to his supplications, O YHWH, my God, to hearken to the cry and the prayer that your servant is praying before you today.
תהי נא אזנך־קשבת ועיניך פתוחות לשמע אל־תפלת עבדך	ופנית אל־תפלת עבדך ואל־תחנתו יהוה אלהי לשמע אל־הרנה ואל־התפלה אשר עבדך מתפלל לפניך היום
Neh 1:11	1 Kgs 8:52
O YHWH, let your ear be attentive to the prayer of your servant, and to the prayer of your servants...	Let your eyes be open to the supplications of your servant and to the supplications of your people, Israel, to hearken to them whenever they call to you.
אנא אדני תהי נא אזנך־קשבת אל־תפלת עבדך ואל־תפלת עבדיך	להיות עיניך פתחות אל־תחנת עבדך ואל־תחנת עמך ישראל לשמע אליהם בכל קראם אליך

Deuteronomic language abounds in vv. 7-9. The people have not kept YHWH's "commands," "statutes," and "ordinances." This trio appears in Deut 5:31; 6:1; 7:11; and 26:17. Nehemiah then introduces a "word" from Moses which recalls YHWH's warning that the people will encounter exile if they are unfaithful. The word "to be treacherous" (מעל) (v. 8), occurs in Lev

---

[146]The word חסד has proved to be an extremely problematic term. For a summary of its meanings, see H.-J. Zoebel, חסד, *TDOT*, vol. 5, 44-64.

[147]Reading the plural with the LXX.

5:15, 21; 26:40; Num 5:6, 12; and Ezr 9:2, 4; 10:6.[148] Except for this term, the rest of vv. 8-9 is vintage Deuteronomy. The verses, in fact, contain a composite of Deuteronomy 4:27 and 30:2 and 4.

Neh 1:8	Deut 4:27
And I will scatter you among the people...	And YHWH will scatter you among the people...
אני אפיץ אתכם בעמים	והפיץ יהוה אתכם בעמים

Neh 1:9	Deut 30:2
But if you return to me, and keep my commandments...	And you will turn to YHWH your God and obey his voice according to all that I have commanded you today...
ושבתם אלי ושמרתם מצותי	ושבת עד־יהוה אלהיך ושמעת בקלו ככל אשר־אנכי מצוך היום

Neh 1:9	Deut 30:4
And even if you have been driven to the ends of the heavens, from there I will gather them.	Even if you are driven to the ends of the heavens, from there YHWH your God will gather you...
אם־יהיה נדחכם בקצה השמים משם אקבצם	אם־יהוה נדחך בקצה השמים משם יקבצך...

The reference in v. 9 to the place where God makes his name dwell matches the ideology and phraseology of Deuteronomy 12 and 1 Kings 8.[149]

Near the close of the prayer, Nehemiah alludes to the Exodus: "They are your servants and your people whom you ransomed by your great strength and strong hand" (והם עבדיך ועמך אשר פדית בכחך הגדול ובידך החזקה) (v. 10). Penitential prayers frequently recall the Exodus in order remind YHWH of his unique relationship with Israel. Nehemiah hopes that this reference to the event and to the relationship that it establishes between YHWH and Israel might move YHWH to turn back his wrath.

Besides his use of deuteronomic language and ideas, the author also places himself in line with an important facet of Deuteronomy's ideology. He

---

[148]Ezra 10:2 and 10 use the verb form. The term is popular in 1 and 2 Chronicles (1 Chron 2:7; 5:25; 10:13; 2 Chron 12:2; 26:16, 18; 28:19, 22; 29:6; 30:7; 36:14). It is used only once in Deuteronomy (Deut 32:51).

[149]Deut 12:21; cf. 12:5, 11, 26; and 1 Kgs 8:26.

believes that the people remain in exile and Jerusalem continues to suffer because of the nation's sin. Further, like 1 Kings 8, the author presumes that the proper response to the situation includes repentance and a penitential prayer. However, the prayer's deuteronomic material is somewhat incongruous to Nehemiah's situation. Deuteronomy's words, which the author quotes in Neh 1:8-9, have to some extent been fulfilled. God has gathered some of the people and returned them to the land. Apparently, for the author, the complete restoration has not occurred and this leaves Deuteronomy unfulfilled. Israel remains under foreign rule and Jerusalem's walls lie in ruins. Those who escaped the captivity "are in great trouble and shame" (v. 3). Thus, like Third Isaiah and Ezra 9, Nehemiah 1 wrestles with old traditions in order to explain the incompleteness of the restoration. For an author who accepts the basic tenets of deuteronomic ideology, the miserable conditions linger because of sin.

Summary

Nehemiah's prayer has three functions. First, it is an appeal to YHWH on behalf of the people in Jerusalem who remain in desperate straits. Second, it serves as preparation for Nehemiah's appeal to Artaxerxes I. Third, as the first direct speech from Nehemiah's mouth, the prayer witnesses to Nehemiah's piety. Using penitential prayer for narrative characterization suggests that some members of the post-exilic community are quite familiar with the practice. That is, perhaps both the author and his readers recognize that penitential prayer possesses literary value for characterization. Beginning in the post-exilic period, it was a growing trend to present the righteous person as, among other things, a penitent.[150]

Nehemiah 9

According to the scene in Nehemiah 9, a penitential prayer occurs within a solemn assembly that convenes on the twenty-fourth of the month of Tishri, two days after the end of the Feast of Tabernacles.[151] Although the author wants the reader to relate the prayer to the feast, the setting does not directly influence the content of the prayer. The scene also situates the prayer between the reading of the law (8:1-12, 18) and the people's recommitment to keeping

---

[150] The deuteronomic history also tends to depict a righteous king as one who prays. See S. Balentine, *Prayer in the Hebrew Bible*, 56-64.

[151] H. G. M. Williamson, *Ezra, Nehemiah*, 308.

its ordinances (10:28-39). This literary context proves more important than the setting of the Feast of Tabernacles. The combination of these four practices—reading the law, interpreting it, penitential prayer, and promise of obedience—continues into Second Temple Judaism. While a connection between interpretation and prayer is surely implicit in Ezra 9 as well, Nehemiah 9-10 more clearly relates the two.

Following the LXX, the *NRSV* credits the prayer to Ezra. However, the MT omits the reference to Ezra. Good reasons exist for following the MT and omitting, "And Ezra said."[152] When one omits the phrase, the Levites become the ones who offer the prayer (9:5). The people don sackcloth, engage in fasting, and cover their heads with dirt.[153] Israel offers the prayer after it has separated (בדל) itself from the foreigners (9:2; cf. Ezra 10:11).

Beginning with an acknowledgement of God as creator, the prayer recounts scenes and events from the life of Abraham, the time in Egypt, the Exodus, the convocation at Sinai, the golden calf episode, the wilderness wanderings, the conquest, and the period of the judges. Meyers has made a full list of the prayer's overwhelming number of allusions to biblical traditions.[154] Like several psalms, especially Psalm 106, passages in Third Isaiah, and Deuteronomy 32, the prayer becomes a retelling of Israel's past as a history of sin. The historical retelling depicts the people continuously responding to God in typical deuteronomic style: they are insolent (הזידו) (vv. 16 and 29, cf. Deut 10:16) and rebel and stiffen their necks (ויקשו את־ערפם) (vv. 16, 17, and 29; cf. Deut 9:6, 13). The accusation that the people killed the prophets and rejected their message of warning is another deuteronomic theme (vv. 26 and 30).[155] Despite their deeds, God was always gracious and merciful to them (vv. 17, 19, and 31), slow to anger, and abounding in love (v. 17; cf. Deut 7:9). Whenever God saw their "distress" (עני in v. 9 and צריהם in v. 27), and heard their "cry" (צעק) (vv. 27 and 28), he came to their rescue with saviors. These aspects of the prayer also indicate that the author has structured it according to the sin—punishment—repentance—salvation cycle, which is most prominent in Judges. Vv. 26-31 repeats this cycle three times, but in the third repetition, it breaks off when God hands the people over to their enemies, and they go off to exile. He does not mention their return (v. 30).

The reason for constructing a retelling of Israel's history that contains the tension between Israel's persistent rebellion and God's graciousness to for-

---

[152]See T. Eskenazi, *In an Age of Prose*, 143.
[153]Ezra 9:3; Neh 1:4; cf Joel 1:8, 13, and 14.
[154]J. M. Myers, *Ezra-Nehemiah*, AB 14 (Garden City: Doubleday, 1965) 167-169.
[155]Cf. 2 Kgs 17:13-14; 2 Chr 36:15-16; Jer 2:30; Ezra 9:11.

give comes in v. 32. The author is trying to establish a correlation between the community's present situation and Israel of the past. He leaps from the past generations to the present community with ועתה, a frequent rhetorical formula in penitential prayers that moves the prayer to the suppliants present problems and the petitionary section. The author implores YHWH to recognize that the community is once again *in distress*: "... do not consider our hardship insignificant" (אל־ימעט לפניך את־כל־התלאה) (v. 32). The prayer's final words carry the same theme: "We are in great distress" (ובצרה גדולה אנחנו) (v. 37). While Israel encountered "distress" in the past, this theme also frames the portion of the prayer that deals with the post-exilic community.[156] Besides this, the prelude to the prayer even has the Levites "crying out in a great voice" (ויזעקו בקול גדול)(v. 4), which may signify the people's pain and not simply function as a reference to the Levites' vigorous performance.[157]

Foreign domination causes the distress. Like Ezra 9:8-9, the people are slaves in their own land. The gift of the land that the ancestors enjoyed (vv. 23-25) including its produce, is now controlled by foreign kings. No matter how beneficent Ezra-Nehemiah depicts the Persian kings to be—and they are beneficent in Ezra-Nehemiah!—their control over Israel signifies in deuteronomic ideology that the people remain sinners (vv. 36-37, especially 37!). Even though the prayer mentions no specific sins, according to deuteronomic ideology, foreign domination indicates that sin exists among the people. Thus, the situation demands their confession of sin and recognition that God is righteous in the punishment he has brought upon them (*Gerichtsdoxologie*)(v. 33).

Summary

The argument that Israel's past correlates to its present dominates the logic of Nehemiah 9. Just as YHWH came to the ancestors when they were in distress and cried out, even though they were sinful, he should now deliver the post-exilic people from their distress. With their confession, the people seek to break the cycle that has plagued Israel from its earliest days. To demonstrate their sincerity, the people pledge obedience to the law.[158] The scene presents an ideal Israel—joined in reading and studying Torah, praying penitential

---

[156]Although my conclusions closely resemble H. G. M. Williamson (*Ezra, Nehemiah*, 300-319), I arrived at them independently.

[157]H. G. M. Williamson, *Ezra, Nehemiah*, 311.

[158]J. Blenkinsopp (*A History of Prophecy*, 188 and 312) discusses pledges to keep specific legal regulations.

prayers, and obedience. How can God resist their cry for deliverance from their overlords?

2 Chronicles

Another text from the late Persian period contains data about penitential prayer—2 Chronicles. Of course, 2 Chronicles recasts the material from the deuteronomic history, including the passages that relate to penitential prayer. It also introduces several penitential ideas into the deuteronomic penitential traditions. The discussion that follows examines the penitential texts in 2 Chronicles in order to indicate how it recasts the tradition. Both deletions from and additions to the deuteronomic history reveal the tendencies of the author of 2 Chronicles.

Until recently, critical scholars generally believed that Ezra-Nehemiah and 1 and 2 Chronicles had a common author,[159] which they labelled as "the Chronicler." Recent scholarship, though, has overturned this old position. T. Eskenazi, who has succinctly summarized the issues related to this critical problem,[160] demonstrates through literary analysis that most of the former "alleged hallmarks" of 1 and 2 Chronicles are missing in Ezra-Nehemiah.[161] In the end, Ezra-Nehemiah espouses a very different ideology from 1 and 2 Chronicles. In fact, occasionally the two works even stand in direct opposition to one another.[162] She concludes that the works are similar because they originate in approximately the same era and draw from similar traditions.

In regard to the date of 1 and 2 Chronicles, their placement after Ezra-Nehemiah in the Hebrew Bible suggests that the editors of the Bible believe that Ezra-Nehemiah is older. Further, recent arguments have established with some probability that 2 Chronicles' ending depends on Ezra rather than *vice versa*.[163] Ezra-Nehemiah's date depends on the date of Ezra's return and several other historical factors.[164] A date sometime after 400 BCE is most likely.[165] 2 Chronicles, then, originates after Ezra-Nehemiah, near the close of the Persian period.

---

[159]See S. J. De Vries (*1 and 2 Chronicles*, FOTL 11 [Grand Rapids: Eerdmans, 1989] 7-8) for a listing of dates in the secondary literature.

[160]T. Eskenazi, *In an Age of Prose*, 11-36. Cf also S. J. De Vries, *1 and 2 Chronicles*, 7-12; P. R. Ackroyd, "The Historical Literature" *HBMI*, 305-308.

[161]T. Eskenazi, *In an Age of Prose*, 33.

[162]E.g., on mixed marriages. See ibid., 32-33, 185-192.

[163]Ibid., 17-18.

[164]See H. G. M. Williamson, *Ezra and Nehemiah*, 45-46.

[165]H. G. M. Williamson, *Ezra, Nehemiah*, xxxv-xxxvi; *Ezra and Nehemiah*, 46; S. J. De Vries, *1 and 2 Chronicles*, 7-8.

Because 2 Chronicles 6 extensively relies upon 1 Kings 8, and, thus, includes Solomon's prayer. This text provides a useful place to begin an inquiry into 2 Chronicles and its understanding of penitential prayer. Some of the variations in 2 Chronicles simply result from its use of plene vowels and different prepositions.[166] Otherwise, 2 Chronicles adds the material in 6:13 and 41-42 to the text found in 1 Kings 8, and omits 1 Kgs 8:50-51.[167] The only tendentious change in 2 Chronicles is the insertion of material similar to Ps 132:8-10. The author does this in order to emphasize his hope in the Davidic covenant and the importance of David.[168] This aside, the author's preservation of the prayer testifies that penitential prayer remains important for him.

2 Chr 7:13-15 contains an important addition to 1 Kings 9 that confirms the prominence of penitential prayer in the author's ideology. In this scene, Solomon receives a revelation that does not appear in 1 Kings. God instructs him that when the people face disaster, they should do the following:

> If my people who are called by my name will *humble themselves* and *pray*, and *seek* my face and *turn* from their wicked ways, then I will hear from heaven and forgive their sin and heal their land (2 Chr 7:14).

ויכנעו עמי אשר נקרא־שמי עליהם ויתפללו ויבקשו פני וישבו מדרכיהם הרעים ואני אשמע מן־השמים ואסלח לחטאתם וארפא את־ארצם:

The form of the language, like 1 Kings 8 and 2 Chronicles 6, is casuistic with God once again the subject of the apodosis.[169] Thus, God promises to act if Israel meets the requirement of repentance and prayer. This divine promise establishes a literary pattern in 2 Chronicles whereby repentance becomes the means for averting punishment.[170] The word "humble one's self," כנע, in the Niphal, which appears more frequently in 2 Chronicles than in any other biblical book, becomes the primary metaphor for this repentance. For example, Rehoboam and the officers of Israel humble themselves to avoid destruction from Egypt (2 Chr 12:6-7), and Hezekiah humbles himself to avert God's wrath (32:26).

---

[166] S. L. McKenzie, *The Chronicler's Use of the Deuteronomistic History*, HSM 33 (Atlanta: Scholars, 1985) 95; S. J. De Vries, *1 and 2 Chronicles*, 258-259.

[167] R. Mason, *Preaching the Tradition: Homily and Hermeneutics after the Exile* (Cambridge: Cambridge University, 1990) 107.

[168] S. L. McKenzie, *The Chronicler's Use of the Deuteronomistic History*, 89.

[169] S. J. De Vries, *1 and 2 Chronicles*, 263.

[170] T. Eskenazi, *In an Age of Prose*, 26-27.

"Humbling" one's self even works for Manasseh. Because he is the idolater *par excellence*, he must be punished as Deuteronomy teaches. Thus, God sends Assyria to capture him and take him to Babylon (33:10-13). There, "in his distress" (וכהצר לו), Manasseh "humbles" (כנע) himself and "prays" (פלל)(v. 12). The author has combined 2 Chr 7:14 with the old formula present in Hosea 6:1 and Deut 4:30: "In your distress you will..."[171] God "hears" (שמע) "his supplications" (תחנתו) and returns him to his kingdom (cf. 2 Chr 6:40). The summary of Manasseh's rule again refers to Manasseh humbling himself and praying (33:18-20).

Although the scene contains no specific reference to a prayer, Josiah's and the people's responses to the words of the newly found book of the Law provide another example of intense penitence (34:13-18). They humble themselves, have a "softened heart," i.e. a penitent heart,[172] mourn, tear their clothes, and weep (34:27). With these actions the people avert God's wrath.

The nation falls in 2 Chronicles 36 after the people and their king have refused "to humble" themselves (36:11-14). The author evokes the metaphor of the stiff neck and hard heart (ויקש את־ערפו ויאמץ את־לבבו) (v. 13), a metaphor popular in deuteronomic ideology, in order to characterize Zedekiah's stubborn refusal to repent. Zedekiah's and the people's stubbornness reaches its apex when they reject the messages of Jeremiah and the other prophets (vv. 12, 15-16; cf. also 20:20), whom God persistently sent them (ושלוח ... השכם). God has no choice but to bring Babylon against the people (v. 16). The theme of rejecting the prophets' warnings predates 2 Chronicles. In the summation of the northern kingdom's sins, 2 Kgs 17:13 mentions that the prophets warned Judah and Israel about their sin.[173] In his Temple sermon, Jeremiah, speaking for God, indicts the people for having rejected the word of the prophets, whom God persistently sent (Jer 7:25-26). Jeremiah also speaks of their obstinateness with the metaphor "stiff neck":

> ... *I sent to you all my servants the prophets continuously*, but they did not listen to me, nor did they incline their ear, rather, *they stiffened their necks* worse than their ancestors.

This same theme appears in Jer 7:25; 25:4; 26:5; 29:19; 35:15; and 44:4. Thus, 2 Chronicles' vocabulary is formulaic and the result of rejecting the

---

[171]Cf. Hos 5:15; Deut 4:30; Jer 14:8; Neh 9:9, 37; M. Weinfeld, *Deuteronomy*, 220.

[172]*BDB*, 940.

[173]Cf. 2 Kgs 17:23 which implies that the people refused the prophetic warning. For discussion of 2 Kings 17, see O. H. Steck, *Israel und das gewaltsame Geschick Propheten*, 66-74.

prophetic message is predictable—God sends punishment. 2 Chronicles builds upon a long standing tradition.

Summary

A distinct pattern emerges as the author unites the old traditions of "seeking" God in "distress" with his own ideology and accompanying vocabulary. Using the revelation to Solomon, the author establishes that the people can turn back God's wrath when they "humble" themselves and pray. Such penitence always allows the people to escape retribution. Even the wicked Manasseh, whose evil reign seals Judah's fate in 2 Kings, receives forgiveness and deliverance when he "humbles" himself and prays. With these scenes, 2 Chronicles' formulates its ideology: anyone, no matter how wicked, can receive God's forgiveness through repentance and prayer.[174] Even when the person's "distress" is exile, where Manasseh finds himself, repentance and prayer provide the way out. While 2 Chronicles makes no explicit reference to prayer when describing the disaster of 586 BCE, the catastrophe descends upon the people because they refuse to "humble" themselves. This literary pattern functions both to explain the past and to give hope to the people living in the late Persian period because a specific method for securing the nation's situation is available.

Conclusion

The penitential prayers that appear in Ezra-Nehemiah stand within a tradition that stretches back to Deuteronomy 4 and 30. Deuteronomy teaches that Israel suffers exile because of sin. Restoration comes only after the people repent. However, Deuteronomy says nothing about prayer as the proper expression of repentance. A key moment of transition in this tradition comes when the author of 1 Kings 8, by reinterpreting Deuteronomy 4 and 30, presents the notion that the people could enact Deuteronomy's demand for repentance through penitential prayer. By addressing the ambiguities of how one repents, and offering a way to remove sin without the Temple and its cult, his message is especially suited for the exile.

Third Isaiah, a document that comes from the restoration period, proves that the idea of repentance, prayer, and confession survive the exile. This text has several ideas that are similar to Deuteronomy and the deuteronomic history, e.g., the vocabulary for repentance, the idea that Israel must repent before it will know blessing, the notion that YHWH is not confined to the

---

[174]Cf., S. J. De Vries, *1 and 2 Chronicles*, 399-400.

Temple, and that the Temple is a place of prayer. The multiple attestations of these ideas suggests their popularity in the post-exilic period. Third Isaiah also reinterprets the penitential traditions in order to explain why the restoration to the land did not occur as Second Isaiah describes it. Simply stated, the restoration is a disappointment because the people have not properly repented. Accordingly, Third Isaiah stresses that only repentance would please God and bring complete deliverance from foreign rule, and Israel does not need a Temple to perform this. Further, the two penitential poems in Third Isaiah, which contain confessions of sins, connect the epiphany of the Divine Warrior with penitence. In this manner, they model how the people can experience deliverance. Finally, Third Isaiah uses penitence to distinguish between groups *within* Israel. That is, salvation is no longer national, but limited to a specific group, the penitent.

The authors of the prayers in Ezra-Nehemiah agree with Third Isaiah that the restoration is incomplete. Ezra 9 maintains that Israel has only known a partial reviving. The presence of foreign rule proves this, even if the overlords are benevolent. The prayers in both Ezra 9 and Nehemiah 9 hope to maintain the restoration already achieved and to build upon it. The prayer in Nehemiah 1 prepares for more improvements in the restored community's life. Deuteronomic thought and language again form the bases of these prayers. However, the texts incorporate other traditions and themes. Under the influence of priestly traditions, for example, the authors refer to the prayers as "confessions." The prayers spring from a conscious interpretive process.

Data from the texts demonstrate that the prayers function as a religious institution. Ezra-Nehemiah's lack of explanation for the prayers indicates that the readers know of the practice and have accepted it. Further, coupling the prayers with rituals like tearing clothes, fasting, and putting on sackcloth suggests that a whole penitential practice has developed, which has prayer as its center. Joel's internalization of some of these acts attests to their fixed place in Israel's religious life (Joel 2:13). One can instruct people to perform an internalized action only when the audience already practices the physical act. The placement of the prayer in Nehemiah 8-10 in connection with a feast, even though the prayer does not contain themes from the particular feast, might also mean that penitential prayer became a part of various special worship occasions. Further, putting a prayer in the mouth of Ezra, a priest (Ezra 9), and the Levites (Nehemiah 9) suggest that penitential prayer is not isolated to fringe groups, but stands at the center of Israel's religious system.

In the exilic and post-exilic periods, Israel expands the use of penitential prayer. Deuteronomy 4 and 30 teach that idolatry is the "quintessential sin" that leads to certain punishment—exile. The deuteronomic history shares this position when it attributes Israel's fall to Assyria and Judah's fall to Babylon to the two kingdoms' idolatry. However, Solomon's prayer in 1 Kings 8 exhibits some ambiguity about what sins bring punishment, and, thus, marks a shift in the idea of which sins have devastating consequences. A development in the use of penitential prayer surfaces in Ezra 9. The offense in Ezra 9 is not idolatry, but intermarriage. Thus, as the practice of penitential prayer becomes more established in the post-exilic period, its applications also increase.

While the prayers themselves reinterpret previous traditions, they are also a part of a larger interpretive enterprise. For example, Third Isaiah consciously reinterprets Second Isaiah. Ezra 9 claims to have a prophetic word, which does not appear in any text, but is the author's own creation from a compilation of texts. Nehemiah 9 closely associates penitential prayer with reading authoritative texts by setting the prayer within the context of reading the law. Therefore, a close relationship exists between penitential prayer and the study of authoritative texts.

CHAPTER TWO

The Prayers in Daniel 9:1-27 and Baruch 1:15-3:8

Introduction

Even though penitential prayer is a widely accepted religious institution by the close of the Persian period, the language and content of the prayers are not fixed. Authors feel free to alter the traditional language in prayers in order to serve their own agendas. Preserving the prayers' deuteronomic centers, their changes typically address Israel's changing historical situations and the people's evolving religious dilemmas. The Jews' problems with the Seleucids, especially Antiochus IV, present a particularly difficult set of religious and political crises. When Antiochus IV orders extensive Hellenistic reforms in Jerusalem and establishes a heretical Jewish cult in the Jerusalem Temple, Jews who refuse to submit to Antiochus' decrees face martyrdom.[175] Even after the Jews rebel and recapture the Temple, and Antiochus dies, they still disagree over religious and political issues. How far should the rebellion go? Who should rule? These tumultuous shifts in the nation's life influence the penitential prayer tradition.

Adapting a penitential prayer to a new situation requires only minor, if not subtle, adjustments. Even slight changes give penitential prayers entirely new meanings and functions. Moreover, whenever penitential prayer acquires a new literary, social, or historical context, its traditional and formulaic phrases assume new force in meaning.

This chapter tests these assertions by analyzing two prayers°Dan 9:1-27 and Bar 1:15-3:8.[176] Written during the historical crisis described above,[177] these two prayers so extensively resemble one another in language that some

---

[175]For a discussion about Antiochus IV's actions and intentions, see J. Goldstein, *I Maccabees*, AB 41 (Garden City: Doubleday, 1981) 104-160.

[176]Because commentators on Daniel have basically only canonical interests, they do not always explore the similarities between the texts. See e.g., W. S. Towner, *Daniel, Interpretation* (Atlanta: John Knox, 1984); S. E. Balentine, *Prayer in the Hebrew Bible: The Drama of Divine Human Dialogue* (Philadelphia: Fortress, 1993) 104-109.

[177]See below for discussions about the dates of these prayers.

literary dependency must exist between them. Despite their similarities, these prayers also exhibit significant differences, which also influence the meaning of the prayers' language. The prayers appear in very different genres. Daniel 9 is an apocalypse.[178] The prayer in Baruch is part of a pseudepigraphical letter claiming to originate in Babylon from the hand of Baruch, Jeremiah's scribe. The letter joins its penitential prayer to a wisdom poem, a Zion poem, and an apostrophe to Jerusalem. While both prayers draw on Jeremianic traditions, they refer to different passages. Daniel is interested in the meaning of Jeremiah's notion of the exile's duration—"seventy weeks of years" (Jeremiah 25:11, 12; 29:10). Besides the pseudonym that attaches the prayer to Jeremianic tradition, the author of Baruch focuses on a Jeremianic idea about how Israel must relate to its foreign lords. The authors' interpretations of their respective historical situations and their approaches to Israel's problems account for many of the prayers' differences.

The Two Prayers' Literary Relationship[179]

As already mentioned, the extensive similar language between the prayers raises the question of literary dependency.[180] First, because Daniel seems to have been written before Baruch, one may exclude the possibility that Daniel is dependent upon Baruch.[181] Few critics support this solution.[182] Second, Baruch may be dependent upon Daniel. The majority of critics accept this as the most likely solution because Baruch not only follows Daniel's wording, but also

---

[178]See J. J. Collins (ed., *Apocalypse: The Morphology of a Genre. Semeia* 14 [1979]; *The Apocalyptic Imagination: An Introduction to the Jewish Matrix of Christianity*, (New York: Crossroads [1987] 1-8) for a definition of the literary genre apocalypse. See J. J. Collins (*Daniel: With an Introduction to Apocalyptic Literature*, FOTL 20 [Grand Rapids: Eerdmans, 1984] 6-10 and 91-91) for an explanation of the subcategories which fit this chapter.

[179]I am not interested in the relationships between the ancient versions. For this problem, see E. Tov, "The Relation between the Greek Versions of Baruch and Daniel," *Armenian and Biblical Studies* (ed., M. Stone; Jerusalem: Armenian Patriarchate, 1976) 27-34. Tov concludes that there is no relationship between Baruch and either Daniel Theodotion or Daniel LXX. For a discussion of Baruch's relationship to Jeremiah 29-52, see E. Tov, *The Septuagint Translation of Jeremiah and Baruch: A Discussion of an Early Revision of the LXX of Jeremiah 29-52 and Baruch 1:1-3:8*.

[180]See C. A. Moore's ("Toward the Dating of Baruch," *CBQ* 26 [1974] 314) caveats about the problem of literary dependency.

[181]For more on a date for Baruch, see below.

[182]For this position, Whitehouse ("The Book of Baruch" *APOT*, vol. 1, 574) lists Ewald.

maintains Daniel's order.[183] Further, Daniel may preserve more ancient language than Baruch,[184] and the material in Baruch that differs from Daniel is intrusive.[185] If this second alternative about literary dependency is correct, then Baruch would have followed Daniel's order and inserted his own material. While these arguments accurately describe the two texts, they still do not confirm Daniel's priority because a third possible solution also explains these data—the prayers may share a common source.[186] Thus, the material in the two prayers is in the same order because they both preserve the order of their common source. Daniel's alleged more ancient language, then, might have resulted from the author of Baruch altering the ancient language in a common source.

As the review of the two arguments reveals, the evidence for deciding literary dependency is insufficient because it can be easily used to argue in either direction.[187] No conclusion is certain. This impasse, though, does not prevent making significant observations about the texts.

Interpretation of Daniel 9

Introduction

Daniel 9 divides into three parts: the narrative introduction (vv. 1-4a); the prayer proper (vv. 4-19); and the narrative conclusion (vv. 20-27). The prayer has a loose organizational scheme. For example, a confession of sin appears in what is otherwise the prayer's petitionary section. Consequently, a thematic treatment of the prayer provides the most useful interpretive approach.

---

[183]R. H. Pfeiffer, *History of New Testament Times with an Introduction to the Apocrypha* (New York: Harper, 1949) 415; O. Eissfeldt, *Introduction to the Old Testament*, 593; J. Goldstein, "The Apocryphal Book of I Baruch," 196-199; A. Lacoque, "The Liturgical Prayer in Daniel 9," *HUCA* 47 (1976) 126-127; B. B. Wambacq, "*Les prieres de Baruch (1,15-2,19) et de Daniel (9,5-19),*" *Bib* 40 (1959) 463-475.

[184]J. Goldstein ("The Apocryphal Book of I Baruch," 197 n 49) presents these arguments.

[185]Ibid.

[186]See O. H. Steck, *Israel und das gewaltsame Geschick der Propheten*, 115. E. Tov ("The Relation between the Greek Versions of Baruch and Daniel," 27 n 4), while siding with Wambacq, recognizes that Baruch may have relied on an independent source. W. O. E. Oesterley (*Books of the Apocrypha: Their Origin, Teaching, and Contents* [New York: Fleming, 1914] 503), who dates the prayer after 70 CE era, believes that the prayer was an "extract" from the Temple liturgy.

[187]In contrast, J. Goldstein ("The Apocryphal Book of I Baruch," 197-199) argues that the author of Baruch knows Daniel and is responding to it.

The Narrative Introduction (vv. 1-4a)

The narrative introduction depicts Daniel offering the prayer while in Babylonian exile, also the book's fictional setting. Actually, the author's historical setting is the time of Antiochus IV's reign of terror in Palestine in 167-164 BCE.[188] The author chooses his fictional setting, in part, because of the correspondence between Judah's loss of the Temple to Babylon and the second century BCE Jews' loss of the cult and Temple to Antiochus' religious program for Palestine. This historical setting influences the prayer's petitions and function.

The introduction also connects the prayer to Daniel's quest to understand Jeremiah's prophecy about the length of the exile (Jer 25:11 and 12; 29:10). This interest results from the author's cognitive dissonance. Jeremiah seems to state clearly that the exile will end after seventy years. While Persia allows the Jews to return to Palestine after about seventy years after Babylon's invasion in 604 BCE,[189] the Jews continue to have problems; their life does not neatly return to normal as Jeremiah promises. The author of Daniel struggles to explain that Jeremiah's prophecy means something different from what it obviously says.

Finally, the introduction establishes the passage's penitential tone by depicting Daniel enacting several penitential rituals, which resemble those of Ezra and Nehemiah. He puts on sack cloth, pours ashes on himself, fasts, and states that he is offering "prayer" and "supplication" (Ezra 9:3-5; Neh 1:2; and 9:2; cf. Greek Esther 14:2). Also as in Ezra 9, the prayer takes place at, or at least continues until, the evening offering, the *Tamid* (Dan 9:21). Daniel uses the term "to confess" to describe his prayer (ידה) (v. 4). By this time, the term has completely separated from its Levitical origins and stands on its own, with the basic meaning to acclaim God's righteousness and Israel's sinfulness.

The Prayer (vv. 4b-19)

The prayer proper contains four basic components: an address to God; confessions of sins; recognition that God's punishment is just; and petitions. Deuteronomic language strongly influences Daniel's prayer and its presence

---

[188] J. Goldstein ("The Apocryphal Book of I Baruch," 197; *I Maccabees*, 43) dates the latest form of the prayer to the autumn of 164 BCE.

[189] I take Jeremiah's use of "seventy" simply as a round number. Therefore, even though Cyrus makes his decree in 538 BCE, roughly seventy years pass between Babylon's invasion in 604 BCE and this event.

testifies that this language has become formulaic as penitential language. Into this traditional rhetoric the author inserts his own ideas about Israel's sins and the role of penitential prayer.

Address to God

Even though invoking God is vital to the prayer and the author, the opening address accomplishes more than attracting God's attention. It also introduces a basic vocabulary and ideological framework that dominate the remainder of the prayer. The author's language closely resembles Nehemiah's address in Neh 1:5

Dan 9:4	Neh 1:5
Now, O YHWH, the great and awesome God who keeps the covenant and is faithful to those who love him and to those who keep his commandments.	Now, O YHWH God of heaven, the great and awesome God who keeps the covenant and is faithful to those who love him and to those who keep his commandments.
אנא אדני האל הגדול והנורא שמר הברית והחסד לאהביו ולשמרי מצותיו	אנא יהוה אלהי השמים האל הגדל והנורא שמר הברית וחסד לאהביו ולשמרי מצותיו

This formula is a combination of Deut 7:9 and 21 (cf. Neh 9:32 and 1 Kgs 8:23: "... keeping the covenant and faithfulness to your servants who walk before you with all their heart"). With it, the author sets the prayer within the context of covenant theology. According to biblical authors, God always proves faithful to this agreement, while Israel typically violates it. In this prayer, Daniel follows this same assertion of other biblical authors.

The Jews' violation of the covenant explains the troubles that they are facing when the author of Daniel 9 writes. As stated above, the author constructs this prayer while Antiochus IV is attempting to install a heretical Jewish cult in Jerusalem. The author interprets these problems as the activation of the covenantal curses that descend upon the Jews when they sin. Later in the prayer, he makes this explicit identification of the religious and political turmoil.

Confessing Sins

The author juxtaposes God's covenant faithfulness with a confession that the Jews have violated the agreement. Once again, his language is typical deuteronomic rhetoric and closely parallels the confession in 1 Kgs 8:47. Daniel's expansion of the threefold confession into a fourfold confession marks the only difference between the two texts:

Dan 9:5	1 Kgs 8:47
We have sinned, we have committed iniquity, we have acted wickedly, we have rebelled.	We have sinned, we have committed iniquity, we have acted wickedly.
חטאנו ועוינו והרשענו ומרדנו	חטאנו והעוינו רשענו

The author's additional confession is another deuteronomic expression that focuses on the Jews' violation YHWH's commandments:[190]

Dan 9:5 ... turning from your commandments and ordinances.
וסור ממצותך וממשפטיך

Deut 17:20 And do not turn aside from the commandments either to the right or to the left.
ולבלתי סור מן־המצוה ימין ושמאול

As the author prepares to speak of the covenantal curses that have come upon the people, he again explicitly states that the people have violated the Torah: "For all of Israel has forsaken your laws (עברו את־תורתך) turning (סור) so as not to obey your voice" (v. 11). The final phrase in this accusation is vintage deuteronomic language as well.

Another confession of sins appears at the beginning of the petitionary section. Like other prayers, the formulaic expression ועתה marks the beginning of this section (v. 15; cf. e. g., Neh 9:32). A reference to the Exodus follows this formula:

And now, O YHWH our God, who brought your people from the land of Egypt with a strong hand, and made a name for yourself, as it is to this day ...

He then moves directly to the twofold confession: "We have sinned and have done wickedness" (חטאנו רשענו) (v. 15). This combination of the Exodus, which generally epitomizes God's past salvation, and confession occurs in other penitential prayers.[191] With it, the author contrasts this past glorious deliverance to the nation's present dismal situation; now salvation eludes the people.[192] As Chapter One explains, God might withhold salvation because of the people's persistent sin. Daniel most certainly agrees.

---

[190] J. Montgomery, *Daniel*, ICC, 363. Cf. Deut 2:27; 4:9; 5:29, 32; 9:12; 11:16, 28; 17:11; 28:14; 31:29.

[191] Cf., e.g., 1 Kgs 8:51; Neh 9:9-11; Isa 63; Bar 2:11.

[192] See 1 Kgs 8:51, 53; Neh 1:10; 9:9-25; Isa 63:7-14.

The author mentions the "iniquities of the ancestors" in this confession (v. 16; cf. Neh 9:2 and Jer 14:20). The category "ancestors" applies to ancestors in general, not to any particular group with whom the author disagrees. Thus, the suppliant maintains that the Jews suffer the consequences of the accumulated sins of past generations and their own generation.

Rejection of the Prophetic Message

In speaking of the people's misconduct, Daniel claims that they have refused to heed prophetic warnings. As Chapter One explains, this is a traditional formula that occasionally appears in penitential prayer tradition. Daniel takes its language from 2 Kings and Jeremiah:

Dan 9:6	2 Kgs 17:13b-14
For we did not listen to your servants, the prophets...	... and that I sent to you by the hand of my servants, the prophets. But they would not listen.
ולא שמענו אל־עבדיך הנביאים...	ואשר שלחתי אליכם ביד עבדי הנביאים: ולא שמעו
	Jer 7:25b-26a
	And I sent to you all my servant, the prophets, ... yet they did not listen to me...
	ואשלח אליכם את־כל־עבדי הנביאים ולוא שמעו אלי ...

The reference to the prophets in Dan 9:10 recalls Jer 26:4 and Ezr 9:10:[193]

Dan 9:10	Jer 26:4-5
We did not listen to the voice of YHWH our God, by following his laws which he placed before us by the hand of his servants the prophets.	... If you do not listen to me by following my laws which I placed before you to obey the words of my servants the prophets...
ולא שמענו בקול יהוה אלהינו ללכת בתורתיו אשר נתן לפנינו ביד עבדיו הנביאים	אם־לא תשמעו אלי ללכת בתורתי אשר נתתי לפניכם לשמעו על־דברי עבדי נביאים

---

[193]Cf. 2 Kgs 17:13, 23; Jer 7:25; 25:4; 29:19; 44:4.

> Ezr 9:10b-11a
> For we have forsaken your commandments which you commanded by the hand of your servants the prophets.

> כי־עזבנו מצותיך אשר צוית ביד עבדיך
> הנביאים

Although Daniel's confession that the people have failed to heed the prophetic word is traditional, it relates well to the context of Daniel 9. As the introduction explains, Daniel prays because he is trying to understand a *prophetic* text—Jeremiah 29. Further, the chapter climaxes with the explanation of Jeremiah's prophesy. Through the inclusion of the rejected prophetic message tradition, the author reminds his readers that disobeying the prophets has serious consequences. This also, then, becomes his tactic for persuading them to accept his interpretation of Jeremiah as the proper explanation for the Jews' difficulties with Antiochus IV.

The confession of sins, then, in Daniel's prayer closely follows traditional and formulaic language. Through the confession he directly states that the people have disobeyed YHWH's commandments, violated the covenant, and disobeyed the prophets.

Although Daniel's confession that the people have failed to heed the prophetic word is traditional, it relates well to the context of Daniel 9. As the introduction explains, Daniel prays because he is trying to understand a *prophetic* text—Jeremiah 29. Further, the chapter climaxes with the explanation of Jeremiah's prophesy. Through the inclusion of the rejected prophetic message tradition, the author reminds his readers that disobeying the prophets has serious consequences. This also, then, becomes his tactic for persuading them to accept his interpretation of Jeremiah as the proper explanation for the Jews' difficulties with Antiochus IV.

The confession of sins, then, in Daniel's prayer closely follows traditional and formulaic language. Through the confession he directly states that the people have disobeyed YHWH's commandments, violated the covenant, and disobeyed the prophets.

Identification of the People's Sins and the Maskilim

Despite its intense concern about sin, the prayer seems vague about the precise sins that the Jews have committed. In fact, the author's formulaic language contributes to this problem. The idea of what sin might bring God's wrath can change from text to text. As Chapter One argues, Deuteronomy identifies idolatry as the "quintessential sin" that leads to exile. While 1 Kings 8 is ambiguous concerning specific sins that bring punishment, Ezra 9 shows that penitential prayer becomes an acceptable response to sins besides idolatry. What sins does the author of Daniel have in mind?

In the confession in v. 13, the author lists a specific failure: the people did not "ponder" (שׂכל) God's truth (v. 13). The term, "to ponder," does not occur in the prayers Chapter One analyzes. This word is an example of the author's own terminology and ideology slipping into his otherwise traditional deuteronomic rhetoric. "To ponder" (שׂכל) is a key term in Daniel.[194] Other passages in Daniel employ the noun form of this word in order to identify the Danielic apocalyptic circle; the members function in the role of *maskilim* (משׂכלים).[195]

Passages in Daniel depict the *maskilim* as those who acquire wisdom and instruct others in this wisdom.[196] Daniel, the character, functions as the model *maskil* for the community and demonstrates to the readers the value of the quest for wisdom. From the beginning of the book, Daniel and his companions have "insight into all wisdom" (ומשׂכילים בכל-חכמה), "knowledge" (וידעי דעת), and "understanding", (ומביני מדע)(1:4). This kind of knowledge enables Daniel to interpret dreams and heavenly visions about human events. In imitating their hero of old, the *maskilim* claim to be recipients of wisdom and interpreters of mysteries.

Like Daniel, the *maskilim* engage in instructing others in wisdom and explaining mysteries to them. As Daniel 11 indicates, this is part of the *maskilim's* eschatological role. As the end approaches, they instruct others: "The *maskilim* of the people will give understanding to many" (יבינו לרבים) (11:33).[197] In the resurrection scene in Daniel 12, where the *maskilim* receive a place of special honor, the text describes them as those who made many righteous (מצדיקי הרבים) (v. 3). This phrase, as well, may imagine the *maskilim* as teachers.[198] Their primary pedagogical task lies in instructing Israel

---

[194]Dan 1:4; 9:23, 25; 11:33, 35; 12:3, 10.
[195]See J. J. Collins, *Daniel*, 66-67.
[196]Ibid., 70.
[197]Cf. Ibid.
[198]For the special honor God accords the *maskilim*, see G. W. E. Nickelsburg, *Resurrection, Immortality*, 24-26. For the influence of Isaiah 53 on this text, see H. L. Ginsberg, "The Oldest Interpretation of the Suffering Servant," *VT* 3 (1953) 400-404; see also, J. J. Collins, *Daniel*, 66-67, 70. The *maskilim* as those who "justify the many" (ומצדיקי הרבים) (12:3) alludes to the Servant who "justifies the many" (יצדיק צדיק עבדי לרבים) (Isa 53:11). Note in Dan 11:35 that some *maskilim* become martyrs.

about the signs of the arrival of the last days and how one should live during them.[199]

Daniel 9 extends wisdom to include not only dreams and visions, but the proper interpretation of Jeremiah's prophetic word (Jer 29:10-14), an oracle that unlocks the meaning of Israel's predicament under Antiochus IV. In Daniel 7-12, Antiochus' reign of terror in Palestine is the problem that especially vexes the Jews. The Temple sacrifices have ceased and Antiochus' desolating sacrilege stands in the Temple (11:31). Some within Israel, probably the "Hellenizers," have violated the covenant (11:32). Similarly, Dan 7:25 refers to Antiochus attempting to change "the sacred seasons and the law."[200] Through this crisis, the *maskilim* firmly hold to the Law and encourage others to do same. Their steadfastness even results in martyrdom (11:35).[201]

As Daniel interprets Jeremiah in light of these historical circumstances, terms for wisdom and understanding frame the prayer, and, consequently, connect the prayer to the basic activity of the *maskilim*. Daniel prefaces his prayer with a word to the reader that he "understands" (בין) Jeremiah's prophecy (Dan 9:2). He discerns the meaning of the prophecy because Gabriel brings him "wisdom" (חכמה) and "understanding" (להשכילך בינה), i.e., the interpretation (v. 22). Vv. 23 and 25 repeat the terms: "Then, understand (ובין) the word and understand (והבן) the vision" (v. 23); "And know and understand (ותדע ותשכל)" (v. 25). Therefore, the community subsumes the acquisition of the meaning of difficult and mysterious prophetic texts under the rubric of wisdom.

This description of the activity of the *maskilim* and the meaning of the verb שכל helps us understand the meaning of the confession: "they did not ponder your (i.e., God's) truth" (Dan 9:13). The author is criticizing fellow Jews for failing to accept the *maskilim's* teaching. This is sin because it is a rejection of divine revelation. Because the Jews as a whole have failed to accept the *maskilim's* instruction, they must confess this sin along with any of Israel's other sins.

Daniel 9, then, continues to add to the categories of sin for which the Jews offer penitential prayer. Its use is not limited to idolatry (Deuteronomy 4 and 30) or intermarriage (Ezra 9). According to Daniel 9, penitential prayer

---

[199]For a discussion of *maskil* as teacher, see G. W. E. Nickelsburg, *Resurrection, Immortality*, 24.

[200]The author of this chapter may be different from chapters 8, 10-12 (J. J. Collins, *Daniel*, 103), but the representation of Antiochus as the desolator of the Temple is consistent with the other chapters.

[201]Daniel draws on Isa 53:5 and 7 for his language and image of the righteous sufferer.

applies when an author believes that fellow Jews have failed to adopt his own peculiar wisdom and world view. This adaption of penitential prayer means that various groups in Palestine could call rival groups to penitence and penitential prayer. The simple insertion of the phrase "they do not ponder your truth" displays how easily an author can adapt penitential prayer for his agenda.

Gerichtsdoxologie

Since the author admits that the people have sinned, he feels that he must also acknowledge God's right to punish the people. The prayer contains two declarations of God's righteousness, both of which employ deuteronomic language. With these the author ascents to the basic tenets of deuteronomic ideology.

The author unites the first declaration with a statement about Israel's shame (vv. 7-8). This has a precedent in Ezra 9:7:

Dan 9:7	Ezra 9:15
Righteousness is to you, O YHWH,	O YHWH, God of Israel, you are righteous...
לך אדני הצדקה	יהוה אלהי ישראל צדיק אתה
	Ezra 9:7
but to us is shame of face to this day.	From the days of our fathers to this day, we have been in great guilt ... and shame of face, even to this day.
ולנו בשת הפנים כיום הזה	מימי אבתינו אנחנו באשמה גדלה ... ובבשת פנים כהיום הזה
Dan 9:8	
O YHWH, to us is shame of face...	
יהוה לנו בשת הפנים ...	

The rhetoric of shame originates from the scene of the condemned standing before the judge.[202] This language, like the deuteronomic *Gerichtsdoxologie*, has become another formulaic expression in penitential prayer.

---

[202] See Chapter One and the discussion on Jeremiah. G. W. E. Nickelsburg, *Resurrection, Immortality*, 14.

Those "near" in v. 7 are those in Jerusalem, while those "far in all the lands to which" God "drove (נדח) them" refers to the exiles. The author borrows this language from Deut 30:1 and 4 where Moses speaks of God "driving" (נדח) the people into exile.

Dan 9:7
... in all the lands to which you drove them...

... בכל־הארצות אשר הדחתם שם ...

Deut 30:1
... among all the nations to which the YHWH your God will drive you.

...בכל־הגוים אשר הדיחך יהוה אלהיך שמה

Deut 30:4
And though you are driven to the end of the heavens...

...אם־יהיה נדחך בקצה השמים

Daniel lists groups of leaders and people in v.6 who share in this shame. Accusations against groups, especially leaders, in ancient Israel form part of the prophetic oracles of judgment, e.g., Jer 32:32 (cf. 2:26), and Zeph 3:1-3. The prayer in Nehemiah 9 also incorporates a similar list of leaders who have sinned (v. 32). The following table compares Neh 9:32; Jer 32:32 (cf. Jer 2:26); Zeph 3:1-3; Dan 9:6; and Bar 1:15-16:

Table 2. *A Comparison of Lists of Religious Leaders*

Leaders	Jer 32	Neh 9	Zeph 3	Dan 9	Bar
kings	x	x		x	x
officials	x	x	x	x	x
priests	x	x	x		x
prophets	x		x		x
judges			x		x
ancestors				x	x
inhabitants of Judah	x			x	x
inhabitants of Jerusalem	x			x	x
people of the land				x	

Inserting a list of sinful leaders into a penitential prayer has transformed the rhetoric of prophetic judgment into an expression of penitence. This transformation is logical since the penitential prayer tradition, including Daniel 9, claims that rejection of prophetic warnings is a sin that the Jews should confess.[203]

In comparison to the other lists in the chart, and consistent with their conscious relationship to Jeremiah, the prayers in Daniel and Baruch most closely resemble Jeremiah. Of these two prayers, however, Baruch's list stands closer to Jeremiah than Daniel, a feature that one can probably attribute to the author claiming to be Jeremiah's scribe. Thus, the pseudonymous author makes the scribe sound like his master.

The second declaration of God's righteousness, Dan 9:11, concludes with an explicit reference to the covenantal curses (see Deuteronomy 28 and Leviticus 26): "The curse and the oath which were written in the Law of Moses are poured out on us." Montgomery holds that the metaphor "to pour" (ותתך) comes from the image of God "pouring out" his wrath.[204] He compares Daniel's language to Jer 7:20; 42:18; 44:6; 2 Chr 12:7; and 34:25. The wording of vv. 12-14 is similar to both Jer 1:11-14 and Neh 9:8:

Dan 9	Neh 9:8
v. 12 And he established his word[205] which he spoke against us.	And you established your word ...
ויקם את־דבריו אשר־דבר עלינו	ותקם את־דבריך
v. 13 ... that all this evil would come upon us ...	
את כל־הרעה הזאת באה עלינו	
v. 14 And YHWH kept watch over the disaster, and he brought it upon us.	Jer 1:12 I am keeping watch over my word to do it.
וישקד יהוה על־הרעה ויביאה עלינו	כי־שקד אני על־דברי לעשתו

---

[203]A. Lacocque ("The Liturgical Prayer in Daniel 9," *HUCA* 47, 119-142) claims that the omission from Daniel of the groups "priests" and "prophets" represents a Judean perspective just after 587 BCE.
[204]Montgomery, *Daniel*, 365.
[205]Reading with the *qere*.

Following his observation that the curses are in effect, the author acknowledges that God has rightly unleashed them upon the people. His language corresponds to the prior declaration: "... YHWH our God is righteous in all his deeds that he does" (כי־צדיק יהוה אלהינו על־כל־מעשיו אשר עשה). The author is not only employing deuteronomic language, but is also accepting deuteronomic ideology.

Summary

Amid the traditional deuteronomic confessional language in Daniel 9 stands a phrase that reveals the author's own particular ideology. The Jews have failed to listen, "to ponder" (שכל), God's truth, i.e., they have not heeded the teachings of the *maskilim*. As a result, they do not properly understand scripture and current political crises. This offense is serious and requires repentance. Because of the Jews' sins, God is just in bringing the covenantal curses upon the nation.

The Desecration of Jerusalem and Petitionary Language

Despite his recognition that God has correctly punished the people, the author proceeds to petition God for help. His confession of the Jews' sins in the petitionary section once again reflects the author's intense feeling of guilt. His petitions relate to Jerusalem and the Temple's desolation, forgiveness of sin, and reproaches from neighbors that the people must endure.

The Petitions' Literary Forms

The rhetoric of Daniel's plea for God to hearken to his prayer resembles petitions from prayers examined in Chapter One. Using formulaic language, the prayers form petitions with anthropomorphic verbs in the imperative and jussive forms.

Dan 9:17
And now hearken, O God, to the prayer of your servant and to our supplications.

Compare the repetition of "hear in heaven" (השמים שמעת) in 1 Kgs 8:30, 34, 36, 45, and 49.

ועתה שמע אלהינו אל־תפלת עבדך
ואל־תחנוניו

Chapter Two

Dan 9:19
Hear, O Lord ...

אדני שמעה

Dan 9:18
Incline your ear, my God, and hear...

הטה אלהי אזנך ושמע

Ps 31:3
Incline your ear, my God...[206]

הטה אלי אזנך

Neh 1:6
Let your ears be attentive...

תהי נא אזנך־קשבת

Neh 1:11
And now, O YHWH, let your ears be attentive to the prayer of your servant...[207]

אנא אדני תהי נא אזנך־קשבת אל־תפלת עבדך

Dan 9:18
Open your eyes and see...

פקחה עיניך וראה

1 Kgs 8:29, 52
Let your eyes be open...

להיות עינך פתחות

Neh 1:6
And let ... your eyes be open...

ועיניך פתוחות

Dan 9:19
O Lord, hear, O Lord, forgive, be attentive, and act...

אדני שמעה אדני סלחה אדני הקשיבה ועשה

1 Kgs 8:39
And now, hear ... forgive... act...

ואתה תשמע... וסלחת... ועשית

Another example of a collection of short imperatives appears in Isa 37:17:

---

[206]Cf. Pss 17:6; 45:11; 71:2; 78:1; 86:1 88:3; 102:3; 116:2.
[207]Cf. Pss 5:3; 10:17; 17:1; 55:3; 61:2; 66:19; 86:6; 142:7.

Incline your ear, O YHWH, and hear, open your eyes, O YHWH, and see, and hear all the words of Sennecharib...

הטה יהוה אזנך ושמע פקח יהוה עיניך וראה ושמע את כל־דברי סנחריב...

These imperatives form part of Hezekiah's prayer, which is a plea of desperation as the Assyrian armies approach. He appeals to God to recognize what Sennacherib is planning and executing. Thus, the petitionary language in Daniel 9 is formulaic.

Petitions on behalf of the Temple

Concern for Jerusalem and its Temple stands at the heart of the petitionary formulae. According to the prayer, Antiochus IV's deeds have left both the city and the sanctuary "desolate" (שמם, vv. 17, 18), a word which also occurs in the narrative introduction and conclusion. In the introduction, Daniel specifically mentions the "desolation of Jerusalem" (v. 2), and in the conclusion, Gabriel uses the word when explaining the prophecy of Jeremiah. In the prayer, the shock of Antiochus's actions against Jerusalem also occupies the second half of v. 12, and then dominates vv. 16-19. This concern for Jerusalem pervades the whole chapter.

The author introduces the city's desolation in order to persuade God to act. According to the author, while the people deserve punishment and cannot ask a favor based on their own goodness, the city and Temple partake in God's holiness and bear his name.[208] Any assault on them affects God's reputation as well. For this reason, Daniel can ask God to turn back his "anger" and "wrath" from Jerusalem (v. 16). The author does this in v. 17 by a play on the Aaronic blessing: "And make your (i.e., God's) face shine" upon the Temple.[209]

Petition about Reproach from Neighbors

In v. 16, the petitioner states that Israel's neighbors insult the people. Psalmists make similar observations or complaints in laments. However, since Daniel's language closely parallels Deuteronomy, the author probably forms his petition with the curses and warnings with deuteronomic literature in mind.

---

[208]Cf. especially 3 Macc 2:9-10, 14-18.
[209]See Num 6:25; Ps 80:4, 8, 20. I emend the text in v. 17 by reading למענך for למען. This agrees with the LXX, Theodotion, and v. 19.

Dan 9:16 Your people have become a by-word to all those who surround us. ועמך לחרפה לכל־סביבתינו	Deut 28:37 ... and you will be an object of terror, a proverb, and a by-word among all the people where YHWH will drive you. והיית לשמה למשל ולשנינה בכל העמים אשר ־ינהגך יהוה שמה
	1 Kgs 9:7b Israel will become a proverb and a by-word among the peoples. (Cf. Jer 24:9-10; 29:18) והיה ישראל למשל ולשנינה בכל־העמים

Thus, the prayer's petitionary section is also conscious of the covenantal curses. However, this traditional language aptly addresses the Jews' current problems since their neighbors, the Syrians, are oppressing them.

The People as Bearers of God's Name

Like his statement about the Temple bearing God's name, i.e., his holiness, the prayer asserts that the people bear his name (v. 19). Consequently, their problems also endanger God's reputation among the nations, and, for this reason, God should act. The author, though, carefully distinguishes between this kind of holiness and the people's own goodness. God alone confers holiness; the people have not acquired it on their own. The people cannot base their petitions on their own goodness because they are sinners who can only rely on God's mercy (v. 18). Still, because they are called by God's name, they enjoy a special status in comparison to other peoples.

Summary

Daniel 9, then, presents the following image. A wise and understanding person, a *maskil*, meditates on the meaning of a cryptic and problematic scripture—a prophecy. In the process, the *maskil* prays a penitential prayer. Immediately, as the prayer begins, God sends an angel to reveal the text's meaning. The angel arrives and gives the interpreter "knowledge" and "understanding" about the meaning of the text. Combining this scene with the rest of Daniel, the *maskil* would most likely instruct others in this interpretation of Jeremiah, and, of course, the author instructs others about the meaning of the Jeremaic prophecy by writing Daniel 9. Casting the prayer in deuteronomic language and ideology, the author also criticizes Israel for its sin and petitions for God's forgiving mercy to deliver Israel. Deliverance will come, Gabriel reveals, but only according to God's apocalyptic time table.

Penitential Prayer and Interpretation: A Comparison of Daniel 9 to Sirach 38:24, 34-39:11 [38:24, 39:1-11 (LXX)]

Another example of penitential prayer functioning as a prelude to interpretation appears in a text prior to Daniel 9—Sir 38:24, 34-39:11. A comparison of the two texts yields several striking similarities, especially because the texts belong to different literary *genres* and spring from groups with disparate world views. Sirach is designated wisdom literature[210] and Daniel 9 is an apocalypse.[211] These similarities are possible because penitential prayer is a widely practiced religious institution in Second Temple Judaism that crosses literary, social, and ideological boundaries.

Ben Sira' refers to penitential prayer within the context of his description of the activity of the *sopher*, which he discusses in comparison to other occupations. Determination of penitential prayer's function begins by examining this context. According to Ben Sira', every city requires a variety of artisans in order to operate (Sir 38:32, 34). The combination of their skills makes daily life easier and fuller. The *sopher*, however, contributes in more important areas. He assumes prominent national and international roles and provides religious and moral guidance (38:32-33).

Instead of focusing on a technical skill related to a craft or trade, Ben Sira' says that the *sopher* "considers" (διανοουμένου) the "Law of the Most High" (ἐν νόμῳ ὑψίστου) and "makes his occupation" (ἀσχοληθήσεται) the "prophets" (39:1). The terms, "law" and "prophets," most likely refer what

---

[210]J. L. Crenshaw, *Old Testament Wisdom: An Introduction* (Atlanta: John Knox, 1981); G. von Rad, *Wisdom in Israel* (New York: Abingdon, 1972); B. L. Mack, *Wisdom and the Hebrew Epic: Ben Sira's Hymn in Praise of the Fathers* (Chicago: University of Chicago, 1985); R. E. Murphy, *Wisdom Literature: Job, Proverbs, Ruth, Canticles, Ecclesiastes and Esther*, FOTL 13 (Grand Rapids: Eerdmans, 1981); R. A. Argall, *1 Enoch and Sirach*, 1-13.

[211]See, e.g., J. J. Collins, *The Apocalyptic Imagination*, 1-8; J. J. Collins, *Daniel*, 6-10, 91-92.

Israel, or at least Ben Sira', considers scripture at this time.[212] Besides this, the *sopher* "seeks" (ἐκζητήσει) "the wisdom of all the ancients." His investigation into "the wisdom of all the ancients" (σοφίαν πάντων ἀρχαίων) includes wisdom traditions not only from Israel, but from other parts of the Ancient Near East and Greece.[213] The word "to seek" (ἐκζητεῖν) most certainly translates בקש or דרש, as it does in 51:13-20 for which both a Greek and Hebrew text exist.[214] He is especially attracted to the more difficult teaching forms of the wisdom tradition, as his work with "parables" (παραβολῶν) (v. 2) and "hidden proverbs" (ἀπόκρυφα παροιμιῶν) indicates.[215] As in v. 1, Ben Sira' returns to the metaphor "to seek" (ἐκζητήσει) in vv. 2b-3 in order to describe the *sopher's* activity. By the time of Ben Sira', studying these forms of wisdom is already a long standing tradition.[216] Such wisdom remains unavailable to average people and the artisans because, according to Ben Sira', it requires training, study, time for such study, and travel.[217] Consequently, the *sopher's* ability to interpret and teach these forms places him among the social religious elite.[218]

---

[212]In the prologue to the book, Ben Sira's grandson uses the designation "the Law and the Prophets" several times to refer to Israel's scripture. See also, G. W. E. Nickelsburg, *Jewish Literature*, 58.

[213]Cf. G. W. E. Nickelsburg, *Jewish Literature*, 58. Several scholars identify elements in Ben Sira' that are similar to the Stoics, Egyptian aretalogies to Isis, and the Egyptian concept *ma'at*. See, e.g., G. W. E. Nickelsburg, *Jewish Literature*, 60; M. Hengel, *Judaism and Hellenism*, 158; B. Mack, *Wisdom and the Hebrew Epic*, 91; P. W. Skehan and A. A. Di Lella, *The Wisdom of Ben Sira*, 46-50, 452; J. T. Sanders, *Ben Sira and Demotic Wisdom* (Chico: Scholars Press, 1983) 26-106.

[214]For the Hebrew text, see S. Schechter and S. Singer, *The Wisdom of Ben Sira: Portions of the Book Ecclesiasticus Hebrew Text, Edited from Manuscripts in the Cairo Genizah Collection* (Amsterdam: APA-Philo Press, 1979). A Hebrew text containing Sirach 51:13-20 also exists among the Qumran Scrolls, 11QPsa Sirach. See J. A. Sanders, *DJDJ IV: The Psalm Scroll of Qumran Cave 11* (Oxford: Clarendon, 1965) 79-85. See below for more on the relationship between Ben Sira' and 11QPsa Sirach. For more on textual issues related to Sirach, see A. A. Di Lella, *The Hebrew Text of Sirach: A Text-Critical and Historical Study* (London: Mouton, 1966); M. D. Nelson, *The Syriac Version of the Wisdom of Ben Sira Compared to the Greek and Hebrew Materials*, SBLDS 107 (Atlanta: Scholars, 1988).

[215]For more on wisdom forms, see, e.g., P. W. Skehan and A. A. Di Lella, *The Wisdom of Ben Sira*, 21-30.

[216]See, e.g., E. Bickerman, *The Jews in the Greek Age*, 168.

[217]P. W. Skehan and A. A. Di Lella (*The Wisdom of Ben Sira*, 452) compare visits to foreign countries to Daniel in Dan 1:3-4, 17-21; 2:49; 3:30; 5:29-30.

[218]B. Mack (*Wisdom and the Hebrew Epic*, 101-107) shows that the image of the "scholar-sage" in Ben Sira' places the wisdom teacher into the role of the Hellenistic heroes. Studying, teaching, and writing become heroic endeveavors.

Within this context of investigation of scripture and tradition, Ben Sira' says that the *sopher* confesses his sins in prayer:

> He gives his heart to rising early,
> to (seek) the Lord who made him,
> he petitions before the Most High,
> and opens his mouth in prayer,
> and he petitions concerning his sins.

> τὴν καρδίαν αὐτοῦ ἐπιδώσει ὀρθρίσαι
> πρὸς κύριον τὸν ποιήσαντα αὐτὸν
> καὶ ἔναντι ὑψίστου δεηθήσεται
> καὶ ἀνοίξει στόμα αὐτοῦ ἐν προσευχῇ
> καὶ περὶ τῶν ἁμαρτιῶν αὐτοῦ δεηθήσεται (39:5).

By combining study and penitential prayer, the *sopher* hopes that God will "fill" him with a "spirit of understanding" (πνεύματι συνέσεως) so that he may discern the meaning of difficult sayings and scripture (v. 6). In v. 7, the *sopher* relies on the continuing presence of this "spirit of understanding" to assist in further interpretation and meditations on scripture and tradition. In turn, the *sopher* fills others with wisdom through his instruction (v. 6). Therefore, God's pouring out of a "spirit of understanding" follows close to the *sopher's* confession. It seems that the confession is prerequisite for, or preparatory for, or leads to the interpretation of scripture and sayings of ancient sages. In turn, this "spirit of understanding" then pours forth from Ben Sira' in the act of instructing his students (v. 6), an image similar to his self-description as a teacher of *Torah* in Sir 24:30-34.

Prayer as a means for acquiring wisdom in general also appears in the autobiographical poem in Sir 51:13-30, an appendix to the book. The Qumran community possessed a Hebrew version of this poem. The canticle is part of a collection of psalmic material. As the differences between the two texts suggest, the Qumran community probably did not lift the poem from Sirach. Instead, the Qumran community and Sirach share a common canticle, which they may have both reworked.[219]

Whatever the history of these texts, the poem in Sirach provides another example of prayer as prelude to acquiring wisdom. It depicts Ben Sira' in a quest as a young man: "I sought wisdom openly in my prayer" (ἐζήτησα σοφίαν προφανῶς ἐν προσευχῇ μου/...ובקשתיה). Another image of prayer

---

[219]Cf. J. C. VanderKam, *The Dead Sea Scrolls Today*, (Grand Rapids: Eerdmans, 1994) 35; D. J. Harrington, *Wisdom Texts from Qumran* (London: Routledge, 1996) 28-30.

appears in v. 19, as the texts states: "I spread out my hands to the heavens" (τὰς χεῖράς μου ἐξεπέτασα πρὸς ὕψος/[...פתח]תי ידי).[220] As a result of his piety and diligent study, the Lord blesses him with wisdom and the ability to teach it (v. 22), and he concludes his book with a call to prospective students to come study with him. Thus, once again in this text, like chapter 39, prayer and study lead to the acquisition of wisdom and instruction.

According to chapter 39, once the *sopher* completes the interpretive process—he has studied, prayed, understood, and taught—his response is once again prayer, but this time a prayer of thanks: "And in prayer, he will give thanks to the Lord" (καὶ ἐν προσευχῇ ἐξομολογήσεται κυρίῳ)(39:6). Sirach as a literary whole reflects this same pattern. After the author has, in a sense, "poured forth" his written instruction in this book, he praises God in 51:1-12: "I give thanks to you, O Lord and King ..."(ἐξομολογοῦσομαί σοι, κύριε βασιλεῦ).[221] The Cairo Genizah Hebrew text adds another poem of thanksgiving at 51:12.

A Model for Interpretation

From the analysis of Sirach 39 and Daniel 9 emerge some striking similarities. Both Sirach's *sopher* and Daniel's *maskil* attempt to penetrate mysterious texts. While the two may look for different types of knowledge, they agree that text (whatever existed at the respective times of the authors) and tradition contain the needed knowledge. Both authors employ the metaphor "to seek" (בקש/[ἐκ]ζητέω) in order to speak of this activity. While Ben Sira' clearly uses the term for interpretation, Daniel's phrase "to seek by prayer" (v. 3) means something similar to Ben Sira'.[222]

In both texts, God gives the proper interpretation. In Sirach, God fills the *sopher* with a "spirit of understanding," while in Daniel, Gabriel arrives to

---

[220]The Qumran text, though, describes the author as spreading out his hands to wisdom to embrace her. J. A. Sanders (*DJDJ IV: The Psalms Scroll of Qumran Cave 11*, 84-85) believes that this may have erotic rather than prayerful overtones. Cf. also, D. J. Harrington, *Wisdom Texts from Qumran*, 28-30; C. Deutsch, "The Sirach 51 Acrostic Poem: Confession and Exhortation," *ZAW* 94 (1982) 400-409; T. Muraoka, "Sir. 51:13-30: An Acrostic Hymn to Wisdom?" *JSJ* 10 (1979) 166-178.

[221]I agree with Skehan and Di Lella (*The Wisdom of Ben Sira'*, 133) that the two postscript psalms in the Greek text are authentic.

[222]See, however, A. Lacocque ("The Liturgical Prayer in Daniel 9," *HUCA* 47 [1976] 129), who argues that God normally functions as the object of בקש. He recommends supplying the personal pronoun, which is frequently understood in Hebrew. The phrase would then translate: "to seek *him by* prayer and supplications."

relay the proper interpretation of Jeremiah. Thus, in both cases, understanding comes as revelation, but only after both sages offer penitential prayers to prepare for the moment of revelation.

While Daniel records the prayer within the narrative, Sirach does not present the content of the *sopher's* prayer. The function of penitential prayer in the deuteronomic tradition suggests that the language of the prayer of Ben Sira' may not have resembled the prayer in Daniel. Deuteronomic penitential prayers generally occur at moments of impending crises, contemporary problems, or national disasters. As this investigation has shown, while Daniel is in the process of interpretation, he is also experiencing Antiochus IV's reign of terror. However, because Ben Sira' is not responding to a national disaster, a deuteronomic penitential prayer probably would not serve his needs. Perhaps his prayer had a more individualistic instead of corporate focus.

Finally, if one considers the larger contexts of both Sirach and Daniel, both the *sopher* and the *maskil* engage in instruction. The *maskilim* instruct fellow Jews about the events leading up to the eschaton and how to live in the last days, while Ben Sira' shares his knowledge of difficult texts, and wisdom and etiquette, with his students.

Why is such a prayer needed? Since the authors believe that the interpretation of the text comes by divine revelation, the process involves coming into contact with the holy God. In the Bible, when humans encounter God, they typically immediately notice their sin and its dangers. Penitential prayer might anticipate this problem. Further, penitential prayer in this interpretive process tempers the sage's request with humility. In a sense, the sage recognizes that such wisdom can only come from God and not a sinful human. Only could such humility convince God to give divine knowledge. Finally, perhaps the sages thought that sin separates humans from God. This would prevent the possible divine-human encounter in the moment of revelation. Penitential prayer may remove that barrier and allow the revelatory interpretation to happen.

These two texts, then, testify to the function of penitential prayer within the process of interpretation. The act of penitential prayer leads up to and prepares the interpreter for the proper meaning of the text. Further, the presence of penitential prayer in these texts indicates that Jewish sages in the Second Temple period set their interpretive task within the context of piety. For some Jews, interpretation as an exercise cannot stand alone; it must be accompanied by prayer.

Chapter Two 87

Interpretation of Baruch 1:1-3:8

Introduction

Just as the political situation influences Daniel 9, the author of the prayer in Baruch writes in response to contemporary events in Palestine.[223] However, the historical circumstances in which each prayer originates are not the same, which accounts for several of the differences between the two prayers. Written after Daniel 9, Baruch dates to the period when the Jews have experienced success against the Seleucids.[224] Relying on the reference to the destruction that comes in the fifth year of the king's reign, J. Goldstein argues that one should date Baruch to the late winter or early spring of 163 BCE. The author of Baruch, then, writes after Judas has recaptured the Temple and has besieged the Akra;[225] the Hasmoneans are successfully rebelling against the Seleucids.

If one interprets these events by strictly adhering to deuteronomic ideology, the Jewish victories would mean that God has remitted the Jews' sins and is showering his blessings upon them. If this is the case, the proper response to God is no longer penitence, but thanksgiving. However, the author of Baruch reacts to these events with neither thanksgiving or praise—neither to Judas or to God. Rather, in a moment when the people seem to have won God's favor, the author engages in penitential prayer. He must assume, then, that Israel's sins persist and that the Hasmonean victories do not signify that the people now stand in God's favor.

Not all Jews embraced the Hasmonean rebellion against the Seleucids in order to secure the Temple nor their various claims to leadership. Further, many Jews did not accept the Hasmoneans' continued aggression after recapturing the Temple. Baruch's statements that the Jews' guilt and the

---

[223]For the problems with the setting for Baruch, see R. Pfeiffer, *History of New Testament Times*, 413-417; J. Goldstein, "The Apocryphal Book of I Baruch," 179; C. Moore, *Daniel, Esther, and Jeremiah: The Additions*, 255-256.

[224]I rely on J. Goldstein's ("The Apocryphal Book of I Baruch," 179-199) arguments for the date of Baruch. G. W. E. Nickelsburg (*Jewish Literature*, 153 n 43) also adopts this position. For more about the problems associatated with setting and dating, see: D. G. Burke, *The Poetry of Baruch: A Reconstruction and Analysis of the Original Hebrew Text of Baruch 3:9-5:9*, SBLSCS 10 (Chico: Scholars, 1982), 26-28; R. Pfeiffer, *History of New Testament Times*, 413-417; C. A. Moore, *Daniel, Esther, and Jeremiah: The Additions*, 255-256; O. H. Steck, *Das apokryphe Baruchbuch*, 285-303. Steck examines all the possibilities, but finally decides to accept a date during the rule of Antiochus V and Alcimus' priesthood, about late 163 to early 162 BCE (300-301).

[225]Cf. J. Goldstein, "The Apocryphal Book of I Baruch," 195-196.

covenant curses still cling to the people place the book's author among those who oppose the Hasmoneans.[226]

Baruch's prayer, then, reinterprets the tradition in common with Daniel and combines it with other material in order to criticize the Hasmonean policies. The author believes that God's punishment as well as the people's sins continue, and that the Hasmonean policies directly violate a divine ordinance. According to deuteronomic ideology, a violation of this nature spells further doom for the Jews.

Outline of Bar 1:1-3:8

Baruch 1:1-3:8 contains two major sections: a narrative introduction (1:1-14) and a penitential prayer (1:15-3:8). Penitential prayer rhetoric has left its marks on the narrative introduction. The prayer itself has the following outline: (1) confessions of sin (1:15-2:10); (2) petitions (2:11-18); (3) explanation of the prophetic message (2:19-26); (4) promises of restoration and new covenant as reward for repentance (2:27-35); (5) declaration of repentance and cry for deliverance (3:1-8). Comparable to Daniel, Baruch's prayer has a loose organization. Once again, a thematic approach best serves the task of interpreting the prayer.

Original Language

Kneucker and Tov argue persuasively for a Hebrew *Vorlage* for Bar 1:15-3:8.[227] In fact, Hebrew was probably the original language of the entire book.[228] The Greek text may be the work of one translator.[229] Although the

---

[226]J. Goldstein's ("The Apocryphal Book of I Baruch," 195-196) examination of the events during this period leads him to conclude that Baruch was written as a protest against Judas Maccabaeus' besieging of the Akra and "as propaganda for Alcimus and his followers, pious Jews who were loyal to the Seleucid government in the belief that God's time for the liberation of the Jews had not yet come."

[227]J. J. Kneucker, *Das Buch Baruch* (Leipzig: Brackhaus, 1879); E. Tov (*The Septuagint Translation of Jeremiah and Baruch*; *The Book of Baruch*) follows Kneucker. He basically reproduces Kneucker's text, with a few changes, in *The Book of Baruch*.

[228]R. H. Pfeiffer (*History of New Testament Times*, 420), following Whitehouse ("The Book of Baruch," *APOT* I, 589), lists several variants between the Greek and Syriac manuscripts that he believes might have arisen as separate renderings of a Hebrew text. Pfeiffer also lists instances where the Greek text has probably mistranslated a Hebrew original (420-421). J. Goldstein ("The Apocryphal Book of I Baruch," 188-189) asserts that the stylistic changes from the prose to the poetic sections in Baruch, which have served as evidence against the book's unity and the idea that book represents a Greek translation of a Hebrew text that was a unity, resemble the changes between the prose and poetic sections of Jonah.

[229]J. Goldstein, "The Apocryphal Book of I Baruch," 187.

author pulled together material from several traditions, perhaps even preexisting texts, Baruch as it presently exists has a single purpose.[230]

The Narrative Introduction (1:1-14)

The narrative introduction establishes a penitential atmosphere by depicting the exiles engaged in penitential rituals and using penitential rhetoric. As in other penitential contexts, the people weep, fast, and pray. These actions signify both the people's lamentable condition and their contrition (v. 5). The exiles instruct the inhabitants of Jerusalem how to repent and what to pray, and they request that the inhabitants of Jerusalem intercede on their behalf (v. 13). The exiles' confession reveals that they understand their predicament as punishment from God:

> ... for we have sinned against the Lord our God. The Lord's anger and his wrath have not turned away from us to this day (1:13).

The penitential prayer that follows this narrative introduction also emphasizes that God's wrath remains upon the people. Both the introduction and the prayer indicate this through the use of the phrase, "to this day" (ἕως τῆν ἡμέρας ταύτης) (1:13).[231] Thus, the author sees a direct correspondence between his fictional world and the real world. Like the days of the "historical Baruch," the Jews' present problems have arisen because of their sin and provide evidence that the deuteronomic curses remain in effect.

The introduction exhorts the Jews to submit patiently to the foreign king, and pray for the him and his son (1:12). With this behavior they hope to win the king's favor so that Israel will prosper and God will "brighten" their "eyes." This language resembles Ezra's words that describe the Persian kings' favorable disposition toward Israel (cf. Bar 1:12; 3:14; Ezr 9:8).[232] This instruction also ties the narrative to Jeremiah's teaching about submitting to the foreign ruler that comes later in the prayer.[233]

---

[230]See also O. H. Steck, *Das apokryphe Baruchbuch*, 253-265.
[231]Cf. Bar 1:15, 20; 2:16, 11, 26; Ezra 9:7, 15; 9:36; Dan 9: 7 and 16.
[232]For a discussion of this metaphor, see Chapter One.
[233]Baruch's instruction to submit to the foreign ruler reappears in the prayer (2:21-24). He draws this teaching from Jer 27:11-12.

The letter's instructions to the recipients to "confess in the house of the Lord upon feast days and at appointed times" (1:14) is comparable to Neh 9:3:[234]

Bar 1:14	Neh 9:3
And read from this book which we have sent you, and confess in the house of the Lord on feast days and at appointed times.	And they stood in their place and read from the book of the law of the Lord their God making confession and praising the Lord their God.

However, the two texts differ in regard to the book that the people read. Baruch refers to this letter that he has written to Jerusalem's inhabitants, while Nehemiah means "book of the law." Like the previous texts in this discussion, Baruch at least testifies to a close relationship between reading a text and penitential prayer.[235]

The introduction, then, contains several significant ideas, namely, that the covenantal curses continue, that the people remain in their sins and must repent through confession, and that they must submit to the foreign ruler. For the author, it is acceptance of these ideas that will bring deliverance. Consequently, the Jews must not continue to support the Hasmoneans' aggressive policies.

The Prayer (1:15-3:8)

The author moves from the narrative introduction to the prayer by a simple narrative transition: Baruch instructs the people to pray the prayer he has written for them. Therefore, the people not only receive instruction *to pray*, but also *what to pray*. The prayer becomes more than a simple confession because it also identifies the Jews' sins, tells them what to say in regard to these sins, and how they should think and act. In other words, despite its traditional and formulaic language, the prayer bears the mark of the author's ideology that he also wants his readers to adopt.

---

[234]E. Tov, *The Book of Baruch*, 15.

[235]Reading from various books, which eventually ended up in the Hebrew Bible, on festival days later became prescribed in Judaism. See C. A. Moore, *Daniel, Esther, and Jeremiah*, 274. The author of the hymn that closes 1QS agrees that one should observe certain days with prayers and praise to God (1QS 10-11). See also, B. Nitzan (*Qumran Prayer*, 49-63) for fixed times for prayer at Qumran and early Judaism.

Recognition of Punishment and Confession of Sin (1:15-18)

The prayer immediately indicates that the Jews are guilty of sin. The author expresses this through the use of a *Gerichtsdoxologie* and by an acclamation of the petitioners' shame. Baruch's language is traditional and closely parallels Dan 9:7, which also resembles Ezr 9:7:

Bar 1:15	Dan 9:7
To you, O Lord our God, is righteousness, but to us is shame of face as to this day, to the men of Judah and the inhabitants of Jerusalem.	To you, O Lord , is righteousness, but to us is shame of face as to this day to the men of Judah and the inhabitants of Jerusalem...
τῷ κυρίῳ θεῷ ἡμῶν ἡ δικαιοσύνη, ἡμῖν δὲ αἰσχύνη τῶν προσώπων ὡς ἡ ἡμέρα αὕτη ἀνθρώπῳ Ιουδα καὶ τοῖς κατοικοῦσιν Ιερουσαλημ.	לך אדני הצדקה ולנו בשת הפנים כיום הזה לאיש יהודה וליושבי ירושלם...

Another *Gerichtsdoxologie* and declaration of shame conclude the first section of the prayer (Bar 2:6-10). These verses join phrases from earlier portions of the prayer to material in common with Daniel 9:13-14. In these verses, the author connects the calamities (i.e., the covenantal curses), that have visited the people to the people's refusal to repent and their continued wickedness.[236] Thus, from the beginning, the prayer displays "strong consciousness of sin, guilt, and punishment."[237]

In both examples of the *Gerichtsdoxologie* the author emphasizes the continuation of the Jews' guilt with the phrase, "as to this day" (1:13, 20; 2:6, 11, and 26). Its repetition suggests that the author believes that this is true of both his fictional world and his real world. According to the prayer, as long as the Jews refuse to submit to the foreign powers, God's punishment will continue. Since some of the author's contemporaries are engaged in rebellion, God's punishment continues to the author's time.

Israel's Sinful History (1:19-22)

The prayer traces the Jews' problems with sin to the early days of Israel's history—the Exodus. In fact, he casts Israel's history as a history of sin:

---

[236]For the description of the people's refusal to repent, the author draws on Jer 7:24. Cf. also Jer 3:17; 11:8; 16:12; 18:12; Pss 33:11; 81:13.

[237]G. W. E. Nickelsburg, *Jewish Literature*, 113.

From the day that the Lord our God brought our fathers out from the land of Egypt, even to this day, we have been disobedient to the Lord our God, and have rebelled so as not to obey his voice (Bar 1:19).

ἀπὸ τῆς ἡμέρας ἧς ἐξήγαγεν κύριος τοὺς πατέρας ἡμῶν ἐκ γῆς Ἀιγύπτου, καὶ ἕως τῆς ἡμέρας ταύτης ἤμεθα ἀπειθοῦντες πρὸς κύριον θεὸν ἡμῶν καὶ ἐσχεδιάζομεν πρός τὸ μὴ ἀκούειν τῆς φωνῆς αὐτοῦ.

A comparison with Jer 7:25 and Deut 9:7 indicates the formulaic character of the above language:

Jer 7:25	Deut 9:7
... from the day that your ancestors came out of the land of Egypt to this day...[238]	... from the day that you came out of the land of Egypt until you came to this place...
למן־היום אשר יצאו אבותיכם מארץ מצרים עד היום הזה	למן־היום אשר־יצאת מארץ מצרים עד־באכם עד־המקום הזה

The statements in Baruch evoke images of Israel's rebellions in the wilderness.[239] The two admissions of disobedience in Bar 1:19, "we have been disobedient to the Lord our God, and have rebelled so as not to obey his voice," are deuteronomic expressions.[240] Thus, while this language does not originate in the Exodus formula, it is still formulaic.

---

[238]Cf. 2 Kgs 21:15; Deut 9:7.
[239]See Chapter One's discussion of Third Isaiah and Nehemiah 9.
[240]C. A. Moore, *Daniel, Esther, and Jeremiah*, 279; J. J. Kneucker, *Das Buch Baruch*, 224. The final phrase contains an odd word, σχεδιάζω. It means "to act hastily," and would represent the Hebrews words קלל or מהר. The term σχεδιαζεῖν is a *hapax legomenon* in the LXX and makes little sense in this context. Kneucker suggests that Baruch follows Dan. 9:11 which means that the Hebrew text of Baruch probably contained סור in the form of an infinitive absolute. E. Tov (*The Book of Baruch*, 16-17) accepts Kneucker's Hebrew retroversion without explanation. In his concordance in the appendix (44), Tov lists σχεδιάζω as corresponding to סור. Whitehouse ("The Book of Baruch," *APOT*, I, 578) argues that the text might have originally read מרדנו, "we rebelled," but someone mistakenly misread the text as מהרנו. Whitehouse's position has more to commend itself than Kneucker's arguments. Against Kneucker, Baruch does not follow Daniel 9 in this verse. As shown above, the language in the rest of the verse comes from elsewhere. Terms like "rebel," "sin," and "turn" are so common in these prayers that one could hardly determine that Baruch has borrowed from Daniel 9 at this juncture in the text.

Chapter Two

Disregarding the Prophetic Word (1:21 and 2:24-26)

This concern about the nation's persistent guilt raises a fundamental question: Of what is it guilty? As the expositions of Daniel and Ezra show, authors sometimes use penitential prayers as a way to criticize something occurring at the time in which they write. Baruch's prayer condemns the Hasmonean rebellion. The prayer asserts that as long as the rebellion persists, the Jews stand in violation of Jeremiah's message. In anticipation of his argument that the people have disobeyed this Jeremianic instruction, the author includes Israel's rejection of the prophetic word in his enumeration of the nation's sins. With language that originates in Deuteronomy and Jeremiah, and that also resembles Daniel 9, v. 21 levels this indictment against the people.

Dan 9:10	Bar 1:21
And we did not obey the voice of YHWH, our God, to walk in his laws that he gave to us by the hands of his servants the prophets	And we did not obey the voice of the Lord, our God according to all the words of the prophets whom he sent to us.
ולא שמענו בקל יהוה אלהינו ללכת בתורתיו אשר נתן לפנינו ביד עבדיו הנביאים	καὶ οὐκ ἠκούσαμεν τῆς φωνῆς κυρίου τοῦ θεοῦ ἡμῶν κατὰ πάντας τοὺς λόγους τῶν προφητῶν, ὧν ἀπέστειλεν πρὸς ἡμᾶς.

Baruch's additions of the words "to walk in his laws which he gave to us" and the phrase "whom he sent to us" derive from traditions about God sending the prophets to Israel, for example Jer 26:4b-5a:

> If you do not obey me to walk in the laws that I give you, to obey all the words of my servants the prophets whom I sent to you...
>
> אם־לא תשמעו אלי ללכת בתורתי אשר נתתי לפניכם: לשמע על־דברי עבדי הנביאים אשר אנכי שלח אליכם...

Baruch expands the tradition of Israel rejecting the prophetic word by providing the specific teaching that the nation has violated. Using the following passages from Jeremiah, he claims that the prophet instructs the people to submit to foreign overlords: Bar 2:22 comes from Jer 27:9; Bar 2:23 derives from Jer 7:34; 16:9; 33:10-11; Bar 2:24 draws on Jer 27:11-12; Bar 2:24-25 originates in Jer 8:1-2; and the terms "famine," "sword," and "pestilence" in Bar 2:25 frequently appear in Jeremiah.[241] According to the author of Baruch, the prophet's foreign political policy remains in effect even in the Second

---

[241] See Jer 14:12; 24:10; 32:36; 38:2; cf. 1 Kgs 8:37.

Temple Period. Just as Israel should not have rebelled against the Babylonians, so the Jews of the author's time must not rebel against the Seleucid king, Antiochus V.[242] If the reader doubts whether or not Jeremiah's instructions remain applicable to the Seleucid problem, the author once again employs the phrase "as to this day" in v. 26. To resist the king becomes tantamount to revolt against God, an act that always leads to disaster for Israel.

The Covenantal Curses (1:20 and 3:4)

Since the Jews' guilt remains, God's punishment continues as well. This punishment is a manifestation of the covenantal curses. In order to stress that the curses are a persistent problem, he draws on an image from Deuteronomy: the curses "cling" to the people. The prayer contains two instances of this metaphor:

    Bar 1:20   Therefore, to this day the evils and the curses have *clung* to us...

                  καὶ ἐκολλήθη εἰς ἡμᾶς τὰ κακὰ καὶ ἡ ἀρά...

    Bar 3:4   ... the evil *clings* to us.

                  ... ἐκολλήθη ἡμῖν τὰ κακά.

The author borrows his image from Deut 28:21 and 60:

    v. 21   The Lord will make the plague *cling* to you.

                  ידבק יהוה בך את־הדבר

    v. 60   And he will bring against you all the sickness of Egypt ... and it *will cling* to you (ודבקו בך).

Just as the Jews are in shame "to this day," God's punishment "remains to this day" through the curses that "cling" to them.

    The notion that the nation remains under the covenantal curses has important ramifications for the author's view of Israel's history. The author

---

[242]This is J. Goldstein's argument in "The Apocryphal Book of I Baruch," 195-196.

omits a reference to the period of restoration under Persian rule as a sign of the end of God's punishment for Israel's sins.[243] This type of omission occurs elsewhere in the literature of Second Temple Judaism (see e.g., the Apocalypse of Weeks, the *Damascus Document*, and *Jubilees*); the time of restoration under Persia was a period of sin. Therefore, according to Baruch, the restoration as Deuteronomy and the prophets had promised never arrived. As in Daniel 9, the author of Baruch recognizes a dissonance between the divine promises and historical reality.

Punishment (2:1-5)

According to the author, Antiochus IV's violence against the Jews validates the claim that God remains angry at the Jews' for their sinfulness (2:1-5, see especially v. 5). In order to allude to Antiochus IV's desecration of the Temple, the author returns to the material in common with Daniel.

Bar 2:1-2	Dan 9:12-13
And the Lord established his word which he spoke against us, and upon our judges who judged Israel and upon our kings and upon our rulers and upon the men of Israel and Judah.	And he established his word which he spoke against us, and against our judges who judged us
For is was not done under all the heavens as he did in Jerusalem. As it is written in the Law of Moses...	to bring upon us a great evil that was not done under all the heavens as was done in Jerusalem. As is written in the Law of Moses...
καὶ ἔστησεν κύριος τὸν λόγον αὐτοῦ ὃν ἐλάλησεν ἐφ᾽ ἡμᾶς καὶ ἐπὶ τοὺς δικαστὰς ἡμῶν τοὺς δικάσαντας τὸν Ισραηλ καὶ ἐπὶ τοὺς βασιλεῖς ἡμῶν καὶ ἐπὶ τοὺς ἄρχοντας ἡμῶν καὶ ἐπὶ ἄνθρωπον Ισραηλ καὶ Ιουδα.	ויקם את־דבריו אשר־דבר עלינו ועל שפטינו אשר שפטונו
	להביא עלינו רעה גדלה...
οὐκ ἐποιήθη ὑποκάτω παντὸς τοῦ οὐρανοῦ καθὰ ἐποίησεν ἐν Ιερουσαλημ κατὰ τὰ γεγραμμένα ἐν τῷ νόμῳ Μωυσῆ.	אשר לא־נעשתה תחת כל־ השמים כאשר נעשתה בירושלם כאשר כתוב בתורת משה

---

[243]Cf. J. Goldstein ("The Apocryphal Book of I Baruch," 198): "Daniel confesses only sins of the past before the destruction of the temple. Bar. 1:19 unambiguously states that the sins have continued into the present."

By listing the judges with other figures from Israel's past, Baruch casts them as historical personalities, not judges in general or contemporary leaders. In contrast, the LXX in Daniel 9 employs κριτής, which depicts the judges as rulers in general.[244] Baruch's representation of the judges as historical figures fits his notion that Israel has been sinful since its early days.

When Baruch's author writes, the Temple no longer remains under Seleucid control. Because of these historical realities, the author cannot continue to focus on the Temple's profaned status as Daniel does. This, in fact, would weaken the author's position that God's punishment continues. To compensate for this, he incorporates an account of cannibalism during Antiochus V's siege. The author works this account into Bar 2:3-5 by expanding upon Daniel's statement: "For it was not done under the heavens as he did in Jerusalem. As it is written in the Law of Moses..."[245] Did the author know of an actual case of this during Antiochus's reign of terror, hear circulating rumors about such a scene, or assume it occurred since the Law (and Jeremiah) predicted it?[246] Three passages, Lev 26:29, Deut 28:53, and Jer 19:9, speak of Israelites eating the flesh of their sons and daughters. Since the author mentions that the "Law of Moses" warns about this, Deuteronomy and Leviticus, instead of eyewitness accounts, probably influence his insertion of reports of cannibalism. He includes this horrific image in order to depict the magnitude of the Jews' sins. Only sincere contrition and repentance can remove the guilt of deeds that lead to such an unbelievable end.

Syria's most recent siege and the horrors connected with it lead the author to conclude that the surrounding nations have no esteem for the Jews as a nation. According to deuteronomic tradition, this diminished status is a manifestation of the covenantal curses. While Dan 9:16 referred to suffering the nations' reproaches, Baruch's language more closely resembles Jer 29:18 (cf. also Deut 28:37):[247]

---

[244] C. A. Moore, *Daniel, Esther, and Jeremiah*, 280.

[245] I have punctuated the text differently from the NRSV, which places a comma after "Jerusalem" and a period after "Law of Moses." This punctuation directly associates the account of cannibalism with what is written in the Law of Moses. The NRSV's punctuation connects "the Law of Moses" to the previous description of Jerusalem.

[246] Josephus relates a famous story about cannibalism during the Jewish War with Rome in 66-70. See *Jewish Wars*, 6.3.4

[247] For the linking of these sorts of terms, see Jer 19:18; 25:9, 18; 51:37; Mic 6:16; 2 Chron 29:8 (*BDB*, 1056-1057). Cf. Deut 28:25.

Bar 2:4	Jer 29:18b
And he gave them to subjection to all the kingdoms around us for a reproach and for an object of horror	Giving them as an object of horror all the kingdoms of the earth for a curse, and for a desolation, and an object of hissing, and a reproach
among all the surrounding people among whom the Lord scattered them there.	among all the nations among which I scattered them there.
καὶ ἔδωκεν αὐτοὺς ὑποχειρίους πάσαις ταῖς βασιλείαις ταῖς κύκλῳ ἡμῶν εἰς ὀνειδισμὸν καὶ εἰς ἄβατον ἐν πᾶσι τοῖς λαοῖς τοῖς κύκλῳ, οὗ διέσπειρεν αὐτοὺς κύριος ἐκεῖ.	ונתתים לזועה לכל ממלכות הארץ לאלה ולשמה ולשרקה ולחרפה בכל־הגוים אשר־הדחתים שם

Thus, as long as other nations hold Israel in reproach, the author could argue that God's wrath remains against the Jews. According to the book of Baruch, the era of God's blessing will include the Jews' elevation over all the nations, and especially salvation from their enemies (see e.g., Bar 4:21-5:9). Only repentance will ease God's anger, lead to respect from the nations, and alter their situation. The armed aggression that the Hasmoneans propose will not bring these results. Following their plan will provoke God to wrath.

The Deuteronomic Cycle (2:27-35)

Despite the author's critical perspective on the nation's religious condition, he still has hope. Just as he employs deuteronomic ideology and language to criticize the nation, he also uses these to encourage the readers that salvation remains possible. This combination of sin—punishment—repentance—restoration provides another example of a complete deuteronomic cycle, which occurs in the petitionary section of the prayer (2:27-35). The most important texts for the author are Deuteronomy 4 and 30, 1 Kings 8, and Jeremiah. As Chapter One demonstrates, these texts teach that the people will repent after God drives them into exile. Baruch speaks of the exilic repentance of these characteristically "stiff necked" (σκληροτράχηλος)(v. 30).[248] With the unusual figure of speech "to turn to one's heart" from Deut 30:1 and 1 Kgs 8:47, the author anticipates the people's recognition of sin:

---

[248]See Exod 33:3, 5; 34:9; Deut 9:6, 13; cf Sir 16:11.

Bar 2:30b

καὶ ἐπιστρέψουσιν ἐπὶ καρδίαν
αὐτῶν ἐν γῇ ἀποικισμοῦ αὐτῶν.

Deut 30:1

והשבת אל־לבבך בכל־הגוים אשר
הדיחך יהוה אלהיך שמה

1 Kgs 8:47

והשיבו אל־לבם בארץ אשר נשבו־שם

As Chapter One states, this phrase, "to search one's heart," means to reflect on the nation's difficulties and to understand that these problems have arisen because the people have sinned. Of course, this line of thinking follows the logic of deuteronomic ideology, but he expands the meaning of the phrase so that it incorporates the interpretation of Jeremiah's warning to obey the foreign king. According to Baruch, "to turn to one's heart" also requires the Jews to accept the proper interpretation of the prophetic word and reflect on its meaning and their own behavior.

In the verse that follows, the author borrows an image from Jeremiah in which God gives the people a new heart so that they will acknowledge him:

Bar 2:31

And they will acknowledge that I am the Lord their God. And I will give them a heart and ears to hear.

καὶ γνώσονται ὅτι ἐγὼ κύριος ὁ
θεὸς αὐτῶν. καὶ δώσω αὐτοῖς
καρδίαν καὶ ὦτα ἀκούντα...

Jer 24:7

And I will give them a heart to acknowledge me, that I am Yahweh.

ונתתי להם לב לדעת אתי כי אני יהוה

The text further depicts people's change of heart with a reference to them "praising" God in the exile (v. 32). The word "praise" (αἰνέω) probably translates the Hiph of ידה in the original Hebrew text of the prayer.[249] Recognizing and turning from their stubbornness (v. 33), and, thus undoing the problem mentioned in Bar 2:30, the people will return to the land as Lev 26:42-45; Deut 30:1-5, 20; 1 Kgs 8:48.[250] After God reverses the curse of reducing Israel as a nation, i.e., he makes them increase (v. 34; cf. Deut 30:5; Bar 2:13 and 29), the author alludes to Jer 32:38-40 in order to recall God's promise to establish a new covenant with Israel (Bar 2:35):[251]

---

[249]J. J. Kneucker, *Das Buch Baruch*, 257.
[250]Cf. also Jer 24:6; 30:3, 19.
[251]Cf. Jer 31[38]:33.

Bar 2:35	Jer 32:38b and 40a
And I will establish an eternal covenant. And I will be their God and they will be my people. And I will never again remove Israel from the land that I gave them.	And they will be my people and I will be their God. And I will establish an eternal covenant.
Καὶ στήσω αὐτοῖς διαθήκη αἰώνιον τοῦ εἶναί με αὐτοῖς εἰς θεὸν καὶ αὐτοὶ ἔσονταί μοι εἰς λαόν καὶ οὐ κινήσω ἔτι τὸν λαόν μου Ισραηλ ἀπὸ τῆς γῆς, ἧς ἔδωκα αὐτοῖς.	והיו לי לעם ואני אהיה להם לאלהים ... וכרתי להם ברית עולם

The author's use of the deuteronomic cycle, and its placement at the end of this section, impresses upon his audience that repentance provides the only way out of Seleucid domination.

Summary

The accusation of disobeying the prophets, which is part of the formulaic package from the material in common with Daniel, occupies a key position in Baruch. Baruch takes the word of the prophet very seriously, especially the word of Jeremiah since the author places himself explicitly within that tradition. The author maintains that Jeremiah's teaching that Israel must submit to the foreign overlords remains in effect even in the Second Temple Period. If the Jews continue their aggressive campaign against the Seleucids, they will have violated a specific prophetic teaching of Jeremiah. Consequently, punishment is inevitable. Baruch's prayer, then, directly attacks those supporting the Hasmoneans' aggression. They must not deceive themselves by believing that Hasmonean success means that God has lifted the covenantal curses. The curses are clearly observable. Because the Hasmonean policy directly contradicts the prophetic word, the Jews are in jeopardy.

The Petitions (2:11-16)

The chief concern of the petitionary section is to bring an end to the wrath of God, which previous portions of the prayer describe. According to deuteronomic ideology, the author can only offer his petitions after he has confessed the people's sins. After the people have dealt with their sins, God can help them. Any other order to the prayer would defy deuteronomic ideology.

Past Deliverance: The Exodus (2:11)

The words καὶ νῦν separate the prayer's petitionary section from the previous verses, even though the author inserts confessions into the section. Neh 9:32 and Dan 9:15 contain similar rhetorical indicators which mark the beginning of petitionary sections. Baruch also preserves the tension between God's gracious salvation in the Exodus and Israel's sins found in the material in common with Daniel (Dan 9:15). Thus, before the author asks God to bring deliverance as in days of old, his deep sense of the nation's guilt constrains him to demonstrate to God that he remembers the people's sins even as he petitions for help (v. 12). Baruch's reference to the Exodus follows the material in common with Dan 9:15, to which Baruch adds portions from Jer 32:21, the italicized words in the text from Baruch below:

Bar 2:11
And now, O Lord God of Israel who brought your people out of Egypt with a strong hand *and with signs, and wonders,* and great powers, *and with an outstretched arm* and made for yourself a name as to this day.

Καὶ νῦν, κύριε ὁ θεὸς Ισραηλ, ὃς ἐξήγαγες τὸν λαόν σου ἐκ γῆς Αἰγύπτου ἐν χειρὶ κραταιᾷ καὶ ἐν σημείοις καὶ ἐν τέρασι καὶ ἐν δυνάμει μεγάλῃ καὶ ἐν βραχίονι ὑψηλῷ καὶ ἐποίησας σεαυτῷ ὄνομα ὡς ἡ ἡμέρα αὕτη...

Dan 9:15
And now, O Lord our God, who brought your people out from the land of Egypt with a strong hand

and made for yourself a name as to this day...

ועתה אדני אלהינו אשר
הוצאת את־עמך מארץ
מצרים ביד חזקה

ותעש־לך שם
כיום הזה...

Jer 32:21
And brought your people Israel from the land of Egypt *with signs, and wonders, and with a strong hand, and with an outstretched arm,* and with great terror.

ותצא את־עמך את־ישראל מארץ מצרים
באתות ובמופתים וביד חזקה ובאזרוע
נטויה ובמורא גדול

Neh 1:10 and 9:10 mention God's "mighty arm," and Neh 9:10 also spoke of the "signs" and "wonders" God performed in the event. Like Baruch, Neh 9:9-10 and Isa 63:14 claimed that God "made a name for himself," i.e., established a reputation for himself, in the Exodus. Baruch's claim that God's good reputation continues "until this day" nicely parallels the statements about Israel's sin and punishment persisting "to this day" (ὡς ἡ ἡμέρα αὕτη). This correspondence also offers hope that despite Israel's miserable condition, God might deliver them.

Petition to Remove Wrath (2:12)

The simple threefold confession in v. 12 resembles 1 Kgs 8:47; 2 Chron 6:37; and Dan 9:15. The remainder of v. 12, the prepositional phrase, ἐπὶ πᾶσιν τοῖς δικαιώμασιν σου, and the vocative address to God, goes with the following sentence in v. 13, as Kneucker[252] and Tov[253] translate it, instead of with the threefold confession.[254] Tov suggests that the Hebrew originally read ככל, but had somehow been corrupted to read על כל, the reading that the Greek translator found in the text.[255] Reading the prepositional phrase in this manner makes it lead up to the request for God to remove his wrath. The word Δικαίωμα, which represents צדקה, alludes to God's saving deeds. Δικαίωμα may also translate משפט or חקים instead of צדקה, except that these Hebrew words usually take the verbs שמר or עשה, verbs that this verse does not use. Kneucker's and Tov's position finds further confirmation because Bar 2:12b-13a parallels Dan 9:16, which, in fact, contains Kneucker's and Tov's reconstruction. The whole Greek phrase probably translates the Hebrew phrase יהוה אלהינו ככל צדקתיך.[256]

Petition for Favor before Captors (2:13b-16)

While the prayer teaches the Jews that they should submit to the foreign ruler, it also asks God to allow the Jews to find respect in the eyes of this power. Still, foreign domination is a sign that the covenantal curses remain in effect. Therefore, the author develops these petitions in 2:13b-16 by reversing the warning of Deut 4:27 and the covenantal curse in Deut 28:62.[257]

---

[252]J. J. Kneucker, *Das Buch Baruch*, 352.
[253]E. Tov, *The Book of Baruch*, 20-21.
[254]The RSV, NRSV, C. A. Moore, (*Daniel, Esther, and Jeremiah*, 283), and Whitehouse *OTP*, vol. 1, 5, 85) all place the prepositional phrase and the address to God with the confession. They do not mention an alternative reading.
[255]E. Tov, *The Book of Baruch*, 21 n f.
[256]Ibid., 21.
[257]Cf. Jer 42:3; Pr Az 14.

Corresponding to the hope that the Jews will increase, the suppliant desires to find favor among the nation that captured the people. He sets up this request in v. 14 by using the material in common with Dan 9:17:[258]

Bar 2:14	Dan 9:17
Hearken, O Lord, to our prayer and to our supplications...	And now, hearken, our God, to the prayer of your servant and to his supplications.
Εἰσάκουσον, κύριε, τῆς προσευχῆς ἡμῶν καὶ τῆς δεήσεως ἡμῶν...	ועתה שמע אלהינו אל־תפלת עבדך ואל תחנוניו

The language of the petition asking for favor from the captors sounds like 1 Kgs 8:50:

Bar 2:14c	1 Kgs 8:50b
And give us grace in the presence of those who captured us.	And give them mercy in the presence of those who captured them.
Καὶ δὸς ἡμῖν χάριν κατὰ πρόσωπον τῶν ἀποικισάντων ἡμᾶς.	ונתתם לרחמים לפני שביהם ורחמום

This petition also recalls a theme from the narrative introduction where the exiles explicitly ask the inhabitants of Jerusalem to pray that their overlords would look upon them with favor (1:11-12). The prayer's repetition of this theme confirms that this blessing comes only through repentance. Therefore, even though the petition seeks to resolve a problem in the author's time, his language is thoroughly traditional and formulaic.

The reason for his request for an improvement in the Jews' status before their captors does not seek glory for the Jews themselves. Rather, honor that comes from the Jews' improved condition will go to God: "in order that all the earth might know that you are the Lord our God" (2:15). The author takes the phrase from prophetic pronouncements of judgment where God acts so that the nations might know that he is the Lord God.[259] Also in the Exodus narratives, the Bible incorporates this theme as the Exodus compels the Egyptians to recognize that Israel's God is the only God.[260]

---

[258]Cf. 1 Kgs 8:49; 2 Chron 6:19; and Neh 1:10.
[259]See e.g., Isa 49:26; Ezek 29:6, 9, 16, 21; 30:8, 19, 25, and 26.
[260]Exod 6:7; 7:5, 17; 8:10, 22; 9:14, 29; 10:2; 11:7; 14:4, 8; 16:6, 12; 29:46.

Chapter Two   103

God's Remoteness (2:16-18)

The people's deep contrition and their desperate situation provide the author with another way to persuade God to act (Bar 2:16-18). First, in order to depict God's remoteness, the author evokes the image of God enthroned in the heavens (v. 16). Such speech sometimes guards against the improper belief that God literally dwells in the Jerusalem Temple.[261] While Baruch certainly does not contradict such an idea, the image emphasizes God's distance from Israel as a reuslt of the people's sins. As punishment, God withdraws from Israel into the heavens; he no longer dwells in the midst of the nation.[262] The suppliant's plea in v. 16 for God to incline his ear and hear Israel's cries, and the plea in v. 17 for God to open his eyes and see express this same notion of distance.[263]

The idea of alienation from God continues in vv. 17-18, but the argument shifts from the importance of God receiving appropriate worship to a statement about who is able to ascribe glory and righteousness to God. Since the Jews alone offer God his proper praise, he should relent from his anger before all of them die and descend to Sheol. There, they will be unable to praise him and testify to his glory and righteousness. Consequently, God's glory would go unacknowledged. The author adapts this argument from Ps 30:9, which extensively resembles Baruch.

While the author of Baruch claims that the dead cannot praise God, he recognizes that those who bend beneath the weight of God's discipline can fulfill the task (v. 18). For the portrait of one incurring God's discipline, the prayer returns to Deuteronomy 28:

Bar 2:18	Deut 28:65b
But the soul greatly mourning, the one walking slowly, stooped over, and failing eyes, with a humble soul.	And the Lord will give to you there a quaking heart and failing eyes, and a languishing soul.
ἀλλὰ ἡ ψυχὴ ἡ λυπουμένη ἐπὶ τὸ μέγεθος, ὃ βαδίζει κύπτον καὶ ἀσθενοῦν καὶ οἱ ὀφθαλμοὶ οἱ ἐκλείποντες καὶ ἡ ψυχὴ ἡ πεινῶσα...	ונתן יהוה לך שם לב רגז וכליון עינים ודאבון נפש

---

[261] See Deut 26:15; 1 Kgs 8:27; 2 Chr 6:18; Isa 63:5; Pr Azar 31 [3:53].
[262] Cf. the metaphor "turn your face" in Chapter One.
[263] For the petition "incline your ear and hear," cf. 1 Kgs 8:30, 32, 34, 36, 39, 43, 45, 49; Dan 9:18. For the petition "open your eyes and see," cf. 1 Kgs 8:52 and Dan 9:18.

In language comparable to Baruch, Ps 51:15-17 and Isa 66:2 tell how God accepts the oppressed individual in the stead of a sacrifice. God should not go so far as to destroy Israel completely. Rather, he should properly discipline them so that he receives praise.

Summary

The author carefully writes the petitions so that they fit the prayer's literary and historical context. Using traditional language, the petitions recognize the presence of the deuteronomic curses and ask God to lift them. The author's chief concern is that the Jews will find favor before the Seleucids. Because the prayer assumes that the Jews are sinners, the author cannot appeal to God based upon the nation's goodness or unjust suffering. Therefore, he claims that answering the petitions will result in glory for God, a benefit for him rather than only the Jews. Further, the prayer suggests that God should act because the people have learned from God's disciplining of them that contrition is the only way a sinner might win God's favor.

Baruch 3:1-8

While Deuteronomy and Jeremiah make their mark on Bar 3:1-8, these verses also exhibit extensive influence from the Psalms and other poetic texts. This material gives Bar 3:1-8 a different texture from 1:15-2:35. At some points, 3:1-8 approaches a tone of complaint not present in the previous verses.[264] Further, the problem of sin, which Chapters One and Two see as a problem of the present generation, primarily belongs to past generations in 3:1-8. The present generation admits its sin (v. 2), but claims to be penitent and righteous. The prayer in 1:15-2:35 contains none of these features.

Because these influences are not present in 1:15-2:35, 3:1-8 may have constituted a separate prayer at some time before its appearance in Baruch. Despite these tensions, these verses have connections to Bar 1:15-2:35. The brief discussion that follows examines both the similarities and tensions between these sections.

Following the address to God, the initial phrase, which matches the tone of 2:16-18, has a psalmic resonance: "A soul in distress and a troubled spirit cry out to you" (ψυχὴ ἐν στενοῖς καὶ πνεῦμα ἀκηδιῶν) (3:1b). Psalmists use

---

[264]C. A. Moore (*Daniel, Esther, Jeremiah*, 293) criticizes the prayer by saying that "the prayer in 3:1-8 reflects an innocent, almost self-righteous attitude."

similar self-descriptions in Pss 61:3; 102:11; 142 [143]:4 (cf Job 7:11).[265] Kneucker likens the statement in v. 3 that God lives forever to the proclamations in the psalms and other poetic texts that God is enthroned forever (Pss 9:7; 29:10; Lam 5:19; Isa 57:15).[266] The statement, "We perish forever," evokes passages from the Psalms,[267] Deuteronomy,[268] and Ezekiel,[269] where the wicked or disobedient Israel encounters the same fate.

The prayer distinguishes past from present generations. It originates from the *children* of past generations, whom the children accuse as being sinners (υἱῶν τῶν ἁμαρτανόντων ἐναντίον σου) (v. 4). Claiming that the present generation has turned from the ancestors' unrighteousness (ὅτι ἀπεστρεψέαμεν ... πᾶσαν ἀδικίαν πατέρων ἡμῶν τῶν ἡμαρτηκότων ἐναντίον σου) (v. 7).[270] The prayer again categorizes the ancestors as sinners in v. 8. The author requests that God free the present generation from the sins of the past because the present generation is repentant (v. 5). Consequently, the image of the curses clinging to the people gets a new twist in this section of Baruch. The sins of the past generations have made the curses cling to the present generation: They "did not obey the voice of the Lord their God, so that the evil has clung to us"(καὶ ἐκολλήθη ἡμῖν τὰ κακὰ)(v. 4).[271]

Twice in vv. 6-7 the prayer mentions "praising God," with the second occurrence emphasizing that the praise originates in the exile. The Greek word "praise," αἰνέω, probably translates the Hebrew word ידה in the Hiph.[272] This origin for the praise, of course, fits the fictional exilic origin of the letter. Further, repentance and praise coming from the exiles is the turning point in the deuteronomic cycle, as Deuteronomy 4 and 30 testify. God's warning that he would "scatter" (διασπείρω/נדח) the people into foreign lands in Bar 3:8 clearly reflects Deut 4:27 and 30:3, and proves that the author is conscious of these passages as he writes. Thus, this concluding section of the prayer hopes salvation will result from the people's penitence.

---

[265]Cf. J. J. Kneucker, *Das Buch Baruch*, 264.
[266]Ibid., 265.
[267]Pss 1:6; 2:12; 9:4, 19 (Q); 37:20; 68:3; cf Prov 11:11.
[268]Deut 28:20, 22; 30:18.
[269]Ezek 33:10.
[270]Cf. the Animal Apocalypse in *1 Enoch* and *Jubilees* 23 where the young rebel against the sinful practices of the fathers.
[271]Cf. 1:18; 1:20; 2:10. For the theme of suffering reproach in v. 8 see 2:4.
[272]Cf. Solomon's prayer in 1 Kgs 8:33 and 35 where the people "praise" God in response to punishment (cf. 2 Chr 6:24 and 26).

Relationship of the Prayer to the Rest of Baruch

The themes of sin, repentance, and return tie the prayer in 1:15-3:8 to the remainder of the book (cf. 4:1).[273] If Israel will only recognize its sins, turn back to the Law and obey it, then God will end the exile and restore the nation to Jerusalem. The introduction to the wisdom poem calls Israel to recognize the reason for its exile (3:10): the nation has forsaken God's wisdom contained in Torah (4:1). If the nation turns to this wisdom, it can recover what it has lost: "strength," "length of days," "life," "light for the eyes," and "peace" (3:14), the very blessings for which the exiles hoped in their letter to the inhabitants of Jerusalem: "The Lord will give us strength and light to our eyes..." (1:12). Thus, Baruch instructs the Jews how to regain such a life.

With the return of occasional Deuteronomic language, Bar 4:5-16 again explains the exile as a result of Israel's sin. For example, the notion that Israel provoked God by sacrificing to demons (4:7) comes from Deut 32:16-17, and the description of the ruthless nation descending upon Israel as God's punishment (4:15) alludes to Deut 28:49-50. Although the author works with a different set of biblical texts in this section of the book, he continues to return to deuteronomic idiom in order to refer to Israel's sin and punishment.

In the apostrophe to Jerusalem and description of the city's future glorification in 4:36-5:9, the author weaves together traditions originating mostly from Second and Third Isaiah. The verses, which picture a complete reversal of the nation's situation, recall that for which the penitential prayer hopes—the return.[274] Therefore, the book closes with the resolution of the nation's opening dilemma. From beginning to end, Baruch remains consistent in its thematic interests.

Conclusion

Even though Daniel and Baruch write in chronological proximity to one another, they respond to two different sets of historical circumstances in two different ways. During this time, the Jews' political situation frequently and quickly changes. Daniel's prayer addresses the shock of Antiochus IV's blasphemous actions in the Temple, which justifiably accounts for the contents of the prayer's petitionary section. Baruch's author, in contrast, finds himself at the beginning of what will be a long controversy over the propriety of Hasmonean policies and authority, and, thus, becomes one of the first writers to

---

[273]Cf. G. W. E. Nickelsburg, *Jewish Literature*, 109.
[274]Ibid., 113.

register a protest against them. Daniel 9 and Bar 1:15-3:8 approach their respective problems while standing on the foundation of deuteronomic language, which by this time has become a standard feature of literary expressions of penitential prayer. Still, they are not slavishly reproducing the tradition. Rather, the authors craft their prayers according to their own problems, ideology, and interests.

The basic structure of the penitential prayer—the confession of sin and the petitions—provide an easily adaptable framework into which the author can work his own ideology. For example, the author of Daniel confesses the Jews' sin of failing "to ponder the truth." Other passages in Daniel use the noun that derives from the same root, שכל, in order to designate the role into which some members of the group have cast themselves; they are *maskilim*. The confession, then, becomes a request for God to forgive the Jews for not following the *maskilim's* teaching about the eschaton, and a message to any outside reader that ignoring or resisting the *maskilim's* teaching is serious. The author of Baruch follows a similar strategy by building upon the traditional language that refers to the people not heeding the prophetic word. Since he writes in the Jeremianic trajectory, the author returns to Jeremiah for a specific prophetic word that, at least according to the author, just happens to fit the political situation during the reign of Antiochus V. The Jews are disobeying Jeremiah's strict directive that the people obey the foreign power. Foreign domination comes as a punishment from God. To resist the overlords is tantamount to rebelling against God. The message is clear: "Jews, obey Antiochus V or stand in defiance of the prophetic word. Such disobedience has always brought disaster."

The historical circumstances can also influence prayers' petitionary sections. Daniel 9, for instance, has great interest in the Temple and Jerusalem because of Antiochus IV's desolation of abomination. Baruch, though, writes during a time when the Jews have regained control of the Temple, and, therefore, makes an extremely oblique reference to the Temple's condition (Bar 2:26). To compensate for this, he reports a story of cannibalism during the siege in order to portray the severity of the people's past sins, which he thinks cannot be ignored. He hopes the story will shock the people into repentance.

While these two prayers are interpretations themselves, the contexts in which they stand, or the material within the prayers, show that the authors responsible for the prayers are also engaged in interpretation of authoritative texts. That is, in these two examples, the penitential prayers have a complementary practice: interpretation. Daniel 9 explicitly presents itself as an attempt at interpreting Jeremiah 29. Penitential prayer is part of the activity that leads to the revelation of the text's meaning. The Jeremianic word in Baruch about obeying foreign rulers, which the author inserts into the prayer, also points to an interpretive enterprise. Further, when one relates the prayer to the material that follows in Baruch, the author calls the people to return to studying and practicing Torah. These two texts, then, reveal that the prayer and interpretation of authoritative texts have become the method for understanding and responding to Israel's sins and the people's recurring political crises.

CHAPTER THREE

Penitential Prayer and Biblical Interpretation among the Qumran Sectarians and Similar Groups

Introduction

Several groups within Judaism during the Second Temple period describe themselves in their literature as penitential movements. Frustrated by the persistent problems befalling the Jews, these groups conclude that the Jews have continued in sin for many years and that God's wrath continues upon the people. Unlike their fellow Jews, these groups acknowledge their own sins, and repent of them. They then attempt to share their knowledge of the nation's religious condition with fellow Jews by pointing out the people's errors and calling them to repentance and renewed obedience. However, their fellow Jews resist this message. Despairing of the spiritual condition and practices of fellow Jews who refuse to accept the penitential group's interpretation of current events and their message of repentance, some groups withdraw, in varying degrees, from the rest of Judaism. If the rest of the nation will not join them in repentance, then they must proceed on their own. As the sole representatives of God's faithful, they have become the sole beneficiaries of divine promises. Meanwhile, the rest of the nation, which lives in apostasy, awaits judgment. Thus, penitents have a divisive impulse.

Chapter One discusses this impulse in regard to Third Isaiah, which makes a distinction *within* Israel between those who repent and those who refuse to repent. The Divine Warrior will deliver the penitent, but punish those who persist in sin. After Third Isaiah, though, this divisive impulse does not appear in biblical penitential literature. However, divisiveness is a prominent feature of several Jewish documents that originate during the crisis under Antiochus IV and the problems associated with the Hasmonean dynasty.

The texts from this era that testify to penitential movements that distinguish themselves from the rest of Judaism are *Jubilees* 1 and 23, the "Animal Apocalypse" and the "Apocalypse of Weeks" in *1 Enoch*, *Testament of Moses* 3-4, 5 and 7, and the Qumran Scrolls. Several of these texts employ the deuteronomic cycle of sin—punishment—repentance— restoration and place the origin of their groups within this structure. They also typically transform cycle into an eschatological scheme. While not all these texts contain penitential prayers, they either refer to people praying, allude to prayer, or employ the language of penitential prayer. Thus, these authors know the tradition and reinterpret it for their respective purposes.

Besides containing penitential prayer language, these texts frequently refer to groups interpreting scripture. According to these authors, this act of interpretation has its place in the deuteronomic cycle along with repentance and prayer; true penitents pray and interpret sacred texts. The authors seem to develop this place for interpretation from their understanding of Deuteronomy 4 and 30. Deuteronomy states that the people will one day "seek" (דרש) God. By the Second Temple era, דרש has acquired the meaning "to interpret" a text. Thus, interpretation becomes part of the penitential process. The penitential tradition, then, contains both prayers that are reinterpretations of tradition and interpretation of authoritative texts.

Jubilees 1[275]

Jubilees, a Jewish text which probably acquired its present form around 168 BCE,[276] yields one of the best examples of the reinterpretation and reapplication of deuteronomic material—its language, sin—repentance—restoration cycle, and world view. Consequently, it provides an *entrée* into a discussion about these penitential movements and a basis for an examination of the Qumran Scrolls.

Jubilees rewrites Genesis 1 through Exodus 12 by claiming to contain a secret revelation that Moses received on Mount Sinai. Chapter 1, the preface to the book, follows the outline of the deuteronomic cycle and claims to be a preview of Israel's "future." However, the text actually climaxes in a description of the author's own time. The schema appears as follows:

Sin	1:7-9, 11-12
Punishment	1:10, 13
Repentance	1:15, 22-25
Restoration	1:16-18

After learning that the people will sin, Moses intercedes for them through prayer with the hope of averting the suffering that results from the cycle's

---

[275]The present book relies on the Ethiopic text as it appears in J. C. VanderKam, *The Book of Jubilees, A Critical Text, Scriptores Aethiopici* 88 (Lovanii: Adelibus E. Peeters, 1989).

[276]See G. W. E. Nickelsburg, *Jewish Literature*, 78-80.

Chapter Three

punitive moment (vv. 16, 19-20). Even though he pleads his case on the basis of Israel's election, best exemplified by the Exodus, God rejects his appeal. Fusing determinism and free will, God declares that the cycle is fixed, yet, at the same time, condemns the people for their proclivity to sin (v. 22). After God has punished the nation with exile, Israel's fortunes begin to change when the people decide to "turn" "with all their heart and soul" (vv. 23-25; and "mind" in v. 16), an echo of Deut 4:30 and 30:2. While the text does not record a penitential prayer, the passage indicates that, as a part of this "turning", the people must "acknowledge (*'a'amara*) their sin" and the sins of "their fathers" (v. 22).[277] The term, *'a'amara*, probably represents ידע in Hebrew. Still, the word functions as the equivalent of "to confess," as R. H. Charles translates the text,[278] even though Ethiopic contains a term meaning "confess" (*'amna*, cf. *1 En* 63:1). *Jubilees* borrows its confessional language from Lev 26:40: "If they confess (ידה) their iniquity and the iniquity of their ancestors ..."[279] While nothing in the deuteronomic cycle itself necessarily leads to a division from fellow Jews, a closer inquiry into *Jubilees*' depiction of the group reveals a sharp delineation between the group and other Jews.

In order to speak of the uniqueness of his group, the author draws on more deuteronomic language—Deut 4:29 and Jer 29:13. He depicts God as saying that the people will "seek" him (i.e., God)(vv. 15-16). While Deuteronomy and Jeremiah employ the term "to seek" as a metaphor for "to repent," in the case of *Jubilees* the term means something more than "repent." Earlier in the text (v. 12), the author refers to a group he labels as "those who seek the Law."[280] The phrase most likely represents the Hebrew דורשי התורה[281] and means to study the Law and correctly interpret it. Also, it appears in *Jub* 23:26 and the Qumran Scrolls with this meaning (See e.g., 1QS 6.6; CD 6.7; 7.18; 4QFlor 1.11).

The word דרש occurs frequently in the Hebrew Bible. One of its synonyms, בקש, generally has the meaning "to look for something." The term דרש, though, contains the nuance of "to inquire."[282] On occasion, the individ-

---

[277]Cf. Rabin's revision of R. H. Charles in "*Jubilees*," *AOT* (ed., H. F. D. Sparks; Oxford: Oxford University, 1984), 12; O. S. Wintermute, *OTP* vol. 2 (Ed. J. H. Charlesworth; Garden City: Doubleday, 1983) 54.

[278] R. H. Charles, *The Book of Jubilees*, *OTP* vol. 1 (Oxford: Clarendon, 1913) 6. Cf. the discussion of CD 1.8-9 below.

[279]Cf. Jer 14:20; Ps 106:6; 1QS 1.24b-25.

[280]See R. H. Charles, *The Book of Jubilees*, 4; O. H. Steck, *Israel und das gewaltsame Geschick der Propheten*, 162-164. Cf. 2 Chron 24:19.

[281]Cf. O. H. Steck, *Israel und das gewaltsame Geschick der Propheten*, 160.

[282]Cf. e.g., Gen 25:22; Ex 18:15; Lev 10:18; 1 Kgs 22:5, 7, 8.

ual directs the inquiry to a prophet in order to discover the will of God.[283] In other instances, "seeking God" merely means "to keep his commandments."[284] Since the word has the nuance of inquiry, one can easily conceive how it came to mean "inquire in a book" as it does in 2 Chron 34:21. Along with these possibilities in meaning, דרש develops into a penitential term, which is demonstrated by its placement with שוב. Two texts clearly demonstrate this: Deut 4:29-30 and Isa 55:6-7:

> And from there you will seek (בקש) Yahweh your God and you will find [him] if you seek (דרש) him with all your heart and with all your soul. And in your distress, when all these things have found you in later days, you will turn (שוב) to Yahweh your God and obey his voice (Deut 4:29-30).
>
> Seek (דרש) Yahweh while he may be found,
>   Call on him while he is near;
> Let the wicked forsake his way,
>   and the evil man his devices.
> Let them turn (שוב) so that he will have mercy;
>   and to our God for he greatly forgives (Isa 55:6-7).

If we include Isa 65:1-2, a reworking of Isa 55:6-7, we acquire a third example of דרש in a context of repentance. Thus, the word means both "investigate in a book" and "to seek by repenting." How do these ideas come together in *Jubilees*? Using a deuteronomic scheme for understanding history, the author reads in Deuteronomy 4 that Israel would repent (שוב). Within that same context he also noted that these penitents would "seek (דרש) God." The term דרש appeared in the passage from Deuteronomy because it could function as a metaphor for "to repent." However, by the time of *Jubilees* and the Qumran Scrolls, the term has also acquired the meaning "to inquire in a text." Therefore, the author understands the passage from Deuteronomy to mean that those who repent, "turn" (שוב), will also "seek" (דרש), i.e., study scripture. The same thinking probably lies behind the words "seek with a perfect heart" in CD 1.10.

The context of *Jubilees* 1 also supports the conclusion that the author has biblical interpretation in mind. Verse 12 alludes to the legal disputes, and v. 14 explicitly refers to them. Even a cursory reading of *Jubilees* reveals its interests in calendrical and halakhic disagreements. Thus, when the author states that during the exile a group will arise that will "seek" God, he imagines a penitential group that manifests its repentance by confession and interpreting

---

[283] Cf. 2 Kgs 3:11; 8:8; 22:13.
[284] See e.g., 2 Chron 12:14; 14:3(4); 2 Chron 17:3.

Torah, or other biblical texts. In the penitential scenes prior to *Jubilees*, namely Ezra 9, Daniel 9, and Baruch 1:15-3:8, interpretations of specific passages that were most likely the center of disputes occasionally found their way into the contexts. In this regard, *Jubilees* reveals nothing new. However, its understanding of the term דרש in Deut 4:29 as a reference to biblical interpretation distinguishes *Jubilees* from these prior texts. Interpreting Deut 4:29 in this manner couples penitential prayer with biblical interpretation.

The relationship between prayer and interpretation in *Jubilees*, therefore, differs from in Daniel 9 and Ben Sira. These two documents use penitential prayer as preparation for interpreting notoriously mysterious texts or traditions. In *Jubilees*, though, interpretation and penitential prayer stand side by side as penitential practices; they are constituents of repentance.

This group's disillusionment with the rest of Judaism also influences its recounting of the nation's history. *Jubilees'* history of Israel lacks any reference to Israel's historical return from Babylon, the post-exilic community, and the second Temple.[285] These omissions are tantamount to a total dismissal of the era of restoration and the early Second Temple period as an era of sin. Consequently, the author believes that the fulfillment of Deuteronomy 4 and 30 refers to his own time and not to the Persian period. Further, only he and his people properly obey Torah and are recipients of divine promises.

Jubilees 23

Jubilees 23 contains the second occurrence of the deuteronomic cycle. This cycle stands within a digression about Abraham's death. Like chapter one, it also provides an account of the appearance of the group, whose members the text now calls "servants" (23:30), within Israel's history. The deuteronomic cycle's outline is as follows:

Sin	vv. 16-21
Punishment	vv. 22-25
Turning Point/Repentance	v. 26
Salvation	vv. 27-31[286]

According to the digression, as the people continue in their sin, human life spans decrease. As in chapter 1, chapter 23 identifies the people's sins as calendrical and halakhic (vv. 19 and 21).[287] The Jews become sharply divided

---

[285]Cf. M. Knibb, "The Exile in the Literature of the Intertestamental Period," 266-267.
[286]See G. W. E. Nickelsburg, *Resurrection, Immortality*, 46; *Jewish Literature*, 77.
[287]Hebrew fragments exist for vv. 21-23. See M. Kister, "Fragments of the Book of Jubilees," *RQ* 12 (1987) 529-536.

over these issues. The author seems to picture two stages in these interpretive battles. First, groups align according to various age and socio—economic groups—young and old, poor and rich, etc.—all of which clash over these calendrical and halakhic regulations (v. 19). As the divisions continue, the sons rise up to "convict" the fathers and the elders (v. 19),[288] that is, they denounce the elders for their incorrect interpretations and practices. The author believes that the halakhic violations have caused the Temple's defilement (v. 21). Once the problem has reached this critical point, God sends the Gentiles to punish the nation for its deeds (v. 22). Life spans continue to shorten until even the children have hoary heads. Suffering from the hands of violent Gentiles, the Jews "cry out," "call," and "pray" for salvation (v. 24), but God does not answer.

At this desperate moment, the text reaches the turning point in the deuteronomic cycle that reverses Israel's condition. A group begins to search the Law and repent on the basis of their newly uncovered knowledge:

> And in those days,
> the children will begin to search the laws,
> and to search the commandments,
> and they shall change to the path of righteousness (23:26).

The words "to search the laws, and to search the commandments" parallel the material from chapter one, and, thus, provide additional examples of the term "to search" as a metaphor for investigation, study, interpretation of the Law, and practicing it within a penitential context. The text has clearly identified these "children," undoubtedly the group holding to the ideas of *Jubilees*, as those who turn ("change to the path of righteousness" in *Jubilees*) as Deuteronomy predicted, and, thereby, inherit all the biblical promises. The rest of the Jews who resist the "children's" message remain apostates and are destined for complete destruction.

---

[288]For the attitudes of various groups about armed resistance against the Seleucids, see J. J. Collins, *The Apocalyptic Vision of the Book of Daniel*, 206; P. Tiller, *A Commentary on the Animal Apocalypse of 1 Enoch*, 102-105.

Summary

Jubilees 1 and 23 depict a group in Israel that describes its activities with penitential language. Putting an eschatological spin on the deuteronomic cycle,[289] the author believes that he lives in the last days and is part of a group that Deuteronomy 4 and 30 promised would turn and "seek" God. As *Jubilees* 1 shows, this group also acknowledged its sin, i.e. confessed it. Although Deuteronomy teaches that the entire nation will repent, these passages assert that only a particular group *within* Israel will repent. For this group, "seeking God" means to investigate and interpret the Law, and then to practice what one has found in it. In *Jubilees*, studying an authoritative text has unambiguously become part of penitence.

1 Enoch[290]

The authors responsible for the "Animal Apocalypse" and the "Apocalypse of Weeks" in *1 Enoch* also conceive of themselves as part of an eschatological penitential reform movement whose emergence is divinely predetermined.[291] Like *Jubilees*, the authors indicate that their opinions have brought them into tension with other Jews from whom they clearly distinguish themselves.

The "Animal Apocalypse" (1 Enoch 85-90)

The "Animal Apocalypse," which in its present form comes from the time of the Maccabean revolt, reviews all human history from its origins to the author's time. It divides Israel's history from the exile to the author's own time into four periods under the leadership of seventy shepherds. It depicts various historical personages and groups with a variety of animals.[292] When the author arrives at his own time, he leaves no doubt about his assessment of his generation: it lives in apostasy, or, in the author's metaphor, the people are "blind sheep." Even the Jews' "shepherds," leaders, are blind. Israel has been in this

---

[289]Cf. O. H. Steck *Israel und das gewatlsame Geschick der Propheten*, 157-162; K. Baltzer, *The Covenant Formulary*, 153-163.

[290]The critical Ethiopic text is found in R. H. Charles, *The Ethiopic Version of the Book of Enoch* (Oxford: Clarendon, 1906).

[291]Cf. M. Hengel, *Judaism and Hellenism: Studies in their Encounter in Palestine during the Early Hellenistic Period*, vol. 1 (Philadelphia: Fortress, 1974) 179-180.

[292]G. W. E. Nickelsburg, *Jewish Literature*, 93-94; M. Knibb, "Exile in the Literature of the Intertestamental Period," 256; P. Tiller, *A Commentary on the Animal Apocalypse*, 61-79.

condition during the monarchy, the exile, and the post—exilic period. However, the situation in the author's time seems even more desperate than the time of pre-exilic Israel, whose sins eventually led to exile.[293] Drawing from Mal 1:7 and 10,[294] the visionary exclaims that the Jews' behavior during the Second Temple has resulted in the Temple's profanation (*1 En* 89:73), a pronouncement that *Jubilees* 23:21 also issues. In order to punish the people for their sins, God sends foreign nations against the Jews.

During the desperation of the fourth period,[295] at the turn of the second century BCE, lambs[296] are born who "begin to open their eyes and to see and cry to the sheep" (*1 En* 90:6), a reference to the birth of the author's eschatological community. The image of the young as the penitents parallels *Jub* 23:26, and indicates that this has become a popular way to represent the repentant. They may, indeed, consist of younger Jews who oppose the teachings and behavior of their elders. The multivalent metaphor, "open their eyes," probably imagines several kinds of transformations, including repentance. First, blindness in the previous sheep depicted their idolatry. This malady begins at Sinai when the people worship the golden calf (1 *En* 89:32-33). Consequently, opening the eyes represents the lambs' rejection of idols. Further, the metaphor also envisions the reception of revelation and connotes the "lambs'" proper obedience to Torah, something that their contemporaries lacked,[297] even though the text does not explicitly detail what constitutes proper obedience to Torah. Obviously, the description distinguishes the "lambs" from other Jews.

Following their transformation, the "lambs" call the rest of the nation, the "blind sheep," to repentance. Again, the visionary gives no description of the message, and the earlier complaints in the text about the Temple provide little help. Complaints in texts such as the *Damascus Document*, *Habakkuk Pesher*, *Testament of Moses*, and *Psalms of Solomon* reveal that groups believed that various halakhic violations could profane the Temple and its services, not simply matters related to sacrifice.[298]

---

[293] P. Tiller, *A Commentary on the Animal Apocalypse*, 340.

[294] P. Tiller (ibid.) disagrees with this position and thinks that any author during this era would have generally applied this term to speak of the Temple's impurity.

[295] G. W. E. Nickelsburg's designation in his privately published translation, 29.

[296] For a discussion of the difference between the Ethiopic texts and the Aramaic fragments on this word see P. Tiller, *A Commentary on the Animal Apocalypse*, 350-351.

[297] Cf. Ibid., 350.

[298] See e.g., CD 5.6b-11a. See G. W. E. Nickelsburg's discussions in "1 Enoch and Qumran Origins," *SBLSP* (1986) 352; "Enoch, Levi, and Peter: Recipients of Revelation in Upper Galilee," *JBL* 100 (1981) 584-586; D. W. Suter, "Fallen Angel, Fallen Priests: The Problem of Family Purity in *1 Enoch*," *HUCA* 50 (1979) 115-135.

The emergence of the righteous apocalyptic community signals that the final judgment approaches. Then, both the shepherds and the blind sheep—apostate Israel—are cast into a fiery abyss (*1 En* 90:20-27). The pattern of sin—punishment that appeared throughout the presentation of Israel's history has now reached its climax.[299] With the wicked removed, God establishes a new "house," a Temple, to replace the former defiled one (vv. 28-29). The sheep with opened eyes attain a preeminent place in the new era as all the nations pay homage to them and obey them (v. 30).

The "Apocalypse of Weeks" (1 Enoch 93:1-10; 91:11-17)

A second account about the emergence of an eschatological, penitential reform movement appears in the "Apocalypse of Weeks." The present form of the apocalypse, which divides all of human history into ten weeks, probably originates in the time immediately prior to Antiochus Epiphanes' persecution.[300]

The Apocalypse describes the Jews of the Second Temple period as a "perverse generation." Further, like *Jubilees*, the "Apocalypse of Weeks" completely ignores the return from the Babylon, Ezra's reforms, and Zerubabbel's Temple. These omissions once again amount to the total dismissal of these periods in Israel's history because of the people's sins. As in the case of the "Animal Apocalypse," it is impossible to determine the author's precise contention with his generation.[301] When the "Apocalypse of Weeks" explains the task of the reform movement, it mentions the following: "They (i.e., the members of the reform movement) will uproot the foundations of violence, and the structure of deceit in it" (91:11). As Nickelsburg has shown, one must interpret this statement in light of the "Apocalypse's" larger context, i.e., the "Epistle of Enoch." An examination of this larger context indicates the existence of an halakhic dispute between the Enochic circles and other contemporary Jewish groups.[302] Enoch pronounces "woes" against Jewish

---

[299]G. W. E. Nickelsburg, *Jewish Literature*, 93; J. J. Collins, *The Apocalyptic Imagination: An Introduction to the Jewish Matrix of Christianity* (New York: Crossroads, 1987) 51.

[300]M. Knibb, "Exile in the Literature of the Intertestamental Period," 259; J. C. Vanderkam, "Studies in the Apocalypse of Weeks," *CBQ* 46 (1984) 521; R. H. Charles, *The Book of 1 Enoch*, liii. G. W. E. Nickelsburg (*Jewish Literature*, 150) argues for a date early in the second century BCE because of *Jubilees'* apparent use of passages from *1 En* 92-105.

[301]Cf. G. W. E. Nickelsburg, *Jewish Literature*, 149.

[302]See G. W. E.. Nickelsburg, "The Epistle of Enoch and the Qumran Literature," 333-348; "The Apocalyptic Message of *1 Enoch* 92-105," *CBQ* 39:313-315.

opponents for the following reasons: "They annul the words of the righteous" (98:14); They "write lying words and words of error; They write and lead many astray with their lies" (v. 15); and they "change the true words and pervert the eternal covenant" (99:2). These statements accuse the opponents of constructing improper interpretations of Torah, and supporting them with intentionally fallacious arguments (cf. e.g., 99:11-16). In the Epistle's conclusion, Enoch exhorts the righteous not to "alter the words of truth" (104:9) and to beware of sinners who do (104:10). The Epistle also encourages instructing others about the truth.

The "Apocalypse of Weeks" reaches its climax both structurally and thematically[303] in the transition from the seventh week to the eight week.[304] In that transition, a reform group emerges, which the author calls "the eternal plant of righteousness" (93:10).[305] The reader has been awaiting the arrival of this "plant" because the Apocalypse's introduction states that the Apocalypse seeks to explain this "plant" (93:2).[306] Designating the movement as a "plant of righteousness" links it back to Abraham, to whom the text refers in 93:5 during the third week. Abraham, like his eschatological counterparts, is "chosen," and is a "plant of righteous judgment" (cf. 93:5 and 93:10). Abraham's immediate descendants also join this company as "the plant of righteousness" (93:5), but as Israel grows more sinful, it loses this label. Thus, these "chosen" undoubtedly conceived of themselves as the true representation of the lineage of Abraham that had gone unexpressed for generations.

Besides, their link to Abraham, the "chosen" receive "sevenfold wisdom and knowledge" (93:10). This wisdom disappears in the sixth week when the people stray from it and become "blind." The "Apocalypse of Weeks'" idea that the righteous receive wisdom and enlightenment from God has a precedent in earlier Enochic traditions, namely, *1 Enoch* 5. This chapter stands as a conclusion to the judgment oracle that begins the present Enochic text (*1 Enoch* 1-5). As Hartman demonstrates, echoes from the Aaronic Blessing and Deuteronomy reverberate through chapter five.[307] Therefore, without surprise,

---

[303]See G. W. E. Nickelsburg, "The Apocalyptic Message of *1 Enoch* 92-105," *CBQ* 39 (1977) 313-315; Cf. J. C. VanderKam ("Studies in the Apocalypse of Weeks," 524) who affirms that one should naturally expect the "sabbath" week to be important, as well as the tenth one.

[304]The group's arrival at the end of the seventh week might be an allusion to Daniel 9 and its interpretation of Jeremiah's seventy years as seventy weeks of years. See J. J. Collins, *The Apocalyptic Imagination*, 59.

[305]Cf. *1 En* 10:3.

[306]J. J. Collins, *The Apocalyptic Imagination*, 56.

[307]L. Hartman, *Asking for a Meaning: A Study of 1 Enoch 1-5*, CBNTS 12 (Lund: CWK Gleerup, 1979) 31-38.

the indictment against the wicked includes a charge that they do not keep the commandments and have "turned aside," words which have a deuteronomic flavor:

> But you have not stood firm nor acted according to his commandments; but you have turned aside... (5:4).

For their disobedience, the wicked are cursed and will receive punishment. In contrast, God will bless the righteous (vv. 6d-h, 7-9).[308] One of the blessings God gives the righteous is wisdom:

> Then wisdom will be given to all the chosen ones (v.7a).

This knowledge is unavailable to other humans and allows the righteous to avoid sin for the remainder of their lives (v. 8f-g). Thus, they escape judgment (v. 9).

In Enochic circles, this wisdom has divine origins[309] and a specific function. According to the "Apocalypse of Weeks", once the "chosen" possess this wisdom, they "uproot the foundations of violence and the structure of deceit in it" (91:10). With the Epistle of Enoch exhorting the righteous to "uproot the foundations of deceit" and "instruct" other Jews about the contents of the Enochic books (105:1), this phrase in the "Apocalypse" must allude to the chosen's task of preaching and instruction. That is, this group must reveal the errors of the perverse generation and overthrow it.

Summary

Like *Jubilees*, these Enochic traditions speak of the emergence of movements within Israel that have their origin in penitence. They believe that all the generations of the Second Temple had failed in obeying the Law, and, thus, had profaned the Temple. Designating themselves with titles reflecting youth, these movements use repentance as a method for departing from the mistakes of the ancestors and their contemporaries. God blesses them with divine wisdom, which not only informs them about the last days, but also reveals the proper

---

[308]V. 6d-j is absent in the Ethiopic manuscripts and appears only in the Greek text. See R. H. Charles, (*The Ethiopic Version of the Book of Enoch*, 11 n. 11), and L. Hartman (*Asking for a Meaning*, 35) for a discussion of the problem and reasons for following the Greek and including the lines.

[309]For more on wisdom in this passage and the Epistle of Enoch, see R. Argall, *1 Enoch and Sirach*, 17-49.

interpretation of Torah. *Jubilees'* metaphors about arguments between "the young" and "the old" (etc.), the "Animal Apocalypse's" reference to the "lambs" and the "sheep," and the "Apocalypse of Weeks'" and the Epistle's discussions of clashes among groups, and their allusions to fallacious interpretations of the Law, provide additional evidence for surmising that these movements engaged in interpretive debates. Their exhortations to other Jews to repent, adopt the proper interpretation of Torah, and learn the mysteries of the latter days, met resistance. Yet, each group maintains that it is the promised eschatological group, and claims sole ownership of the wisdom required for living in the last days.

The Testament of Moses[310]

The *Testament of Moses*, which rewrites Deut 31:24-26, contains a creative adaptation of the deuteronomic cycle and penitential prayer. Believing that Deuteronomy's prophecies apply to his own time during Antiochus' persecution,[311] the author uses the deuteronomic cycle to dramatize the events that he thinks will lead to the imminent eschaton, now the conclusion of deuteronomic cycle. Nickelsburg outlines the *Testament of Moses'* adaptation of the deuteronomic cycle of sin—punishment—repentance (or turning point)—salvation as follows:[312]

	Deut	T. Mos.	T. Mos.
Sin	28:15	chap. 2	chap. 5
Punishment	28:16-68	3:1-4	chap. 8
Repentance/Turning Point	30:2	3:5-4:4	chap. 9
Salvation	30:3-10	4:5-8	chap. 10

---

[310] The English text is from J. Priest, "Testament of Moses," *OTP*, vol 1, 919-934. For a summary of the critical issues associated with the *Testament of Moses*, see J. Tromp, *The Assumption of Moses: A Critical Edition with Commentary*, 87-128. Tromp, however, strangely dismisses Nickelsburg's claim that the *Testament of Moses* is a rewriting of Deuteronomy (121-122). For G. W. E. Nickelsburg's position, see *Resurrection, Immortality*, 44-45; *Jewish Literature*, 80-83.

[311] See G. W. E. Nickelsburg, *Resurrection, Immortality*, 43-45; "An Antiochian Date for the Testament of Moses," in *Studies on the Testament of Moses* , 33-37. For an opposing, view see J. Tromp, *The Assumption of Moses*, 116, 120-123.

[312] G. W. E. Nickelsburg, *Resurrection, Immortality*, 44, n. 29; *Jewish Literature*, 80-81.

As the chart indicates, like *Jubilees*, the work contains a dual deuteronomic cycle.[313] The moment of repentance in the first cycle, while it does not include a penitential prayer, resembles the outline and language of penitential prayers that we have examined.

The First Cycle

The first deuteronomic cycle, in typical deuteronomic fashion, identifies Judah's sin as idolatry. God responds to this with the punishments of invasion and exile. Reflecting upon their condition, the two southern tribes call out to the ten northern tribes[314] with language that resembles the *Gerichtsdoxologie* from penitential prayer:

> Just and holy is the Lord. For just as you sinned, likewise we, with our little ones, have now been led out with you (3:5).[315]

An obvious difference between this scene and a penitential prayer is that the humans confess to other humans rather than to God. This image of two nations or individuals confessing to one another springs from the scenes of judgment where the condemned confess to each other.[316] However, like penitential prayers, the conversation juxtaposes God's righteousness with Israel's sins.[317] In order to coax God into responding, the tribes appeal to the covenant with Abraham (cf. Bar 2:34; Pr Azar 12-13).[318] A second recognition that the punishment results from the people's transgressions occurs in 3:10-14 (cf. Dan 9:13). These verses also recall Leviticus 26 and Deuteronomy 4 and 28-30 and prophesy that the people will "remember" God (*Tunc reminiscentur me*) and

---

[313] G. W. E. Nickelsburg, *Jewish Literature*, 80-81.

[314] J. Tromp (*The Assumption of Moses*, 166) translates *pulverati* in the text as follows: "... and they will retire to the fields like a lioness, covered with dust, starving and thirsting." Priest (*OTP* vol 1, 928) and R. H. Charles (*AOT*, revised by J. P. M. Sweet, 608), however, relate the word to "plains." Thus, Priest translates the text: "Then, considering themselves like a lioness in a dusty plain, hungry and parched..." If Tromp is correct, the scene has incorporated the penitential practice of covering one's self with dust as a sign of contrition.

[315] Translation from J. Priest, "*The Testament of Moses*," *OTP* vol, I, 928.

[316] Cf. 1 *En* 62:5; Isaiah 13; *Wis Sol* 5:3, where the condemned wicked look at "one another" and confess. Cf. Antiochus' confession to his "friends" in 1 Macc 6:10.

[317] J. Priest (*OTP* I, 928, n. e) notes that the two southern tribes are not blaming their plight on the ten northern tribes. The sins of Judah have been indicated in 2:7-9.

[318] Also cf. *T. Levi* 15:4 and *T. Ash* 7:7. Cf. J. Tromp (*The Assumption of Moses*, 170) who holds that the author refers more specifically to Exod 32:13.

recognize why such a disaster has come upon them (3.10).[319] "To remember" functions as an equivalent to "to confess."[320] The tribes once again are speaking to one another as they "remember."

Finally, after seventy-seven years, a mysterious figure intercedes for the people (4:1). Most interpreters understand the figure as Daniel.[321] Others propose that the figure is Ezra, who intercedes by prayer for the people in Ezra 9 and again later in the Ezra trajectory in *4 Ezra* 8:31-36.[322] Finally, J. Goldstein proposes that the figure is an angel.[323] If the author is alluding to Daniel, then the text probably envisions the scene in Daniel 9 when he prays for the people. Whatever the identity of the person, he assumes the posture of others who offer prayers,[324] and prays for compassion based on the covenant with the fathers and Israel's election (4:2).

In this first cycle, then, the author has cast the parts of penitential prayer into a drama.[325] The author has simply assigned various parts of the prayer to the scene's *dramatis personae*—groups or individuals—as well as the narrator.

The Second Cycle: Testament of Moses 5 and 7

The second deuteronomic cycle in the *Testament of Moses* begins with a description of the people's apostasy (chaps. 5 and 7). Their misdeeds include idolatry, avarice, oppression, and unacceptable offerings that pollute the Temple and the altar. These improprieties are reminiscent of complaints in the Qumran Scrolls and the *Psalms of Solomon*. According to the *Testament of Moses*, God punishes the people for these sins. During this era of punishment (9:2), the mysterious figure Taxo emerges who, explaining that he does not engage in the sins of fellow Jews, exhorts his sons in following him in holding fast to the Law even though it means martyrdom. Taxo explains that their innocent deaths will spur God to vengeance and bring the kingdom's arrival (chap. 10). Unlike *Testament of Moses*' first deuteronomic cycle, confession

---

[319] J. Tromp, *The Assumption of Moses*, 170.
[320] Ibid., 171.
[321] J. Priest, *OTP*, I. 929, n. a; R. H. Charles, *The Assumption of Moses*, 14.
[322] J. Tromp, *The Assumption of Moses*, 175-176.
[323] J. Goldstein, "The Testament of Moses: Its Content, Its Origins, and its Attestation in Josephus," SCS 4 (Cambridge: SBL, 1973) 51.
[324] Cf. and contrast 1 Kgs 8:22; Ezra 9:5; 2 Macc 3:15; 3 Macc 2:1.
[325] Cf. J. Tromp, *The Assumption of Moses*, 164-165.

and repentance have no place in this second deuteronomic cycle.[326] Tromp, however, proposes that Taxo and his sons fast as a penitential act.[327] The action's intent, though, remains ambiguous because fasting is appropriate on various occasions. In this instance, it probably prepares Taxo and his sons for martyrdom.

For some time, scholarship has noticed the similarities between this scene and 2 Maccabees 7, the martyrdom of the mother and her seven sons. This text produces another set of difficult questions that receive detailed discussion in Chapter Four of this book. In regard to the present discussion of the *Testament of Moses*, however, 2 Maccabees 7 records the death of pious Jews who refuse to deny their faith even under Antiochus' tortures. While going to their deaths, the pious brothers confirm that they are suffering *because* of the rest of the Jews' sins.[328] While the brothers do not die on behalf of the nation, i.e., their deaths do not function as a vicarious atonement, a causal relationship exists between their deaths and Judas' success in turning back the Seleucid oppression. Based upon his interpretation of Deuteronomy 32, the author of 2 Maccabees believes that Judas' accomplishments function as God's vindication of the brothers' deaths. The deaths of Taxo and his sons in the *Testament of Moses* have a similar effect. While they do not atone for the nation, their deaths cause God to bring vindication in the form of his eschatological kingdom (*Testament of Moses* 10).

Summary

While the *Testament of Moses* testifies to how an author could freely adapt the deuteronomic cycle, this text also provides another example of an eschatological movement that criticizes the deeds of other Jews, especially the priests. According to the text, the appearance of these faithful Jews is part of the deuteronomic cycle. While the rest of Judaism wallows in its sins, the innocent deaths of members from this group will incite God to act and bring his kingdom.

---

[326]For the paradox of historical determinism and Taxo as a free agent, see J. Licht, "Taxo, Or the Apocalyptic Doctrine of Vengeance," *JJS* 12 (1961) 99-100. The paradox provides further evidence that the combination of historical determinism and penitential prayer in Daniel 9 is not unusual.

[327]J. Tromp, *The Assumption of Moses*, 226-227.

[328]For a brief discussion on whether the brothers die "because" or "on behalf of" the people's sins, see Chapter Four.

Testaments of the Twelve Patriarchs[328]

The practice of adapting the deuteronomic cycle to speak of the role of penitence and its relationship to the eschaton's arrival continues into the time of the *Testaments of the Twelve Patriarchs*. Critical problems about the provenance of these documents, though, hamper their usefulness. In fact, scholars cannot reach a consensus on whether to understand the *Testaments of the Twelve Patriarchs* as Jewish documents with some Christian interpolations or as entirely Christian documents. R. H. Charles proposed the former position,[329] while M. de Jonge presented and defended the latter position in his dissertation and subsequent publications.[330] The material appears here in full recognition of these unresolved critical problems. Whatever scholarship decides on these issues, the *Testaments* still offer another example of the use of the deuteronomic cycle and the importance of repentance as the turning point that brings the eschaton.

De Jonge constructs a chart that shows the deuteronomic cycle in what he called "Sin, Exile, and Return" passages (S.E.R.) in the *Testaments*. Like the texts from the Second Temple period described above, the *Testaments* convert the S.E.R. pattern into an eschatological schema; the deuteronomic cycle ends with the eschaton.[331] Of the nine instances of this pattern in the *Testaments*, five include repentance. Using Hollander and de Jonge's work, the following list locates the S.E.R. passages and marks the passages in which repentance occurs with an "(r)": *T. Levi* 10, 14, 16; *T. Jud.* 18:1 and chap.

---

[328]The critical text is M. de Jonge in cooperation with H. W. Hollander, *The Testaments of the Twelve Patriarchs: A Critical Edition of the Greek Text*, PVTG 1.2 (Leiden: Brill, 1978).

[329]R. H. Charles, *The Greek Versions of the Testaments of the Twelve Patriarchs* (Oxford: Clarendon, 1908). H. Aschermann (*Die paranetischen Formen der Testament der 12 Patriarchen und ihr Nachwirken in der fruhchristlichen Mahnung* [diss., Berlin, 1955]) basically follows his position, listed in K. Baltzer (*The Covenant Formula*, 142, n. 25) who concurs with Aschermann; Eissfeldt, *Introduction to the Old Testament* (trans. P. R. Ackroyd; New York: Harper and Row, 1965) 634-35; H. C. Kee, "The Testaments of the Twelve Patriarchs," *OTP* I, 777; O. H. Steck, *Israel und das gewaltsame Geschick der Propheten*, 149-150.

[330]M. de Jonge, *The Testaments of the Twelve Patriarchs: A Study of their Text, Composition, and Origin*, 2nd Ed., (Assen: Van Gorcum, 1975); *Studies on the Testaments of the Twelve Patriarchs: Text and Interpretation*, SVTP 3 (Leiden: Brill, 1975); M. de Jonge with H. W. Hollander. *The Testaments of the Twelve Patriarchs: A Commentary*,

[331]O. H. Steck, *Israel und das gewaltsame Geschick der Propheten*, 150-151. De Jonge agrees ("The Testaments of the Twelve Patriarchs: Christian and Jewish," *Jewish Eschatology, Early Christian Christology, and the Testaments of the Twelve Patriarchs*, 239.)

23 (r); *T. Iss.* 6 (r); *T. Zeb.* 9:5-7 (r), 9; *T. Dan* 5:4a-9 (r); *T. Naph.* 4:1-3 (r), 4-5; *T. Gad* 8:2; *T. Ash.*7:2f, 5-7; *T. Benj.* 9:1 f.[332] The texts describe the nation's repentance as follows:

T. Jud. 23:5	Until *you turn* (ἐπιστρέψητε) to the Lord with a perfect heart,[333] *repenting* (μεταμελούμενοι) and walking in all the commandments of God...
T. Iss. 6:3	... so that if they sin, *they will turn* (ἐπιστρέψουσι) quickly to the Lord.[334]
T. Zeb. 9:7	And after these things you will remember the Lord, and *you will repent* (μετανοήσετε), and he will turn you ...
T. Dan 5:9	And when *you turn* (ἐπιστρέψαντες) to the Lord...
T. Naph. 4:3	... *and you will turn* (ἐπιστρέψαντες) and *acknowledge* (ἐπιγνώσεσθε) the Lord your God ...

The reference to repentance occurs in only a few formalized sentences; its meaning is assumed.[335] The statement in *T. Naph.* 4:3 that the people will "acknowledge" God might refer to praying a penitential prayer.[336] The *Testaments* weave the cycle into their broader interests of warning future generations about the disaster of not following the patriarchs' ethical exhortations and Torah.[337] If the nation fails to heed the warning, only repentance brings God's mercy and the return.[338]

---

[332]Hollander and de Jonge, *The Testaments of the Twelve Patriarchs: A Commentary*, 53-54.

[333]Ibid., 226; cf. 1 Kgs 8:61; 11:4; 15:3, 14; 1 Chron 28:9. This may as well be the Greek equivalent of the words "perfect heart" in CD 1.10. This is the preferred metaphor at Qumran because of its hyperbolic force.

[334]For the use of ἐπιστρέφειν to mean "make return" see 1 Kgs 8:34; Tob 14:5; Par Jer 5:8 (Ibid., *Testaments of the Twelve Patriarchs*, 249).

[335]K. Baltzer, *The Covenant Formulary*, 158-159.

[336]Cf. *Jub.* 1:22.

[337]Hollander and de Jonge, *The Testaments of the Twelve Patriarchs*, 249.

[338]Hollander and de Jonge (*Testaments of the Twelve Patriarchs*, 249) compare Deut 4:30 f.

Summary

From the examination of these penitential groups emerge the following observations. First, as Waltzer, Speck, de Jonge, Nickelsburg and others demonstrate, the deuteronomic cycle enjoys a healthy existence during the Second Temple period. During this period the cycle develops into an eschatological schema that culminates in the complete fulfillment of the prophetic promises. In several of these texts, the appearance of a faithful penitential group is part of the events leading to the end. These groups claim that their contemporaries are floundering in apostasy. As in Third Isaiah, the act of repentance and its accompanying blessings no longer apply to the nation as a whole, but only to the penitential group *within* Judaism.

Second, the penitential groups in the "Animal Apocalypse" and the "Apocalypse of Weeks" are recipients of "divine wisdom." With this wisdom they not only understand the mysteries of the end, but also arrive at the proper interpretations of Torah. *Jubilees* makes explicit what was only latent in other penitential contexts: "To seek" means to investigate and inquire from a text in order to reach a proper interpretation and way to act. Locked in interpretive combats with their contemporaries, these groups carry out a teaching mission to the rest of Israel.

The Qumran Community

The Community's Memory of its Origin[339]

The Qumran Scrolls allow a glimpse into a sect that originates in penitence and eventually completely separates from other Jews. Rather than reconstructing the community's historical origins, the following presentation focuses on how the community itself remembered and retold its founding. This methodological approach decisively influences the outcome of the analysis because it assumes that in rehearsing the past the author represents the sect's self understanding at the time of composition, not necessarily the sect's actual historical origins. Therefore, the present task does not include excavating through the strata of the texts in order to describe the literary development of the texts and relate the layers to specific periods in the sect's development. Still, any presentation must maintain some awareness of the texts' history of development and prove

---

[339]I use this language because I am interested in how the community itself retold and remembered the founding of the sect, rather than attempting to reconstruct the historical origins of the community.

cognizant of issues and methodological conundrums related to a particular passage. Of the previous texts, *1 Enoch* and *Jubilees* contain the paradigm that most resembles the Qumran community's description of its origin. In fact, these texts were unambiguously important at Qumran.

The Qumran Scrolls permit more than a discussion of the sect's self-understanding of its origins and the role of penitence in this. Several columns speak directly about the place of prayer, including penitential prayer, in the sect's theology and life. Further, the existence of actual prayers among the Qumran Scrolls allows a glimpse into how a particular sect uses prayer.

Damascus Document Col. 1

The *Damascus Document* opens by giving an account of the group's origins.[340] Because the Qumran sect believed that it alone was the faithful remnant about which the Scripture spoke, the story begins with Israel in apostasy and punishment. The author sums up the punishment for this apostasy with the typical deuteronomic expression: "And he delivered them over to the sword" (ויתנם להחרב)(1.4; cf. 3.11). While the phrase sometimes depicts falling to an enemy army, in this instance the author is probably alluding to the covenantal curses. The explicit reference in ll. 17-18 to the "sword" as the punishment for violating the covenant supports this understanding of these words.

While the nation is in this condition, 390 years after Jerusalem's fall to Babylon, God "visits" the people in order to fulfill the prophecy in Ezek 4:5.[341] As a result of God's "visitation," a "plant root"[342] springs up (l. 7)—the Qumran community's ancestors and founders. With this quote from Ezekiel and the reference to the "plant root", the author declares his own community

---

[340] For the Hebrew text see S. Zeitlin, *The Zadokite Fragments. Facsimile of the Manuscript in the Cairo Genizah Collection in the Possession of the University Library, Cambridge, England, JQRMS* 1 (Philadelphia: Dropsie College, 1952). For discussion of text critical problems special to the *Damascus Document*, see e.g., S. A. White, "A Comparison of the "A" and "B" Manuscripts of the Damascus Document," *RQ* 12 (1987) 237-553.

[341] Several scholars have noted that if one adds the reference to time in this text with others in the Dead Sea Scrolls, the result is 490 years, most likely an allusion to Daniel 9. See S. Talmon, *The World of Qumran from Within* (Jerusalem: Brill, 1989) 283; B. Z. Wacholder, *The Dawn of Qumran: The Sectarian Torah and the Teacher of Righteousness* (Cincinnati: Hebrew Union College, 1983) 177; F. F. Bruce, "The Book of Daniel and the Qumran Community," *Neotestamentica et Semitica* (eds. E. E. Ellis and M. Wilcox; Edinburgh: T & T Clark, 1969) 232-233.

[342] L. Ginzberg (*An Unknown Jewish Sect* [New York: The Jewish Theological Seminary of America, 1970] 5) suggests that Jer 12:2 stands behind the text.

as recipients of the promised deliverance;³⁴³ the Qumran sect is the true Israel. In his retelling of the past, the author completely omits the historical return from Babylon, the rebuilding of the Temple, and the post—exilic community. With these omissions, the author excludes the possibility of understanding the people of these eras as recipients of Ezekiel's prophetic promise.

The examination of *Jubilees* and the "Apocalypse of Weeks" shows that disillusioned authors in this period could recast Israel's history through their own biases in order to make themselves the true restored community. In fact, the *Damascus Document* has verbal links to the "Apocalypse of Weeks" in the use of the metaphor "plant" for the community.

Some of the Qumran sect's initial actions are penitential: "They understood their iniquity and they acknowledged that they were guilty men" (ויבינו בעונם וידעו כי אנשים אשימים הם) (ll. 8b-9a). The community, then, originates in penitence and confession.³⁴⁴ Admittedly, the author expresses the notion of confession with the verb ידע rather than ידה. However, in other texts, like *Jubilees* 1:22, "acknowledging" one's sins is tantamount to "confessing" them.³⁴⁵ This same interpretation applies here in the *Damascus Document*.

Despite the early sectarians' sincere penitence, they did not correctly interpret and practice the Law. To speak of this era of error, the author constructs an image that also occurs in both Isa 59:10 and Deut 28:29 in which God's people grope as if blind. Although in error, the sect's sincerity is not in question because it "searches" with a "perfect heart" (בלב שלם דרשוהו)(l. 10).³⁴⁶ This latter phrase, which appears especially in 2 Chronicles,³⁴⁷ hyperbolically expands the frequent deuteronomic expression "with all your heart."³⁴⁸ In response to their sincerity, and because of their aimless wanderings, God sends a Teacher of Righteousness (l. 11), who instructs the community about how to live in the final age (ll. 11-12). The proximity of the

---

³⁴³See S. Talmon, *Qumran from Within*, 48-52.

³⁴⁴Cf. D. Dimant, "Qumran Sectarian Literature," *Jewish Writings in the Second Temple Period*, *CRINT* 2 (ed., M. Stone; (Philadelphia: Fortress, 1984) 492.

³⁴⁵Cf. Jer 14:20; Isa 59:12; Ps 52:5. The Ethiopic word for "to acknowledge" is *'a'amara*. Cf., *BDB*, 394. Cf. the discussion above on "to remember" in the *T Mos* 3:10.

³⁴⁶The text in Ezek 4:6 reads that Ezekiel was to lie on his other side for 40 days for the punishment for Judah, a day representing one year. The *Damascus Document*, however, pictures the community aimlessly groping for 20 years. S. Talmon attributes the discrepancy to a scribal error in the Ezekiel text on which the author of CD relies.

³⁴⁷See 1 Kgs 8:61; 11:4; 15:3; 2 Kgs 20:3; Isa 38:3; 1 Chron 12:39; 28:9; 29:9, 19; 2 Chron 15:17; 16:9; 19:9; 25:2.

³⁴⁸Cf. *T Jud* 23:5.

Teacher's appearance to the phrase "they searched for him with a perfect heart" strongly suggests that "to search" metaphorically represents Biblical interpretation. As the investigation below argues more fully, the word דרש can mean this in the *Damascus Document*. Further, the discussion of the community's disagreements with the rest of Judaism in the remainder of column 1 includes metaphors that imply halakhic disputes. For example, while the community "searches" for God, the rest of Israel "searches" for "smooth things" (1. 18; cf. 4QpNah 2 and 7), language that, along with "they chose illusion" and "they watched for breaks," originates from Isa 30:10 and 13. In fact, Isaiah 30 also depicts God as promising to send the people a teacher who will instruct them during a period of sin and punishment. The author of the *Damascus Document*, therefore, believes that the appearance of his community and the Teacher of Righteousness fulfills a prophetic promise.[349]

Several other statements in the text suggest that the community is engaged in exegetical battles:

1. 13	They departed from the way.
ll. 15b-16a	... departing from the paths of righteousness...
1. 16b	removing the bound that their forefathers had established...

With these phrases, the author accuses other Jews of manufacturing facile interpretations of scripture to validate their wicked deeds (cf. 1. 19).[350] Metaphors like these resemble the rhetoric from the "Apocalypse of Weeks" (*1 En* 91:18), the Epistle of Enoch (*1 En* 99:10), and *Jubilees* 23:21, where such language distinguishes the wicked from the righteous. The righteous follow the path while the wicked do not follow it. For example, *Jubilees* accuses the wicked of refusing to return to "the path of righteousness" even after escaping punishment. The *Damascus Document* attributes some of the problems to the "Man of Scorn," who, according to the text, preaches (נטף)[351] so that the "waters of falsehood" flow through Israel (l. 14). Therefore, such phrases naturally occur in contexts of halakhic disputes.

---

[349]See G. W. E. Nickelsburg, *Jewish Literature*, 131-132.
[350]Cf., e.g., 1QpHab 1.4-2.10.
[351]The word literally means "drip," but in prophetic texts figuratively means "discourse." See *BDB*, 642-643.

The sect remembered its origins in relation to a disagreement over proper interpretation of a sacred text. Israel, mired in improper interpretation and, consequently, sinful behavior, suffers from the covenantal curses ("sword of vengeance," לחרב נקמת, l. 17; cf. l. 4), which "cling" (דבק) to the people.[352] The sect's stand on these interpretations resulted in persecutions (ll. 20-21). For this oppression, God angrily punishes the opponents (2.1).

Summary

The *Damascus Document's* opening lines envision the sect's origins in association with the following. First, the founding members are penitents who confess their sin. Second, they acquire a teacher who assists them in interpreting Torah.[353] Their interpretations separate them from the rest of Israel which was saturated with falsehood. Third, they propose that they constitute God's remnant that he promised would arise and return to the Law near the eschaton. The group encounters hostility from some sections of Judaism.

Damascus Document 2.17-3.12

The author returns to discuss the history of Israel's errors and sins in 2.17-3.12. Using language similar to col. 1, the people suffer the covenantal curses because of their sins: "he delivered them up to the sword" (3.11-12; cf. 1.4, 17-18). The curses climax in the nation's exile. Also in correspondence to col. 1, and like *Jubilees* 1 and the "Apocalypse of Weeks," col. 2 completely omits any discussion of the restoration under Persia and the post-exilic community. With this silence and the lumping of those eras with pre-exilic Israel, the author dismisses those generations as sinful. As a result, the promised restoration and era of future blessing has remained unfulfilled. Instead of acknowledging post—exilic Israel as the recipient of the prophetic promises, the Qumran sect identifies its early ancestors as constituting the true remnant (3.12-13; cf. 2.4)[354] and recipients of the divine promises.

God establishes a covenant with the sect and reveals to it "the hidden things in which Israel went astray,"[355] the rules about sabbaths, feast days, and other *halakhot* (ll. 13b-16a). These "hidden things" are not the recovery of what the rest of Israel has neglected, but an entirely new revelation delivered

---

[352] Cf. Bar 1:20 and 3:4; 4Q504 3.10b-13a.
[353] Cf D. Dimant, "Qumran Sectarian Writings," 492.
[354] M. Knibb, *The Qumran Community* (Cambridge: Cambridge University, 1987) 19.
[355] Cf. Deut 29:28.

through the Teacher of Righteousness, as other texts testify.[356] As in col. 1, the sect struggles for some time while it holds to improper interpretations (3.17-18).[357] Yet, for this momentary faltering, the members of the sect receive forgiveness: "But God, in his wonderful mysteries, atoned for their iniquity and removed their transgression" (l. 18).[358]

Along with the halakhic regulations, the text alludes to Biblical interpretation: they "dug a well abundant in water" (l. 16). A discussion of this phrase appears below in the treatment of CD 6.4, a text that clearly interprets the well as the Law.[359] Col. 3 also must have the Law in mind for in it the community finds its foundation for *halakhot*.

Summary

While this material may not follow the same order as col. 1, some recurring features appear. First, the sect distinguishes itself from the rest of Israel which is in apostasy. The two columns achieve this by both picturing the nation's past as suffused with sinfulness and condemning the contemporary generation. Both columns refuse to acknowledge the return from exile and the post exilic community, presumably because the author dismisses the people living then as sinful, and wants to depict his own community as the recipients of the promise of divine deliverance. Second, the community relates its origins to differences between itself and the rest of Judaism in the area of Biblical interpretation and halakhic requirements. Finally, the texts remember the community's origin as steeped in penitence, even though the sect in its early days lives in error.

Damascus Document 5.20-6.11a

The people of the community emerge as penitents and interpreters again in the author's discussion of the sect's origin in CD 5.20-6.11a. As in the previous passages, this text portrays the nation in rebellion, exemplified in its rejection of God's commandments as Moses and the prophets delivered them.[360] Despite

---

[356]Cf. M. Fishbane, "Use, Authority, and Interpretation of *Mikra* at Qumran," *Mikra*, 364.

[357]Cf. J. Murphy-O'Connor, "The Essenes and their History," *RB* 83 (1974) 220.

[358]Cf. CD 2.4-5.

[359]Cf. A. Dupont-Sommer, *The Essene Writings from Qumran* (Oxford: Basil and Blackwell, 1961) 126 n 4.

[360]This is how Dupont-Sommer (*The Essene Writings from Qumran*, 131 n 1) understands the words "his anointed of holiness." Cf. 2.12. L. Ginzberg (*An Unknown Jewish Sect*, 9-10) understands CD 2.12 in this way. However, in this passage he emends the text to read "They preached apostasy from *his holy messiah*" (27-28).

Israel's sinfulness, God calls a group and makes them "hear" in order to testify to his faithfulness to the covenant that he made with the patriarchs. The text designates this group as "penitents of Israel (שבי ישראל) who went out from the land of Judah to sojourn in the land of Damascus" (6.5). This phrase stands at the center of a debate between J. Murphy-O'Connor and several other scholars. Murphy-O'Connor argues that the words שבי ישראל should translate as "the returnees of Israel."[361] He proposes this as part of his theory that the Qumran sect originates in Babylon and emigrates from there to Jerusalem. In order to prove this position, he asserts that the geographical references function not as actual geographical locations, but as metaphors. This would mean that the term שוב denotes geographical direction rather than moral transformation. He translates CD 19.33-34: "None of those who entered the covenant in the land of Damascus *and who returned* (emphasis his), but then who betrayed it ..." According to Murphy-O'Connor, the word שוב in this case implies that not all the sect returns to Judah; some stay behind in Babylon.[362]

Knibb justly criticizes Murphy-O'Connor's positions by revealing their inconsistencies. As Knibb notices, Murphy-O'Connor understands the geographical references simultaneously as metaphorical and concrete; i.e., Judah represents Judah while Damascus poses as a cipher for Babylon.[363] Further, and most crucial for the present discussion, Knibb convincingly refutes Murphy-O'Connor's notion that שוב has geographical value. In the six occurrences of שוב in the *Damascus Document*, four times the term undoubtedly has moral connotations (CD 2.5; 8.16; 19.29; 20.17), while in the two other appearances a moral meaning remains highly possible (CD 4.2; 6.5).[364] Comparisons with the use of שוב in 1QH support the conclusion that the word has moral connotations. Knibb's position, along with others who evince his opinion, has more merit: the term שוב signifies moral transformation rather than spatial migration. Thus, the Hebrew phrase שבי ישראל translates into English as "the penitents of Israel."[365]

---

[361] J. Murphy-O'Connor, "The Essenes and their History," 220.
[362] Ibid., 225
[363] J. Murphy-O'Connor, "The Essenes and their History," 221.
[364] M. Knibb, "Exile in the Damascus Document," *JSOT* 25 (1983) 105-107. Cf. S. Talmon, *Qumran from Within*, 39-44; J. M. Baumgarten, "Sacrifice and Worship Among the Jewish Sectarians of the Dead Sea (Qumran) Scrolls," *HTR* 46 (1953) 148 n 20; J. J. Collins, *The Apocalyptic Imagination*, 61.
[365] Cf. also G. Vermes who translates the phrase "converts of Israel" (*The Dead Sea Scrolls in English* (London: Penguin, 1987); A. Dupont-Sommer, *The Essene Writings from Qumran*, 131 (translated from French by Vermes); E. Lohse (*Die Texte aus Qumran*, [München: Kösel-Verlag, 1986]) translates the words with "die Bekerhten Israels."

Chapter Three

These penitents in CD 6, whom the text also designates as "men of understanding" (נבונים) and "sages" (חכמים),³⁶⁶ and later, "princes" (שׂרים), fulfill Num 21:18—they dig a well. Since the well represents the Law, the "digging" can only refer to its study and interpretation. In l. 6, the text sums up this activity with the expression "they sought him (i.e., God)" (דרשוהו).³⁶⁷ Like col. 1, then, the sect frequently uses דרש to refer to interpretation of biblical text. Consistent with cols. 1 and 3, col. 6 also speaks of an individual, in this instance a "stave," who instructs the sect in the Law's proper meaning. Their interpretive conclusions, like col. 1, lead to disputes with the contemporaries and precipitates a break from them. In fact, the language describing the situation is reminiscent of col. 1:

CD 5 and 6	CD 1
5.20 In the time of the desolation of the land, *the removers of the bound* rose up and led Israel astray. ובקץ חרבן הארץ עמדו מסיגי הגבול ויתעו את ישראל	1. 16 *And they removed the bound* that the ancestors established as an inheritance. ולסיע גבול אשר גבלו ראשנים בנחלתם
5.21 ... for they speak rebellion against the commandments of God. ...כי דברו סרה על מצות אל ביד משה	1. 14 And there rose up a Man of Scorn who discoursed to Israel. בעמיד איש הלצון אשר הטיף לישראל
6.1-2a *They prophesy falsehood*³⁶⁸ so as to turn Israel from following God. וינבאו שקר להשיב את ישראל מאחר אל	1. 18 *They chose falsehood* (1. 18). ויבחרו במהתלות

---

³⁶⁶Adopting the terms of Dupont-Sommer, *The Essene Writings from Qumran*, 131.
³⁶⁷The identity of the persons in CD 6.9-11 is the focus of much debate. See J. J. Collins, *The Apocalyptic Imagination*, 125-126.
³⁶⁸Cf. Isa 30:10.

1QS 8 and 9

The *Community Rule* 8 and 9[369] manifests a similar set of ideas as it explains the sect's origins. Several scholars understand the explanation for the sect's migration into the wilderness in 1QS 8.12b-16 as the community's "programme" or "manifesto."[370] The passage is also famous in modern research because of its interpretation of Isa 40:3, which is also important in the John the Baptist pericopae in the New Testament.

Only the ambiguous words, "And when these things came to pass" (l. 12b), hint at the events that precipitate the sect's move. Obviously, eschatological expectations provide some impetus for the move because the sectarians believe that in the wilderness they can "prepare the way" for God, i.e., his arrival, or at least the coming of his eschatological promises. To "prepare the way" for God also means devotion to study of the Law (מדרש)(l. 15). As was characteristic of studying the Law in the *Damascus Document*, in 1QS 8 the sect follows the interpretation of Law by the sect's leading figure.[371] Such a figure appears in ll. 11-12 as the teacher of the initiates: the "Man who searches" (דרש).[372] Though the proper interpretations remain hidden from the rest of Israel, the Holy Spirit has revealed them to the community and its instructors (ll. 11, 16). Therefore, the group's interpretation again distinguishes it from the rest of Judaism.

In col. 9, which contains elements similar to col. 8, the text again quotes Isa 40:3 to speak of the migration into the wilderness in order to dedicate full attention to the study of Torah (9.19-20). A teacher instructs the adherents in "mysteries" (וכן להשכילם ברזי פלא)[373] and "truth" (ואמת) that remain unavailable to the rest of Israel (ll. 18-20).

While neither 1QS 8 or 9 contains a penitential prayer, the passages confirm the centrality of biblical interpretation for the group. The sect consistently depicts itself as breaking away from its contemporaries because it is a peniten-

---

[369]For the Hebrew text see M. Burrows, ed., *The Dead Sea Scrolls of St. Mark's Monastery*, vol. 2, fasc. 2: *The Manual of Discipline* (New Haven: American Schools of Oriental Research, 1951).

[370]M. Knibb, *The Qumran Community*, 127; G. W. E. Nickelsburg, *Jewish Literature*, 156 n 116; A. R. C. Leany, *The Rule of Qumran and its Meaning* (Philadelphia: Westminster, 1966), 211.

[371]M. Knibb, *The Qumran Community*, 134.

[372]The Hebrew could also mean "but which the seeker finds." See A. Dupont-Sommer, *The Essene Writings from Qumran*, 91-92, n 6.

[373]Cf. ll. 20 and 21. For a discussion on the meaning of שכל see the treatment of Daniel 9 in Chapter Two.

tial group living amid a perverse generation. The members are fiercely dedicated to the study of biblical texts. In fact, even an interpretation of a biblical text prompts the sect's retreat into the wilderness. Like the *Damascus Document*, 1QS relates a teacher figure to this era of the sect. His interpretations are the ones to which the sectarians must adhere. With these ideas, the sectarians have drawn a line of demarcation between themselves and the rest of Israel.

Summary

The sect consistently depicts its origins as rooted in penitence and interpretation. These practices distinguish it from contemporaries, and eventually lead to its complete separation from the rest of Judaism. Adherents to the community leave the company of the perverse and convert to the Law as the community interprets it.

Entrance into the Community

Every aspiring member of the sect enters the community through a ceremony that features penitential confession as the moment of initiation, transition, and transformation. The ceremony exists in the opening columns of the *Community Rule*. Penitential prayers influence the content of the ceremony. Thus, the ceremony demands consideration in light of the penitential prayer tradition in order to identify similarities and the relationship between the two.

The Covenant Ceremony in 1QS[374]

The Covenant Ceremony (1QS 1.16-2.18) derives its major components from Deuteronomy 28-30,[375] but, as is common to many penitential prayers, the author of the ceremony also consciously builds upon the ideas of Deuteronomy 4. In fact, although the text is broken, the Rule's first lines probably quote, or at least allude to, Deut 4:29:

---

[374]Murphy-O'Connor ("*La genèse littéraire de la Règls de la Communauté*," *RB* 77 [1969] 539) claims that the service existed separately and was inserted into the text. According to his assessment, the ceremony originates in the Stage IV of the document's development. For a suggestion of an outline of the liturgy with biblical parallels, see K. Baltzer, *The Covenant Formulary*, 188-191.

[375]M. Knibb, *The Qumran Community*, 84; K. Baltzer, *The Covenant Formulary*, 49-50, 188-191.

Deut 4:29b
כי תדרשנו בכל־לבבך ובכל־נפשך

1QS 1.1b-2
לדרוש אל [בכל לב ובכול נפש...]

In the lines that follow, the author explains the penitential transformation that must take place in the initiates: "And no longer walk in the stubbornness of a guilty heart, and lustful eyes to do all manner of evil" (ll. 6-7). Entrance into the sect also marks both a sociological and anthropological transformation that results in a sharp distinction between those inside and outside the community.[376] The initiates join the company of the "sons of light" and must love them, while those outside the community, "sons of darkness," deserve only contempt and hatred. The community is separate from all others. This distinction continues into the ceremony's sections containing the blessings and curses; the penitent and obedient receive a blessing while all those outside the community are cursed. This is an important transformation in the blessing—curse formula. Previously, as Nitzan argues, both blessings and curses applied to the same people and corresponded to this one group's behavior. Now at Qumran, however, the inside group receives the blessings while it reserves the curses for the outsiders.[377]

The ceremony itself begins with the priests blessing God (1.18b-20) to which the congregation responds with a twofold "amen" (cf. 4Q504).[378] Next, the priests recount God's saving deeds for Israel:

> And the priests will recount the saving deeds of God in his mighty works and proclaim all his living mercy to Israel (ll. 21-22a).

In contrast to God's fidelity and graciousness, the Levites juxtapose Israel's sins:

> Then the Levites will recount the iniquities of the sons of Israel and all their guilty rebellions and their sins during the rule of Belial (ll 22b-24a).

Penitential texts, especially Nehemiah 9, Psalms 78, 105, 106, and Isaiah 63:7-64:12, and 4Q504, have the same structure as 1QS 1.16-2.18; they recite God's saving deeds, the people's sins, and a confession. Several scholars have also noted the similarities between the priests' words in the ceremony and the

---

[376] See also B. Nitzan (*Qumran Prayer*, 124-129) on the conformity of the ceremony to the sect's ideology.

[377] Ibid., 124-129.

[378] A. R. C. Leany (*The Rule of the Community and Its Meaning*, 127-128) follows Yadin's theory that we have a parallel between this text and 1QM 12-13.

words pronounced over the scapegoat on the Day of Atonement in Lev 16:21.[379] The terms are even in the same order. This similarity, however, does not mean that the community actually held the ceremony on the Day of Atonement, but may result from a simple literary dependency on Lev 16:21.

As in the penitential scenes from other texts listed in the preceding paragraph, the people respond to the recitation of Israel's sins with a confession:

> [And all] those entering the covenant will confess after them saying: "We have committed iniquity, we have transgressed, we have sinned, we have acted wickedly, we and our ancestors before us when we walked [contrary to the statutes]. True and righteous [is God in sending] his judgment against us and against our ancestors (ll. 24-26).

> [וכול] העוברים בברית מודים אחריהם לאמור נעוינו [פשענו חט]אנו הרשענו אנו
> [ואב]ותינו מלפנינו בלכתנו [קרי בחוקי] אמת וצד[ק   ] משפטו בנו ובאתנ[ינו]

Although the admission of the ancestors' sins is formulaic, it fits the context well since the Levites confess the history of Israel's sins. The multiple confession, the same one that the community makes in CD 20.28-31, reflects traditions like those in 1 Kgs 8:47; 2 Chron 6:37; Jer 14:7; Dan 9:5; and Bar 2:12. While the manuscript is deteriorated at l. 26, it may have contained a *Gerichtsdoxologie*, i.e., the people declared that God rightfully and justifiably sent punishment on the people because they have sinned. This has remained a standard element in penitential prayers; the supplicants accept the deuteronomic explanation for disaster visiting the people. The initiates' speech concludes in 2.1 with their request that God be gracious and merciful toward them forever.[380]

Thus far, the analysis of the ceremony demonstrates how closely it parallels penitential prayers. Using Deuteronomy 4 as the scriptural foundation for their performance, the sect has enumerated Israel's sins, confessed the sins, and declared God's righteousness in his judgments. These actions indeed cover the essential elements of penitential prayer. The only difference is that the author of the ceremony has assigned the various parts of penitential prayer to the participants in the ceremony.[381] Of course, this requires conforming

---

[379]Cf. S. Talmon (*Qumran from Within*, 233-237), who holds that the ceremony must have therefore taken place on the Day of Atonement each year. He suggests comparing the language to 1Q34[bis], a prayer for the Day of Atonement. Cf. J. Murphy-O'Connor ("A Literary Analysis of the Damascus Document xix,33-xx,34," *RB* 79 (1972) 544-564), who notices the same relationship between Lev 16:21 and the confession in CD 20.29-30.

[380]For the language of this line, cf. Isa 63:7; 4Q504.

[381]Cf. B. Nitzan, *Qumran Prayer*, 26-27.

some of the statements to the speaking participant. Beyond these adjustments, though, the ceremony and the contents of penitential prayer present no substantial differences. The phenomenon that appears in the ceremony corresponds to the use of penitential traditions in the *Testament of Moses*, which assigns the various parts of penitential prayer to characters in the narrative. Thus, in formulating the covenant ceremony in the *Community Rule*, the author relies heavily upon the material from the penitential prayer tradition.

The ceremony continues by referring to the results of penitence. The priests respond to the people's confession with a blessing, which recasts for its own purposes the words of the Aaronic Blessing (Num 6:24-26)[382]:

> May he enlighten (ויאר) your heart with understanding of life (בשכל חיים) and eternal knowledge (בדעת)(2.3).

As in several previous texts, the ceremony directly links confessing one's sins to the reception of knowledge. For example, the members of the group responsible for "Animal Apocalypse" and the "Apocalypse of Weeks" believe that divine wisdom was a reward for their repentance. 1 *Enoch* 5:6d-h and 7-9 also depicts God as enlightening the chosen with wisdom. Further, both Daniel 9 and Ben Sira' assumed that penitential prayer led to divine wisdom about perplexing texts or traditions. Also, the *Damascus Document* and 1QS 8 and 9 connect the sect's founding with the acquisition of hidden knowledge. In the covenant ceremony, penitence results in receiving divine wisdom. The numerous recurrences of the combination of these ideas—recognition of sin, declaration of God's righteousness, reception of wisdom or knowledge—testify to the centrality of this teaching in the Scrolls. These passages invite further investigation in order to cull from them a clearer image of the role of these themes.

The Community Rule 10-11

Recalling the obligation to offer prayer and praise at specific times, both during the days and nights, and on special days,[383] the concluding hymn in 1QS

---

[382]M. Knibb, *The Qumran Community*, 86; G. W. E. Nickelsburg, *Jewish Literature*, 135; P. Wernberg-Møller, *The Manual of Discipline* (Leiden: Brill, 1957) 51-52; B. Nitzan, *Qumran Prayer*, 133-135, 146-150.

[383]For more on this, see the discussion about the place of prayer within daily life of the community. See, also, B. Nitzan (*Qumran Prayer*, 52), who suggests that "the community saw the set times of praise as an eternal divine law." Times of prayer especially came at the "transitional points" of the day, evening and morning (53-61).

10-11 juxtaposes recognition of sin, declaration of God's righteousness, and the reception of divine knowledge. In fact, recognition of sin and God's righteousness lies at the heart of his task:

> I will declare his judgment in accordance with my iniquities, and my transgression is before my eyes like a graven decree. I will say to God: "My Righteousness" (1QS 10.11).

Because righteousness belongs to God alone, the hymn traces any such virtue in humans back to God. Thus, ll. 12-13 acknowledge God as the source of the petitioner's righteousness, goodness, holiness, etc. In col. 11 God's righteousness removes the member's sins (1QS 11.3). In place of sin, the hymn declares that God grants knowledge and enlightenment to humans. These metaphors, of course, are similar to those in the blessing in 1QS 2.1-4. According to 1QS 11.5b-9a, such knowledge is hidden and given only to the initiates. Therefore, just as in col. 2, the acquisition of such knowledge distinguishes the members of the group from those on the outside.

Besides this, the reception of knowledge indicates an anthropological transformation for the member. Unlike the covenant ceremony and several penitential prayers, the hymn's declaration of God's righteousness does not refer to his rightful punishment of Israel's sin. Rather, the declaration reflects on God's nature *vis-à-vis* human nature.[384] Righteousness belongs to God alone. Humans cannot possess it on their own. As 11.9b-10a and 11.20b-22 state, humans are by nature creatures of dust. On one hand, the dust metaphor represents human mortality, finiteness, and weakness (ll. 20a-22), while, on the other hand, it depicts humans' moral situation before God (ll. 9b-10a). Human *qua* flesh is riddled with the problem of sin.[385] Given all this, the author stands in wonderment that God has granted to humans knowledge and wisdom that is unattainable by human effort.

Knowledge in the Hodayot

While the ideas in the final hymn of the *Community Rule* clearly parallel those in the covenant ceremony, the question remains whether the hymn's ideas actually have any genetic relationship to the covenant ceremony. An inquiry into the appearances of this particular collection of themes establishes a link to the covenant ceremony and indicates that the ceremony became foundational

---

[384]Cf. E. P. Sanders, *Paul and Palestinian Judaism* (Philadelphia, Fortress, 1977) 278.

[385]J. Becker, *Das Heil Gottes: Heils—und Sündenbegriffe in den Qumrantexten und im Neuen Testament*, SUNT 3 (Göttingen: Vandenhoeck & Ruprecht, 1964) 112-113.

for further theological reflection about the meaning of joining the sect and the role of penitence in the moment of initiation and in the life of the member. The high frequency of this collection of ideas in the *Hodayot* attests that these thoughts held an integral place in the sect's thinking. However, the manifestation of these themes is insufficient proof of a connection between these ideas and the covenant ceremony. The most useful evidence, of course, is an explicit reference to the ceremony in one of the hymns.

The following chart presents the texts that reflect on the combined ideas of human as sinner, God as righteous, and the divine gifts of forgiveness, wisdom, and knowledge. The hymns' numbers follow the new order published by G. Martinez.

Table 3. *Appearance of the Ideas Human as Sinner, God as Righteous, and the Gift of Knowledge in the Hodayot*

Human as Flesh	God as Righteous	Knowledge
4.25	4.20	4.21-22
5.2, 19-21	5.23, 55	5.2-3, 6, 25-26
	6.15-16	6.9-13, 25
7.16, 25	7.17	7.2
9.21-25	9.26-27	9.31-38
11.19-28	-	11.19-23
12.29-30	12.31, 37	12.27-29
15.32-33	(15.28-32) implied	15.26
19.3, 10-12, 20-21, 24	(19.7-8 indirectly) 17-18, cf. 31	19.4, 12-14, 16-17, 28
20.24-27	20.31	20.29
21.6-8, 10, 16 Frag 3.5, 11		21.5
22.4, 8, 13, 15 Frag 4.11		22.7, 14(?)
23.11-13		

Amid all this convincing data about the frequency of these themes are a couple of explicit references to the covenant ceremony: 1QH 21 and 1QH 19. The reference to the covenant ceremony in 1QH 21 stands in a context that reflects retrospectively on the mysterious anthropological shift from sinner to recipient of divine wisdom that results from entering the sect.[386] The hymn also considers the paradoxes that spring from a human, a creature of dust, in possession of such a divine gift.

> For what is flesh? [ ] to do wonders and in your imagination to display might, and to establish all things for your glory. [ ] the host of knowledge to recount to flesh mighty deeds and true precepts to the one born [of woman], *and have brought him into the covenant with you*, and has uncovered a heart of dust to keep [ ] from the snares of judgment, to your mercy. For I am a creature [of clay], a heart of stone. Why should I be considered like this, that [ ] place in the ear of dust, and the eternal occurrences be engraved in a heart [of stone]. *And you converted [him] to bring [him] into covenant with you*, and that he stand [ ] in the midst of eternal things to where the everlasting light of dawn shines [and no] darkness (ll. 6-14).

As the italicized text shows, the author reflects twice on the significance and mystery of entering the covenant. In terms comparable to the priests' blessing in the covenant ceremony, the author marvels that God imparts mercy to weak and sinful humans and transports them into the realm of eternal things. The author's language also borrows from narratives of heavenly ascents where the human moves from the realm of dust to "stand" in the midst of "eternal things" and "eternal light" (l. 29).[387] Thus, entrance into the covenant not only officially admitted a person into the sect, but also marked an anthropological and ontological transformation. In fact, the transformation resembles the blessings that humans receive at the eschaton. Thus, entrance into the community results in realized eschatology.

The reference to the covenant ceremony in col. 19 also envisions the moment of pardon as an ontological change for humans. The author signals that he has the sect's entrance ceremony in mind with the words "joined to your (i.e., God's) sons of truth and in the lot of the people, your holy ones" (להוחד [עם] בני אמתך ובגורל עם קדושיכה) (l. 11). The noun form of יחד frequently designates the community in the Scrolls.[388] According to this hymn, in the moment of expiation and entrance into the community, a person moves from sin/transgression/abomination/dust/spirit of perversity to cleansing holi-

---

[386]Cf. B. Nitzan, *Qumran Prayer*, 337-339.
[387]G. W. E. Nickelsburg, "*1 Enoch* and Qumran Origins: The State of the Question and the Prospect for an Answer," *SBLSP* (1986) 341-360.
[388]Cf. 1QS 1.1; see S. Talmon, *Qumran from Within*, 53-60.

ness/member of the community/lot of the saints/truth/understanding/life in God's presence with the everlasting hosts. The transformation requires two basic elements: penitence, including confession, from humans and God's forgiveness. While the *Hodayot* do not always present the actions of both God and humans together, they should be presumed throughout the hymns.[389]

In fairness to the evidence, not every hymn proves to be a retrospective reflection on entrance into the covenant. Several hymns, like 1QH 12.29-31a, for example, speak generally on God's righteousness in contrast to human sin and weakness without any hint of the covenant ceremony:

> What is flesh [to do]?
> And a creature of clay to declare such wonders?
> For he is iniquitous from the womb...
> For I know that righteousness does not belong to humans,
> Nor to the sons of men perfection of the way.
> To God most high belong all the works of righteousness...

The author's recollection of his sins causes tremendous distress:

> As for me, shaking and trembling seized me,
> And all my bones broke,
> And my heart melted like wax before the fire,
> My knees shook like water descending a steep place,
> For I remembered my guilt, and the unfaithfulness of my ancestors...
> (1QH 12.33b-34a).

Sinners frequently experience such physiological responses to the recognition of guilt.[390] As col. 12 concludes, the author describes how God poured out his mercy and pardon on him (l. 37). The mention of God's righteousness and power *vis-à-vis* human sin and weakness corresponds to the declaration of God's righteousness in 1QS 10-11 where God's righteousness does not specifically relate to God's just punishment but to his nature in comparison to human nature. 1QH 12 also attests to a persistent tension that the sect maintained, namely, that even though God grants forgiveness and anthropologically alters the initiate, a large moral gap remains between God and humans.

---

[389]E. P. Sanders, *Paul and Palestinian Judaism*, 276.

[390]See, e.g., Ezra 9, the angels in *1 Enoch* 13:4-7, and the kings and the mighty in *1 Enoch* 48:8-10; 62:1-12. See also, G. W. E. Nickelsburg, "The Qumranic Radicalizing and Anthropologizing of an Eschatological Tradition (1QH 4:29-40) in *Ernten, was man sät. Festschrift für Klaus Koch*. D. R. Daniels, U. Gleßmer, and M. Rösel, Ed. Neukirchener (1991) 429-431.

Despite the presence of these hymns with no explicit mentioning of the covenant, the position that these ideas sprang from reflection on the meaning of entering the covenant remains tenable. Other authors at Qumran moved from this specific understanding of entrance into the sect through a ceremony that included penitence to more general reflection of God's power and human weakness. Therefore, the other texts may stand within the development of this tradition.

Although the position that 1QH and 1QS 10-11 represent a development of the ideas from the covenant ceremony seems quite plausible, identifying the sect's use of such hymns proves difficult if not impossible. Scholarship has attempted to locate the function of these hymns through form criticism. In regard to their literary forms, scholarship has basically agreed to divide the *Hodayot* into two broad categories: hymns of an individual, often assumed to be the Teacher of Righteousness; and hymns of the community.[391] Beyond this, form criticism's task becomes more difficult and the conclusions more tenuous. In other words, it remains impossible to determine a hymn's *Sitz im Leben*.[392] Form criticism operates under the fallacious presumption that similarity in form indicates the same *Sitz im Leben*. In regard to the *Hodayot*, the similarities between the community hymns and the covenant renewal ceremony in 1QS do not necessarily mean that the sect used the hymns in that particular setting. The sect may have used the hymns as liturgy on various occasions,[393] or personal reflection or remembrance, or even for instruction and study. B. Nitzan argues that a comparison of the prayer and liturgical material from Qumran to 1QH indicates that 1QH is not a liturgical work. It lacks, for example, typical formulae of other liturgical material.[394] Besides this, its individualism and expressions of personal feeling are unlike other liturgical texts.[395] Despite these limitations of the texts and in methodology, the material from 1QS and 1QH verify that penitence continued to function not only as an integral part of community practice, but also community thought. The community basically taught that penitence marks the moment of trans-

---

[391]For a summary of the scholarship see J. Murphy-O'Connor, "The Judean Desert," *EJMI* (eds. R. Kraft and G. W. E. Nickelsburg; Philadelphia: Fortress, 1986) 130-132.

[392]See D. Dimant, "Qumran Sectarian Literature," 523.

[393]H.-W. Kuhn, *Enderwärtung und gegenwärtiges Heil: Untersuchungen zu den Gemeindeliedern on Qumran*, SUNT 4 (Göttingen: Vandenhoeck & Ruprecht, 1966); S. Holm-Nielsen, *Hodayot: Psalms from Qumran* (Aarhus: Universitestsforlaget, 1960); J. Murphy-O'Connor, "La genèse littéraire de la Règle de las Communauté," *RQ* 77 (1969) 544-546.

[394]B. Nitzan, *Qumran Prayer*, 322-324.

[395]Ibid., 328.

formation from sin to righteousness, from death to life, from ignorance to wisdom.

Summary

In order to enter the sect, an initiate must confess his sins. The covenant ceremony in 1QS includes this confession as a key moment. The confession marks the moment of transformation for the initiate. He moves from outside to inside the sect, from ignorance to wisdom, from death to life. The initiate even realizes in the present some of the blessings generally reserved for the eschaton. An examination of 1QH shows that these hymns also reflect back on the entrance to the covenant as a moment of anthropological transformation.

Prayer in the Community's Daily Life

In regard to role of prayer in the community's daily life, the Qumran Scrolls provide some of the most useful data in the literature of the Second Temple period. The Scrolls contain not only discussions of prayer, but also actual daily prayers.[396] Consequently, an examination of these data leads to perhaps the sharpest picture of the function of daily prayer in Second Temple Judaism. Even so, the process of analyzing these texts is not without its pitfalls.

The Community Rule 6.6-8

Just as penitence and interpretation mark the sect's origin, prayer (sometimes penitential) and interpretation serve as the sect's primary daily activities. 1QS 6.6-8 explicitly combines the two activities:

> And in any place where there are ten men, let it not be without a man who seeks (דרש) the Law day and night continually ... And the congregation[397] will watch together a third of every night of the year to read in the book, to search (דרש) the ordinances, and to say the blessings (לברך) together.

The notion of studying the Law day and night arose from the community's reading of Josh 1:8 and Ps 1:2.[398] The people probably kept watch for a third

---

[396] See E. Chazon, "Prayers from Qumran and Their Historical Implications," *DSD* 1 (1994) 265-284; B. Nitzan, *Qumran Prayer*.

[397] A. Dupont-Sommer (*The Essene Writings from Qumran*, 85) translates this "the Many."

[398] Ibid., 85; M. Knibb, *The Qumran Community*, 116.

of each night, rather than for a third of the nights of the year.³⁹⁹ The author here continues the use of דרש to speak of interpreting the Law. The "book," which derives from Josh 1:8, is certainly the Law.⁴⁰⁰ The member of the sect also prays, which the passage refers to with the phrase "to say the blessings" (לברך). The community may have composed a specific group of prayers for this activity or occasion, as they did for so many other facets of their life. 1QS 10 also mentions that the community says blessings at the beginning and the end of days.

The conclusion to the Admonitions in CD 20.26-32⁴⁰¹ unites following the Law as interpreted by the Teacher of Righteousness and penitential confession. The passage summarizes some of the most important ideas of the community, and, as such, affirms again the place of study and prayer.

> All those who hold to these judgments going and coming according to the Law, and those who obey the voice of the Teacher of Righteousness, and those who confess (ויתודו) before God, "We are wicked, indeed both we and our ancestors, in walking contrary to the statutes of the covenant. Righteous and true are your judgments against us..." (ll. 27-30)

The language of the confession parallels the confession in the covenant ceremony in 1QS 1.25b-26:

> ... We are wicked, and our fathers before us in walking contrary to the statutes. True and righteous [is God in sending] his judgment against us and against our ancestors.

Those who practice these things receive strength, forgiveness, and salvation.

The Community Rule 9

Because it eventually separated from the Jerusalem Temple, the community needed a method for atonement besides sacrifice. The community's relation-

---

³⁹⁹M. Knibb, *The Qumran Community*, 117.
⁴⁰⁰Ibid.
⁴⁰¹Cols. 19 and 20 (following Schechter's numbering) come from ms B. They are usually placed between cols 8 and 9 of ms A. In the quest for isolating the sources of the Damascus Document, CD 20.26-34 stands at the heart of the debate. Murphy-O'Connor argued that the compiler of the Damascus Document composed this passage to re-enforce the Admonitions. P. Davies, on the other hand, understands this text, along with CD 1.1-7.9, as part of the original text. For a brief summary of the opinions on the sources, see R. A. Kraft and G. W. E. Nickelsburg, eds., *Early Judaism and its Modern Interpreters*, 127-128.

ship with the Jerusalem Temple, though, can only be partially reconstructed. At some moments during the community's history, the adherents still sacrificed at the Temple. Eventually, however, the sect completely broke from the Jerusalem Temple and was forced to develop another avenue for removing sin. Prayer and obedience came to substitute temporarily for Temple sacrifices.

> To atone for guilty transgressions and unfaithful sin, and loving-kindness for the land, apart from the flesh of holocausts and the fat of sacrifice, and the offering of lips[402] rightly offered will be as a righteous fragrance, and perfection of the way as acceptable free will offering (ll. 4-5).

CD 11.20-21, drawing on Prov 15:8, makes a similar claim.[403] In 4QFlor,[404] which speaks of three Temples, the second Temple, the contemporary Temple, is desolate because of Israel's sin. God consequently establishes a third Temple, a "Temple of men" (מקדש אדם), in which is offered "burnt offerings" and "words of thanksgiving." In this text, the Temple metaphor represents the community itself. The sacrifice metaphors most likely stand for prayer and obedience. In this way, 4QFlor resembles 1QS 9. 1QS 8.1-10,[405] which also depicts the community as a Temple.[406] In this text, though, obedience and suffering become the accepted sacrifices.

The notion that something could replace sacrifice was not new or isolated to Qumran. Using the language of Psalm 51, the petitioner in the Prayer of Azariah asks that God accept brokenness and enduring oppression as sacrifice.[407] Of course, the narrative context prevents the suppliant from traveling to the Temple; he is in a blazing furnace. Ben Sira', who does not boycott the Temple, and Tobit teach that giving alms is a discipline that expiates sin.

---

[402]Vermes' translation, which can be inconstant and too paraphrastic, on this occasion translates the metaphor with "prayer." Where the metaphor appears elsewhere in the text he translates it literally. See 1QS 9.26; 10.6, 14.

[403]See B. Nitzan, *Qumran Prayer*, 47-49.

[404]For the Hebrew text see J. M. Allegro, *DJD V: Qumran Cave 4*, 53-57.

[405]Some take this section as the "manifesto" of the community. See G. W. E. Nickelsburg, *Jewish Literature*, 156 n 116; A. R. C. Leaney, *The Rule of Qumran*, 211; and M. Knibb (*The Qumran Community*, 129) who calls this the "programme" of the community.

[406]Some propose that the "Council of the Community" was a special inner group. M. Knibb (*The Qumran Community*, 129), however, has forcefully argued that the designation simply refers to the whole community.

[407]See Chapter Four.

The Words of the Heavenly Lights (4Q504)[408]

Beyond the discussion of the function of prayers, the desert discoveries have produced a collection of daily prayers that is penitential—The Words of the Heavenly Lights (4Q504).[409]

Baillet dates the scroll to the mid second century BCE for paleographical reasons.[410] He believes that the prayers originate among the ancestors of the community because of the absence of sectarian language and ideas, namely eschatological determinism and dualism. While he correctly notices the absence of these features, he incorrectly attributes the prayers to the Hasidim.[411] Still, determining whether a Qumran document is "sectarian," i.e., a product of the sect and fits its own peculiar ideology and sociology, or whether the group imported a document from some other source, remains a complicated methodological problem. One should not assume that the community could only produce material laden with dualism, eschatological determinism, and separation from the rest of Judaism. Further, B. Nitzan notices that in Qumran prayers the community tends to identify itself with the rest of Israel and generally uses less sectarian language. Nevertheless, references to Israel's sins signifies the community's conflict with the Judaism.[412]

Baillet's theory that the prayers originate among the ancestors of the community encounters one problem. The prayers clearly differ in regard to

---

[408] For the Hebrew text, see M. Baillet, *DJD* VII, *Qumrân Grotte 4* (Oxford: Clarendon, 1982) 137-177.

[409] For more on fixed times for prayer and fixed prayer, see B. Nitzan, *Qumran Prayer*, 49-53. M. R. Lehmann disagrees with Baillet that these were prayers for the days of the week. Instead he tries to show that 4Q504 belonged in the category of *Tahanun*. However, as L. H. Schiffman ("The Scrolls and Early Jewish Liturgy," 40-41) points out, the document's explicit reference to Wednesday and Saturday leaves Lehmann's contentions unfounded. See also B. Nitzan, *Qumran Prayer*, 64-66. Further, Schiffman ("The Scrolls and Early Jewish Liturgy," 40-41) and Chazon ("Is *Divrei Ha-Me'orot* a Sectarian Document?", 9-10) have shown that no evidence exists for holding that the *Tahanun* existed in the Second Temple period.

[410] M. Baillet, "Un recueil liturgique de Qumrân, grotte 4: 'Les Paroles des Luminaires,'" *RB* 68 (1961) 235-238.

[411] At one time it was the concensus and *en vogue* to perceive the Hasidim as the ancestors of many Jewish groups. Subsequently, J. J. Collins (*The Apocalyptic Vision of the Book of Daniel*, 191-224) and G. W. E. Nickelsburg ("Social Aspects of Palestinian Jewish Apocalypticism," *Apocalypticism in the Mediterranean World and Near East: Proceeding of the International Colloquium on Apocalypticism, Uppsala, August 12-17, 1979* [Ed. D. Hellhom; Tübingen, 1983] 641-54) has demonstrated the impossibility ot this theory.

[412] B. Nitzan, *Qumran Prayer*, 328-333.

their view of the return from Babylonian exile. Unlike the *Damascus Document*, which totally disregarded the return and the post-exilic community, 4Q504 5.9-13 explicitly mentions the return from Babylon as the fulfillment of God's promises to the nation. Thus, these prayers may have originated before the community adopted a polemical retelling of Israel's history. Yet, one would think that the sect would have returned to this liturgy to correct its view of the past according to the new polemical ideology. This inconstancy brings into relief a problem which modern critiques at times take too lightly: the Dead Sea Scrolls were an ancient *library*. How works in a library relate to one another and are viewed by the community are complicated issues.[413] Should one expect every document in an ancient library to be ideologically homogeneous?

Still, in the absence of what some would call "typical" Qumranic themes, what made these prayers appealing and useful to the sect? If the members offered these prayers daily, then some aspect(s) of the prayer proved particularly applicable to their theology. An inquiry into these prayers should attempt to identify such feature(s) in the prayers. The following discussion proceeds by column.

Column 1

The first column exists in fragmentary form. Its twofold "amen," which has precedents in Num 5:22; Neh 8:6; Pss 72:19; 89:52, as well as 4Q504 7.2, and the traces of previous lines in the manuscript suggest that the document is missing material. Lines 8-10, however, provide some hints about the topic of this material. The words "miracles," "from Egypt," and "from the desert" are decipherable. These terms figure prominently in the recitations of the Exodus. The fact that other penitential prayers refer to the Exodus allows for even further confidence in assuming that this was the topic prior to the twofold "amen." If this is the case, and in comparison with later extant portions of the prayer, the prayer probably recalled the Exodus in order to introduce the idea of Israel's election. The theme of election, then, has the potential to highlight the severity of Israel's disobedience as well as provide a basis for an appeal for forgiveness and give meaning to Israel's suffering.

---

[413]For a more thorough discussion of the methodological problems related to labelling a prayer or liturgical piece from Qumran "sectarian," see E. Chazon, "Is *Divrei Ha-Me'orot* a Sectarian Prayer?" *The Dead Sea Scrolls: Forty Years of Research* (eds. D. Dimant and U. Rappaport; Leiden: Brill, 1992) 3-17.

Column 2

The words אנא אדני usually begin a petitionary section. In this column, the prayer mainly petitions for God to remember how he pardoned Israel in the past and to repeat it in the present (ll. 7-10), to remove his anger (l. 11), and to bring healing to the nation (l. 14). The prayer argues from historical precedent (i.e., God forgave the fathers' sins) and the covenant relationship. The reference to previous history is reminiscent of Nehemiah 9, Psalm 79, and Isa 63:7-64:12. The prayer remembers that only God's covenant in the past saved Israel from total annihilation. Believing that the covenant remains in effect, the prayer relies upon it for confidence that the Jews can still experience forgiveness and pardon.

The specific sin that 2.8 has in mind remains a mystery because the author conflates the golden calf scene and the people's refusal to attack in Numbers 14. The line, "when they rebelled against your word," recalls Deut 1:26 and 43 where Moses retells the people's refusal to invade Canaan. The language in l. 8, however, reproduces in transposed form the words of Deut 9:8, Moses' recapitulation of the golden calf rebellion. The reference to God's "great might" in l. 10, while present in other passages, appears in Deut 9:29, and Num 14:19 ascribes to God "great power" (כגדול כוחכה, l. 7). Further, Num 14:19 has a close parallel to the statement in ll. 7-8 which reads: "you pardoned our fathers when they rebelled" (נשאת[ה] לאבותינו במרותם) (cf. also l. 11). With this conflation of texts, the author constructs an idealized image from the past of the nation's rebellion. The modern critic has no reason to decide between one or the other scene as the referent for the prayer. The request for healing exhibits the influence of the covenantal curses, which the prayer later explicitly states are in effect. The author takes his images of "madness," "blindness," and "bewilderment" in ll. 14-15 from Deut 28:27-28, and closely relates these problems to Israel's sins (l. 16).[414]

By focusing on past sins through the lens of election and the covenant, the prayer plans to propose a correlation between the past and the present. Since God in his abundant love and mercy forgave the fathers, he could do the same for the author's generation (ll. 7-9).[415] So, the author requests in l. 11 that God turn his wrath from the nation, language that parallels Dan 9:16 and Bar 2:35.[416] The prayer extends the basis for mercy to God's name in l. 12.[417]

---

[414]Cf. B. Nitzan, *Qumran Prayer*, 84.
[415]For God's love for Israel as "election," see Deut 7:8, 13, and 16, which also uses the covenant with the patriarchs as another basis for election.
[416]Cf. also 1 Kgs 8:41; 2 Chron 6:32; Lev 26:18, 24, 28.
[417]See Jer 14:9; 1 Kgs 8:43; Isa 43:7; 63:19; Dan 9:18, 19.

As in other penitential contexts, this theme encourages God to respond on behalf of his people in order to protect his reputation. According to this appeal, the special relationship between God and this people means that their historical status reflects on him.

Although the manuscript has a tear at ll. 12-13, it probably spoke of God leading the people to repentance: "... [to make us repent] with all our heart and soul." The word שוב is not legible in the manuscript. However, the similarities between this line and 1QS 5.8-9 justify its inclusion. Further, later in 4Q504 5, the prayer explicitly states that God causes the people to repent. Following this repentance in column 2, the author imagines a new level of obedience as God "plants" the law in the people's hearts. The prayer draws its language from texts like Jer 31:33, where God "plants" the law in Israel's heart so that it will not turn to the right or to the left (cf. also Deut 28:14)(ll. 13-14).[418]

Column 3

The column begins by relying on the contents of Isa 40:15 and 17.[419] As in the previous columns, this Isaiah text attracts the author because of its possibilities for further contemplation about the meaning of Israel's election and its covenant with God. In contrast to the other nations, God has elevated Israel to a special place. He has made Israel his child, his first-born.[420] The language in 4Q504 3.9-10 clearly employs the vocabulary of election. Although the text contains a lacuna, the wording probably springs from passages like Exod 19:5 and Deut 7:6:

4Q504 3.9-10	Exod 19:5b
... for you chose us for yourself [for a people from all] the earth.	... and you will be my possession for all the peoples...
כיא אותנו בחרתה לכה [לעם מכול] הארץ	והייתם לי סגלה מכל־העמים כי־לי כל־הארץ

Deut 7:6
... YHWH your God chose you to be his possession from all the peoples that are on the face of the earth.

בחר יהוה אלהיך להיות לו לעם סגלה
מכל העמים אשר על־פני האדמה

---

[418] Cf. also Deut 5:32(29); 17:11, 20; Zech 12:6.
[419] For the use of "remembrances" in Jewish prayer traditions, see B. Nitzan, *Qumran Prayer*, 93-99.
[420] Cf. Ex 4:22; Jer 31:9; Hos 11:1; Sir 36:17.

Chapter Three

However, along with the blessing of election comes the responsibility for improper behavior. As the first-born, Israel must also endure God's chastisement when it sins.[421] In line with the allusions to the curses in the previous columns, God punished Israel with the covenantal curses (ll. 8-9 and 10-13).[422] This pattern, a special relationship and incurred punishment, continues in ll. 9-11 where the prayer parallels Daniel and, even more closely, Baruch. Baruch combined the themes of pouring out of God's wrath, the curses clinging to the people, disregarding the prophets' warnings, and disobedience to the Law of Moses. As the italicized words in the following parallel columns indicate, 4Q504 3.10-13 stands close to Bar 1:20-21. The bold italics show the relationship of 4Q504 to Bar 2:20.

Bar 1:20	4Q504 3.10b-13a
Therefore, the curse and the evil which the Lord commanded *through Moses, his servant has clung to us...*	... *therefore you poured out on us your anger and your jealousy with all the fury of your wrath*, and *clings to us [ ] you [ ] which was written in the Law of Moses, and your servants the prophets...*
καὶ ἐκολλήθη εἰς ἡμᾶς τὰ κακὰ καὶ ἡ ἀρά, ἣν συνέταξεν κύριος τῷ Μωυσῇ, παιδὶ αὐτοῦ ...	שפכתה אלינו את חמתכה [ואת קנא]תכה בכול חרון אפכה ותדבק בנו [ ] ותיכה אשר כתב מושה ועבדיכם הנביאים...

Bar 2:20
For you sent your anger and wrath against us just as you said by the hand of your servants the prophets.

ὅτι ἐνῆκας τὸν θυμόν σου καὶ τὴν ὀργήν σου εἰς ἡμᾶς, καθάπερ ἐλάλησας ἐν χειρὶ τῶν παίδων σου τῶν προφητῶν.

The absence of a copy of Baruch among the Qumran Scrolls makes these similarities peculiar.[423] Has the author of 4Q504 read Baruch, or did peniten-

---

[421]Cf. Deut 8:5 and Hos 11:1-7. Cf. also the discussion on the *Psalms of Solomon* in Chapter Four of this book.

[422]Cf. Deut 28:48, 59; 1 Kgs 8:35, 37, 46; Jer 14:16; Bar 2:25.

[423]J. Goldstein ("The Apocryphal Book of Baruch," 199, n 53) argues on the basis of names of months in the two books that Baruch most likely will never be found among the Dead Sea Scrolls.

tial prayers frequently contain this same combination of ideas during this period? These phrases probably only show that such language is formulaic in penitential prayers.

The manuscript is torn at l. 20. This line probably included a *Gerichtsdoxologie*, "You are just," as a climax to the prayer's recognition of God rightfully punishing the nation. The words "and our kings" in l. 15 may have been part of a long litany of rulers who had sinned, like those in Ezra, Daniel, and Baruch. Finally, the phrase, "in the last days," which the author takes from Deut 31:29, assumes eschatological overtones which it did not possess in Deuteronomy. Thus, the author may have fashioned the prayer with the belief that the covenantal curses and the repentance of the community were eschatological events. In this regard, the prayer may contain an inchoate set of ideas that stand at the heart of later Qumran theology.

Column 4

As in all the previous columns, column 4 continues the theme of election. The prayer draws from Deut 7:8 in order to recall God's love for Israel (ll. 4-5). This column, however, expands the theme of election to reflect God's choice of Jerusalem, the Temple, Israel, Judah, and David. Some of the language in the discussion originates from 1 Kings 8, Solomon's Temple dedicatory prayer. For example, the author constructed ll. 2-6 from 1 Kgs 8:16.

1 Kgs 8:16	4Q504 4.2-6
... *have I not chosen a city* from all the tribes of Israel to build a house *for my name to be there. And I chose David* to be over my people, Israel.	... from your dwelling place [ ] resting place in Jerusalem, *the city that you chose from all the earth for your name to be there forever*. For you loved Israel more than all the peoples, and *you chose* the tribe of Judah, and you established your covenant with *David*...
...לא־בחרתי בעיר מכל שבטי את־עמי ישראל לבנות בית להיות שמי שם ואבחר בדוד להיות על־עמי ישראל	מנוחה בירוש[לים העיר אשר בח]רתה בה מכול הארץ להיות [שמכ]ה שם לעולם כיא אהבתה את ישראל מכול העמים ותבחר בשבט יאודה ובריתכה הקימותה לדויד...

Other portions of the text that depict a peaceful time when Gentiles brought gifts to Jerusalem may also allude to the period of Solomonic rule, even though David is the only king the column mentions (see e.g., l. 7). For example, in 1 Kgs 10:1-11 the Queen of Sheba and Hiram bring gifts of gold, silver, and precious stones. Even though the author is reminiscing about the monarchical period, he adapts material from Isa 66:18-19 where the prophet speaks of the nations seeing God's glory and bringing the Jews back to Jerusalem as offerings to God.

Within the context of divine election, the text again raises the problem of Israel's rebellion. The author describes the rebellion by borrowing from Deut 31:20,[424] a text in which God warns Moses that the people will serve idols once they have enjoyed the bounty of the land. This theme carries over to column 5, which begins with condemnation of Israel's idolatry. Combining columns 3 and 4 together would result in a lengthy retelling of Israel's history as a history of sin in contrast to God's covenant faithfulness. In this way, the daily prayers function like other penitential prayers.[425]

Column 5

The recitation of Israel's sins spills over into column 5. The nation forsakes God, "the fount of living waters" (cf. CD 8), a metaphor that Jer 2:13 employs to picture the people's disobedience,[426] to serve idols, a cardinal sin in Deuteronomy and the deuteronomic history. The author's vocabulary for the sin, "serving a foreign God in their land," is influenced by Deut 31:16 and 32:12. And, flowing in the stream of deuteronomic thought, the prayer proclaims that this sin brings punishment as God determines to "pour out his anger, etc."[427] and desolate the land by foreign enemies.[428]

Yet, in harmony with the conception of Israel as God's "first-born" who receives God's punishment, column 5 interprets the disaster that confronts Israel as "chastisement" (l. 17). Therefore, once again, the prayer maintains that God sends punishment in order to discipline Israel as a son in order to steer it back to proper behavior. Despite Israel's unfaithfulness, the prayer affirms that God did not abandon Israel.[429] Instead, he remained faithful to the covenant with the nation. Even in the moment of punishment, God did not reject the people. In ll. 6-11, the prayer pictures this faithfulness as the fulfillment of God's promise in Lev 26:44-45:

---

[424] Cf. Neh 9:25.
[425] See Nehemiah 9; cf. Deuteronomy 32.
[426] Cf. Bar 3:12 and CD 19.34 (B).
[427] Cf. 2.11; 3.10-11; Dan 9:11, 16; Isa 66:15-16.
[428] Cf. Lev 26:23; CD 3.1.
[429] Neh 9:17, 19, 31.

Lev 26:44-45	4Q504 5.6b-11a
Still yet, when they are in the land of their enemies, I will *not reject them* nor abhor them, so as *to put and end to them, to break the covenant with them.* For I am YHWH their God. *And I will remember* for their benefit *the covenant* with the ancestors, whom *I brought* from the land of Egypt *before the eyes of the nations...*	... In all this, *you did not reject* the race of Jacob, and *did not reject* Israel to the end, *so as to break your covenant with them ...* *And you remembered your covenant.* *For you brought us out before the eyes of the nations*, and did not forsake us among the nations...
ואף־גם־זאת בהיותם בארץ איביהם לא־מאסתים ולא־געלתים לכלתם להפר בריתי אתם כי אני יהוה אלהיהם וזכרתי להם ברית ראשנים אשר הוצתי־אתם מארץ מצרים לעיני הגוים...	... בכול זואת לוא מאסתה בזרע יעקוב ולו געלתה את ישראל לכלותם להפר בריתכה אתם כיא אתה אל חי לבדכה ואין זולתכה ותזכור ברית אשר הוצתנו לעיני הגוים ולוא עזבתנו בגוים...

In quoting this portion of Leviticus, the prayer collides with the idea of the return in other Qumranic texts. For example, the *Damascus Document* totally dismisses the return and the post-exilic period as periods of sin. This discrepancy means that these daily prayers either arose before the sect started to rewrite history through polemic, or that not every writer felt compelled to polemicize Israel's past.

While the author returns to the deuteronomic traditions for the description of God driving the people into exile and their eventual repentance, he slightly adjusts the traditions to fit his emphasis on God's faithfulness and graciousness. According to the writer, even the return was the result of God's graciousness.

Deut 30:1	4Q504 5.11b-13a
And it will be when all these things come upon you, the blessing and curse which I set before you, you will turn to your heart[430] among all the nations to which YHWH your God drove you.	... and you were gracious to your people Israel in all the lands to which you drove them, to return to their heart, to return even to you and to obey your voice according to all which you commanded by the hand of Moses your servant...

---

[430] See Chapter One for a discussion of this metaphor.

ותחון את עמכה ישראל בכול [ה]ארצות
אשר הדחתם שמה להשיב אל לבבם
לשוב עודך ולשמוע בקולכה [כ]כול
אשר צויתה ביד מושה עבדכם...

והיה כי־יבאו עליך כל־הדברים האלה
הברכה והקללה אשר נתתי לפניך
והשבת אל־לבבך בכל־הגוים אשר
הדיחך יהוה אלהיך שמה

Deut 30:2
You will turn to YHWH your God
and obey to his voice.

ושבת עד־יהוה אלהיך ושמעת בקלו

Deut 4:30
In your distress, when all these
things have found you, in the latter
days, you will return to YHWH
your God and obey his voice.

בצר לך ומצאוך כל הדברים האלה
באחרית הימים ושבת עד־יהוה אלהיך
ושמעת בקלו

1 Kgs 8:47
And if they turn to their heart in the
land to which they have been
driven...

והשיבו אל־לבם בארץ אשר נשבו־שם

Recounting the return with this nuance confirms the author's contention that God sends punishment upon Israel as one "chastises" a "son." God primarily intends for the punishment to restore Israel to the land and to himself. Ll. 15-21 seem to explain how God leads Israel to repentance. Borrowing from Isa 44:3, the author claims that God has poured out his holy spirit on the people, which results in the people "seeking" (פקד) God in the midst of their distress (צר)(l. 16).[431] The formula "to seek in distress" is old.[432] While the author may have Deut 4:30 in mind in this case, "In your distress ... you will return to the Lord your God," Deuteronomy uses בקש instead of פקד.[433]

---

[431] For this meaning for פקד, see *BDB*, 823.

[432] M. Weinfeld (*Deuteronomy 1-11*, 48-49) notices the presence of this formula in the Dead Sea Scrolls, but did not note the use of פקד instead of בקש. See Chapter One for fuller description of the formula.

[433] The final discussion between God and Moses before the Song of Moses also discusses the "distress" that will come to Israel. Cf. 4Q504 5.17 and Deut 31:21.

Column 6

The existing beginning lines (ll. 2-3) read as if forgiveness has been announced and the people are responding to it.[434] Ll. 5-6 confirm that the community offered these daily prayers in order to remove sin. Throughout ll. 5-6 the author leans heavily on Leviticus 26:

Lev 26:40-41[435]	4Q504 6.5-6
And when they confess their iniquity and the iniquity of the ancestors, and the treachery (מעל)[436] moreover, that they continued in their contrariness (הלכו ... בקרי) against me, so that I continued contrariness (אלך ... בקרי) with them...	... we expiate our iniquity and the iniquity of our ancestors, along with our treachery (מעל) when they did against me, and, we continued in contrariness (הלכו בקרי).

Woven into the language of expiation is a full expression of the *Gerichtsdoxologie* (ll. 3-4). As in the *Community Rule* and the *Hodayot*, the declaration of God's righteousness assumes an emphatic form by doubling the second person address: "To you, to you, O Lord, is righteousness" (לכה אתה אדוני הצדקה). To remove any doubt that the author has God's punitive and restorative deeds in mind, he includes: "because you have done all this." Appropriate to the themes of these daily prayers, the people acknowledge God's punishment as discipline, "scourges," to which they must submit.[437] They affirm that God punishes them only to make them more faithful.

Even so, the people request that God turn back his wrath from Jerusalem.[438] They introduce this petition with a typical phrase: "and now" (ועתה).[439] The diaspora's existence probably suggests to the petitioners that God's wrath lingers. The deuteronomic words "where [you drove them] there" (Deut 30:1) show that the suppliants conceive of this phenomenon as part of the residue of the covenantal curses.[440] Consequently, a request for a return

---

[434]M. Baillet (*DJD*, VII, 149) believes that l. 2 alludes to Ezek 18:31. He further notes that the nouns חטאה and פשע are parallel to one another in Ps 51:3 and 4. Cf. also Isa 43:25.

[435]Cf. also Lev 26:21, 23, 24, 27, 41.

[436]See the discussion in Chapter One. See Lev 5:14, 21; 26:40; Num 5:6, 12, 27; Neh 1:8; 9:4.

[437]See 1QH 4.8; 8.15; 9.18, 32, 33; 10.7; 12.36; 13.28, 16.27; 17.6, 10, 12, 25; 18.19, 19.8, 22; 20:9 (following Martínez's numbering); 1QS 3.14; 3.23; 4.12.

[438]Cf. Dan 9:16.

[439]Cf. 2.7; Dan 9; Bar 2:11.

[440]Cf. Tob 3:4; Bar 3:8.

from exile serves as the main interest of ll. 12-14. Only the resolution of this problem could indicate that God has completely removed his wrath.

Column 7

The vacant line after l. 2 means that the prayers end here.[441] The prayers close by returning to the theme of God as the one who delivers from distress, and signifies that the community's requests await fulfillment.

Summary

Isolated from the Temple, the Qumran community must devise a method for dealing with sin. The Jews of the Second Temple Period have already considered this problem and have determined that giving alms, obedience, oppression, and prayer could remove sin. The Qumran sectarians include several of these methods in their religious system. They also make prayer and biblical interpretation daily practices.

"The Words of the Heavenly Lights" is a collection of daily prayers. Because the prayers do not contain the "typical" sectarian features of the sect's thought, the prayers probably originate from the community's ancestors. At least in their understanding of the Babylonian exile, the prayers conflict with the ideology of the *Damascus Document*. However, the prayers' dominant covenantal theology make them especially useful for the community. The Qumran sectarians believe that they are God's covenant people. Thus, daily penitential prayers with a strong covenantal theme fit nicely into their ideological system. The group probably reads the language of election and covenant as referring to its own status before God. Consequently, even though the prayers might produce some tensions with other parts of the sect's ideology of history, they still satisfactorily express the sect's idea of its unique relationship with God.

Conclusion

Several groups that this Chapter examines distinguish themselves from the rest of Judaism based upon their reinterpretation of Deuteronomy and reapplication of the deuteronomic schema. When deuteronomic language does not dominate the texts, as in the case of the "Animal Apocalypse" and the "Apocalypse of

---

[441]M. Baillet, "Un recueil liturgique de Qumrân, grotte 4: Les Paroles des Luminaires," *RB* 68 (1961), 233.

Weeks," the pattern of sin—punishment is still prominent. Having given up on their contemporary Jewish brothers and sisters, each group transforms the predictions that anticipate the repentance of all Israel, and limits the salvation to a specific group *within* Israel, namely, the group itself. In other words, the scope of the deuteronomic cycle shifts from national to sectarian. At the same time, these groups make the SER pattern an eschatological framework. Deliverance is an eschatological event, along with the emergence of the group. The moment of repentance is the turning point in the scheme which leads to the end. The deuteronomic cycle and the penitence it contains assume a sectarian function. They legitimate the founding of these groups and distinguish them from their Jewish neighbors.

The reception of wisdom also follows the moment of repentance in texts like those in *1 Enoch* and the Qumran Scrolls. Groups like those responsible for *1 Enoch* and the Qumran Scrolls taught that the group itself possessed wisdom unavailable to other Jews. The group acquires this wisdom in various ways—dreams, visions, tradition, interpretation of texts through a divinely appointed interpreter or teacher. When an initiate enters the group, the group shares its divine gift of knowledge with the initiate. The Qumran Scrolls leave no doubt that penitence is the bridge from outside to inside the group, from sin to forgiveness, from ignorance to wisdom, from death to life.

The texts of *Jubilees*, the *Testament of Moses*, the *Testaments of the Twelve Patriarchs*, and the Qumran Scrolls all bear marks of influence from the language of penitential texts, if not penitential prayer. The most recognizable adaptation of penitential prayer occurs in the *Testament of Moses* and the Covenant Ceremony in 1QS. Both these works take the main components of penitential prayer and distribute them among either various characters (*Testament of Moses*) or worshipping participants (1QS).

The author of *Jubilees* and the Qumran sectarians understood both penitential prayer and interpretation as constituents of repentance. That is, besides some form of inward transformation, genuine repentance is expressed in prayer and searching sacred texts, namely the Law and the prophets. How does "seeking God" by interpretation become enmeshed in the penitential context? As 1QS 1.1-2, the author read Deut 4:29-30 to mean that a group in Israel would repent (שוב) and "seek (דרש) God." The term דרש in Deuteronomy actually functions as a metaphor for "to repent." However, by the time of *Jubilees* and the Qumran sect, the term means "to inquire in a text." Therefore, these authors understand the passage from Deuteronomy to mean that those who repent, "turn" (שוב) will also "seek" (דרש), i.e., study scripture.

Study of the Law flows naturally from repentance. Since the people assume *a priori* from their national problems, namely the presence of foreign domination, that the nation has sinned, they must have neglected the Law either by disobeying it or misinterpreting it for a personal agenda. Those who repent and pray would naturally adopt a serious position about understanding and obeying the Law. This idea is not new. It naturally grows out of scenes like Ezra 9-10 and Nehemiah 9-10, where, after confessing its sins, the nation promises fidelity.

The Qumran sectarians' declaration that the rest of the nation is in error meets serious and threatening opposition. Unless the texts are metaphorically exaggerating their struggles, the disputes may have even turned physically violent, or were expected eventually to turn violent. The group at least perceived itself as oppressed.

At Qumran, prayer dominates community life. The sect remembers its origins as conceived in penitence and penitential prayer. One enters the community through confession of sin. The sect annually renews their covenant with God in part by confessing its sins. If the Words of the Heavenly Lights (4Q504) are daily prayers as they seem, the community weekly repeats the cycle of rehearsing Israel's sins and confessing them. The sectarians believe that they are surely "the penitents of Israel" (שבי ישראל) who have gone out into the wilderness. Thus, prayer functions to define the community's origin and to distinguish between those on the inside and those on the outside of the community; prayer has become a sectarian activity. The community's identity is embedded in repentance, penitential prayer, and repentance's other constituent, biblical interpretation.

CHAPTER FOUR

Penitential Prayers of Pious Sufferers and those Oppressed by Arrogant Rulers

Introduction

In deuteronomic ideology, the nation suffers as a whole for its sins, and experiences deliverance for its repentance. As Chapter Three explains, several groups from the Second Temple Period readjust these basic tenets of the deuteronomic world view in order to address their respective situations. The presence of foreign domination unambiguously signifies that the covenantal curses are "clinging" to the people as God's punishment for their refusal to repent. Attempting to explain these harsh historical and social realities, these groups alter the deuteronomic scheme so that it pictures their repentance instead of the repentance of the nation as a whole. Accordingly, the blessings of the scheme are for them. Thus, standard deuteronomic language and ideology underwent a thorough reinterpretation.

The events of the Second Temple period pose a serious challenge to deuteronomic ideology because the righteous, or pious, often suffer severely at the hands of the brutal, dominating foreign power. Since the righteous frequently include penitence as one of their religious virtues, how does deuteronomic ideology account for their suffering? If deuteronomic ideology has at its heart a cause and effect principle, the righteous should experience blessing instead of suffering. The deuteronomic sin—punishment ideology cannot explain suffering in every situation. Because of this, several authors adjust deuteronomic ideology in order to deal with this inadequacy. In the discussions that follow, Tobit and the Prayer of Azariah especially wrestle with this problem.

God's decision to employ a human, a *foreign* king no less, to punish the nation causes another problem for the deuteronomic sin—punishment scheme. Since these authorities typically have inflated egos and fiercely strong, independent wills, their vanity typically entices them to excess. As a result, "the rod of God's anger" might punish the Jews too severely and exceed his bounds by taking credit himself for the success. As a result, the means of God's punishment threatens his sovereignty, glory, and the existence of his people. Several prayers in this chapter, the Prayer of Azariah, 3 Maccabees, Greek Esther, and the *Psalms of Solomon*, adapt their contents to this particular issue.

Therefore, this chapter groups prayers that share one or both of these problems—a pious person is suffering or an arrogant ruler is on, or about to go on, a rampage in total disregard to God's sovereignty. Authors must construct their prayers with these pressing crises in mind and appropriately adjust the deuteronomic penitential prayer tradition.

Tobit 3:1-6[442]

The Predicament, Confession, and Complaint

The book of Tobit relates the story of a righteous sufferer, Tobit. His dedication to his people leads him to burying his fellow Israelites who have died. Because he is also pious, he observes the rules on cleanness associated with burying the dead by sleeping outside the city (2:1-10). During the night, sparrow droppings fall into Tobit's eyes, leaving him blind. Tobit's burial practices also arouse Sennacharib's ire, who wants to kill Tobit for his deeds. After threats on his life, four years of blindness, and a quarrel with his wife, Tobit cries out to God: "And becoming deeply grieved in [my] soul and moaning, I cried out and I began to pray with groaning" (Tob 3:1).[443] The prayer that follows is penitential, but, oddly, a person suffering for his piety delivers the prayer. However, Tobit is not without fault or sinless. His harsh, unfounded, and *unjust* criticism of his wife (2:11-14) proves that he sins.[444] Considering the emphasis that the book places on family, especially in Tobit's charge to Tobias about honoring his mother, affronting the dignity of another family member is not a light problem.[445] However, Tobit commits this *faux pas*

---

[442]The text has two major recensions. Studies have concluded that the longer text represented in Sinaiticus is more reliable. Consequently, I follow Sinaiticus in my discussion of this prayer. See Nickelsburg, "Stories of Biblical and Early Post-Biblical Times," *CRINT* vol. 2, 45; J. T. Milik, "La patrie de Tobie," *RB* 73 (1966) 523-530. See especially C. A. Moore (*Tobit* AB 40A [New York, 1996] 53-64) for the most current and thorough discussion of these problems. Moore also reviews and analyzes the Tobit texts from Qumran (33-39). See also J. A. Fitzmyer "The Hebrew and Aramaic Fragments of Cave Four," *CBQ* 57 (1995) 655-675; *Tobit, DJD* 19 (Oxford: Oxford University, 1995).

[443]For the construction περίλυπος γενόμενος, cf. Gen 4:6 and Dan 2:12 (LXX). For the use of περίλυπος with ψυχή see Pss 41 (42):6 and 42 (43):5.

[444]Cf. G. W. E. Nickelsburg, *Jewish Literature*, 33; C. A. Moore, *Tobit*, 31.

[445]Cf. Tobit's testament where he exhorts Tobias to honor his mother after Tobit's death (4:3-4). For a discussion on the social roles of family members in Tobit and the way in which Tobit attempts to bring social order into exilic life, see A-J. Levine, "Diaspora as Metaphor: Bodies and Boundaries in the Book of Tobit," in *Diaspora Jews and Judaism: Essays in Honor of, and in Dialogue with A. Thomas Kraabel* (ed., J. A. Overman and R. S. MacLennan; Atlanta: Scholars, 1992) 105-117.

after he has run from the king and has become blind. Thus, his blindness and threats against his life do not result from his sin, but from his piety.

Despite suffering for his piety, in his prayer Tobit asserts that God has rightfully judged him because he and his nation have sinned (vv. 2-3, 5). His prayer begins with a *Gerichtsdoxologie* that acclaims God's righteous punishment of the people: "You are righteous, O Lord" (Δίκαιος εἶ, κύριε)(v. 2).[446] God's "deeds" are "just" (καὶ πάντα τὰ ἔργα σου δίκαια)(v. 2), and his "ways" are "merciful and true" (αἱ ὁδοί ... ἐλεημοσύνη καὶ ἀλήθεια)(v. 2; cf. Deut 32:4).[447] Tobit applies the three terms, δίκαιος, ἐλεημοσύνη and ἀλήθεια, to himself in 1:3: "I, Tobit, walked in the ways of truth and in righteousess all the days of my life, and performed many deeds of mercy."[448] While other penitential prayers praise God for his mercy and judgment as Tobit does in v. 2, these two ideas fit nicely in Tobit. As Nickelsburg explains, "to scourge" (i.e., to punish or discipline), "to afflict," and "to have mercy" are key themes in the book.[449] Although the prayer does not include the word "to scourge," the combination of judgment and mercy matches the book's ideology.

Tobit's prayer lacks the simple confession of sin, "I have sinned," as one finds in other prayers. Instead, his request for mercy acknowledges his sin: "Do not punish me for my sin and for my sins done in ignorance..." (v. 3). He confesses his ancestors' sins: "... those (sins) of my fathers who sinned against you" ... "and they disobeyed your commandments" (vv. 3c-4a). In v. 5, his praise of God's true judgments controls his reference to his sin: "And now your many judgments are true in exacting penalty from me for my sins." Tobit then switches to first person plural to include himself with the disobedient nation to confess its sin. Therefore, Tobit's situation has developed from a combination of past generations' sins and Tobit's own sins.[450]

When speaking of the judgment that has befallen the nation, Tobit draws from deuteronomic traditions. According to the prayer, the primary judgment

---

[446] Cf. Ezr 9:15; Neh 9:8, 33.

[447] F. Zimmerman, *The Book of Tobit, Jewish Apocryphal Literature* (New York: Harper, 1958) 60. BA read καὶ κρίσιν ἀληθινὴν καὶ δικαίαν σὺ κρίνεις εἰς τὸν αἰωνα, "You judge with true and right judgment forever."

[448] Di Lella, "The Deuteronomic Background of the Farewell Discourse in Tobit 14:3-11," *CBQ* 41 [1979] 386; P. Deselaers, *Das Buch Tobit: Studien zu seiner Entstehung, Komposition und Theologie* (Göttingen: Vandenhoeck & Ruprecht, 1982) 78. Deselaers argues that the Hebrew for δίκαιος is צדק, ἔλεος renders חסד, and ἀλήθεια translates אמת (77 n. 45).

[449] G. W. E. Nickelsburg, *Jewish Literature*, 33-34; "Stories of Biblical and Early Post-Biblical Times," 41.

[450] Cf. Neh 1:6.

that the nation must endure includes exile and reproach: "You delivered us over ... to be a proverb, a by-word, and a curse (καὶ εἰς παραβολὴν καὶ λάλημα καὶ ὀνειδισμὸν) among all the people among whom you have scattered us" (v. 4). The language certainly alludes to the covenantal curse in Deut 28:37: "You will become an object of terror, a proverb, and a by-word among all the peoples where YHWH will drive you" (והיית לשמה למשל ולשנינה בכל העמים אשר־ינהגך יהוה שמה). The theme also occurs in Solomon's prayer in 1 Kgs 9:7, as God warns the people: "Israel will become a proverb (משל) and a by-word (שנינה) among the peoples."[451] Israel's dispersion among the nations in v. 4 for disobeying the commandments recalls Deut 4:27 and 30:3.[452] Further, their experience of "plunder,[453] exile,[454] and death," are also deuteronomic curses. Tobit takes the phrase, "for we did not walk in faithfulness before you," from the conditions of the Davidic covenant in 1 Kgs 2:4 and 3:6,[455] which he applies to the nation instead of the king.[456]

Even though the author clearly enunciates that Deuteronomy's punishments are in effect just as God warned, Tobit's prayer unmistakably emphasizes personal anguish more than most of the previous prayers studied in this book.[457] This tone, which the text even establishes in the prayer's preface (3:1), remains consistent throughout the prayer. In the prayer's conclusion Tobit wishes for his death so that he might be released from his "distress" (ἀνάγκη),[458] a theme that is also related to the formula from Deuteronomy 4 ("In your distress, you will cry...").[459] In correlation to the nation, Tobit must endure personal reproaches: "For I hear lying reproaches ... For it is better for me to die than to see great pain in my life and not to hear lying

---

[451]Cf. Jer 23:40; 24:9-10 and 29:18.

[452]For a fuller discussion of these passage in Deuteronomy, see Chapter One. See also Di Lella, "Deuteronomic Background," 382.

[453]See Deut 28:29, 31.

[454]See Deut 28:41; 32:42. Cf Ezr 9:3, 4, 5; Neh 1:2, 3; Tob 1:3; 3:15. For cognates of αἰχμαλωσία in Tobit see 1:9, 10; 2:2; 7:3; 14:4, 15.

[455]The two recensions display a slight difference in wording. BA reads οὐ γὰρ ἐπορεύθημεν ἐν ἀληθείᾳ ἐνώπιόν σου, and Siniaticus reads καὶ οὐκ ἐπορεύθημεν ἀληθινῶς ἐνώπιόν. In this case, BA may render the Hebrew or Aramaic Vorlage more literally. The Hebrew in both 1 Kgs 2:4 and 3:6 states: ללכת לפני באמת.

[456]Ps 86:11 also speaks of "walking in faithfulness."

[457]Cf. Neh 1:3 (LXX) where the people have suffered "exile" (αἰχμαλωσία) and are in "shame" (ὀνειδισμός).

[458]The term appears only once in BA in v 6. In the longer Sinaiticus, the word appears twice in v 6.

[459]See Chapter One.

reproaches."[460] Laments in the psalms complain that the enemy is either taunting or plotting against the psalmists.[461] The theme nicely fits Tobit's narrative context, since he faces reproach in 2:14b, and, later, Sarah endures reproach in 3:7, 8b-9.[462] Thus, the narrative legitimates his complaint. This intense personal struggle is also reminiscent of Job 3 except that Job maintains that he is innocent while Tobit admits his sins. Even so, Tobit's language borders on lament,[463] as he states that the insults directed against him are "lies," i.e., undeserved and untrue accusations. With this final reference to Tobit's suffering in the prayer's conclusion, distress and anguish form a thematic *inclusio* in the narrative context (3:1 and 6). Therefore, throughout the prayer, the author maintains the tension of a pious person confessing sin, yet simultaneously suffering for deeds of charity.

The Prayer's Function in the Plot

Tobit's prayer, along with Sarah's, marks the first major turning point in the narrative.[464] The two make their prayer on the same day, and God hears both in heaven. God commissions Raphael, whose name means "God heals," to attend to their situations and to heal them. Although the reference to "healing" has an immediate relationship to the characters' predicaments—Tobit is blind and Sarah is possessed by a demon—the choice of this word corresponds to God's response in other penitential contexts where "to heal" functions as a metaphor for deliverance.[465] Therefore, in line with deuteronomic ideology, and parallel to several of the literary creations from chapter three of this book, penitence serves as the first step toward resolution of a predicament. As the narrative works itself out for the good of the main character, the prayer also assumes the function of resolving the tension between the pious sufferer theme and deuteronomic ideology. In the end, as Deuteronomy teaches, the pious experience God's vindication and blessing.

---

[460]The final sentence does not appear in BA.
[461]See Pss 13:1-3; 69(68):7, 9, 10, 19, 20; 79(78):12; 88(87):50; 119(118):39. Cf. also Wis Sol 5:4.
[462]G. W. E. Nickelsburg, *Jewish Literature*, 30. For further appearances of the word ὀνειδισμός in Tobit see 3:10, 13, 15.
[463]Cf. P. Deselaers, *Das Buch Tobit*, 83-85.
[464]For more on the importance of prayer in the story, see C. A. Moore, *Tobit*, 30, 141.
[465]See Hos 6:1-2; Jer 14:19 (2 times); Isa 57:18; Jub 23:30.

Correlation between Tobit and the Nation

The book of Tobit's notion that repenting through penitential prayer effects change plays out in the life of an individual. However, how does a story about an individual relate to the nation? Nickelsburg argues persuasively that the narrative establishes a correlation between Tobit's fate and the nation's destiny.[466] Just as Tobit was "scourged" for his sins and "received mercy" because he repented, scourged Israel can "receive mercy" if it repents (cf. 11:15 and 13:2, 5). In chapter 13, Tobit exhorts Israel to repent with the language of Deuteronomy. As in Tobit's prayer, he reminds Israel that God is the one who has "scattered them among the nations" (v. 3; cf. Tob 3:4; 14:4; Deut 4:27 and 30:3), and he will also gather them from the nations (Tob 13:5; 14:5; Deut 30:3-4).[467] This restoration becomes possible when the people, in the metaphor of Deuteronomy, "turn" with all their "heart and soul:" ἐν ὅλῃ τῇ καρδίᾳ ὑμῶν καὶ ἐν ὅλῃ τῇ ψυχῇ ὑμῶν (v. 6). The results of the repentance also correspond to the petitions of Tobit's prayer in chapter 3. God will no longer "hide his face" from the people (13:6; cf. 3:6) and he will look upon the people "with favor" and show them "mercy" (13:6; cf. 3:3). While chapter 13 does not include a penitential prayer, the call for repentance and the themes of Tobit's speech lead the reader back to chapter 3 and Tobit's moment of contrition. If the nation would respond to its sin as Tobit did, a glorious new era would begin (13:9-17). A major difference between Tobit's prayer in chapter 3 and chapter 13 is that chapter 13 establishes no tension between the themes of the pious sufferer and deuteronomic ideology. According to chapter 13, Israel is unquestionably in exile because of its sins.

The Prayer's Function: Model for a Pious Life in the Exile

Scholars remain uncertain about Tobit's date and place of composition. The rebuilding of the Temple in 515 BCE is the final historical reference in the book, and, consequently, establishes the *terminus a quo*.[468] The discovery of Hebrew and Aramaic fragments of Tobit among the Dead Sea Scrolls establishes a *terminus ad quem* of at least 100 BCE.[469] The lack of a reference to the persecution of Antiochus IV, though, moves the *terminus ad quem* to a

---

[466] G. W. E. Nickelsburg, *Jewish Literature*, 32-33. Cf. also C. A. Moore, *Tobit*, 32-33.
[467] Cf. also C. A. Moore, *Tobit*, 278-279.
[468] Ibid., 35.
[469] J. T. Milik, "La patrie de Tobie," 522; E. Bickerman, *The Jews in the Greek Age* (Cambridge: Harvard University, 1988) 57.

date prior to 175 BCE Within these parameters, scholars have proposed dates ranging from the fifth to third centuries BCE.[470]

The narrative's exilic setting has led some scholars to conclude that the book was written in the diaspora.[471] If this is the case, Tobit instructs the readers how to order life in the exile and deal with its desperation and anguish.[472] Recognizing that even the most pious can experience suffering, and, in fact, occasionally become the main targets for persecution, Tobit's prayer creates a tension between the themes of the pious sufferer and the deuteronomic ideology of history, refusing to give up either one. As the model for a pious life within the deuteronomic scheme, Tobit explains that the pious must not presume that they are sinless. In fact, the text in part teaches that penitence expressed in prayer is an important attribute of the pious. Prayer and praise in general mark the lives of the pious in this book (cf. 8:4-9, 15-17; 11:14-15; 13:1), and even the angelic escort, Raphael, acknowledges the value of prayer (even though giving alms is better)(12:8; cf. 14:11). Penitence is a virtue that distinguishes the pious from others.

Summary

Tobit's story gives cause for hope. The people pray to a God who is not only just, but merciful. Di Lella correctly summarizes Tobit's message: "Despite the enormity of Israel's past sins, the people addressed by the Book of Tobit were offered the possibility of repentance and the assurance of divine mercy (13:5-6)—two consoling doctrines derived from Deuteronomy."[473] Further, the

---

[470]E.g., E. Bickerman (*The Jews in the Greek Age*, 57) dates the book to the Persian period based on the statement that Media will have "real peace." D. Flusser ("Psalms, Hymns, and Prayers," *CRINT* vol. 2, 555-556) also proposes a date during the Persian period, the fifth to fourth centuries, based on the conclusion that the fragments of Tobit from Qumran contain an Imperial Aramaic earlier than the Aramaic of Daniel. G. W. E. Nickelsburg ("Tobit," *HBD*, 792) dates the book to the third century BCE. See C. A. Moore ("Tobit," *ABD* VI, 591; *Tobit*, 40-43) for further discussion on the problems and proposals associated with dating the work.

[471]G. W. E. Nickelsburg, *Jewish Literature*, 35; "Tobit," *HBD*, 792. For discussion on an Egyptian or Mesopotamian provenance, see C. A. Moore, "Tobit," *ABD* VI, 591.

[472]Di Lella ("The Deuteronomic Background," 388) categorizes Tobit as "fundamentally nomic literature in parenetic form." That is, Tobit as literature instructed exilic readers how to order their lives in the midst of chaos. See also A-J. Levine, "Diaspora as Metaphor: Bodies and Boundaries in the Book of Tobit," 105-117.

[473]Di Lella, "The Deuteronomic Background," 388. For more discussion on the influence of Deuteronomy on Tobit, see C. A. Moore, "Book of Tobit," 589. See also W. Soll ("Misfortune and Exile in Tobit: The Juncture of a Fairy Tale Source and Deuteronomic Theology," *CBQ* 51 (1989) 209-231) for a treatment of the transformation of misfortune to joy according to modern theory about fairy tales.

story explains to the oppressed pious that their struggles may also end if they confess and maintain their righteousness.

The Prayer of Azariah

The Prayer of Azariah, which probably derives from a Hebrew *Vorlage*,[474] along with a narrative bridge and The Song of the Three Young Men, appears in the Greek versions between Daniel 3:23 and 24 of the MT.[475] This addition provides another example of a suffering pious person offering a penitential prayer. In this scene, the king forces three righteous men to choose between obedience to Torah and his law,[476] a predicament that in some ways resembles Tobit. In both stories, the sufferers carefully practice Torah and face persecution because of their obedience (Tob 1:3-20; Dan 3:8-12, 16-18). Both include accusations against the righteous heroes (Tob 1:19; Dan 3:8-12), and both encounter problems with a pagan king (Tob 1:15-20; Dan 3:13-15, 19-20). Finally, both experience deliverance and vindication. Therefore, as Nickelsburg asserts, the story fits the pattern of the persecution and exaltation of the righteous.[477]

Gerichtsdoxologie and Themes from Deuteronomy

The prayer begins with the ברוך אתה formula: Εὐλογητὸς εἶ, κύριε ὁ θεὸς τῶν πατέρων ἡμῶν (v. 3 [3:26]). The hymn that follows the Prayer of Azariah and Tobias' prayer in the wedding chamber begin similarly:

Εὐλογητὸς εἶ, κύριε ὁ θεὸς τῶν πατέρων ἡμῶν (Pr Azar 29 [3:52]);

Εὐλογητὸς εἶ,   ὁ θεὸς τῶν πατέρων ἡμῶν (Tob 8:5)[478]

---

[474]J. J. Collins, *Daniel*, 199, 202; C. Kuhl, *Die drei Männer im Feuer*, BZAW 55 (Giessen: Töpelmann, 1930). C. A. Moore (*Daniel, Esther, and Jeremiah*, 25-26; "Additions to Daniel," *ABD* II, 19) follows Kuhl's conclusions as well. R. Doran ("The Additions to Daniel," *HBC*, 863) disagrees: "There are no compelling linguistic arguments for assuming the Greek to be a translation of an originally Hebrew or Aramaic text."

[475]The two Greek versions of the Prayer of Azariah, the LXX and Theodotion, are basically identical. No Hebrew or Aramaic text or fragment of the prayer have been discovered.

[476]G. W. E. Nickelsburg, *Resurrection, Immortality*, 53.

[477]Ibid., 48-111.

[478]Cf. Pss 28:6; 31:22; 84:53; 106:48; 124:6; 135:21; Tob 3:14; 8:15; Jdt 9:2; and Pr Man 1.

Chapter Four 169

Despite the young men's innocence, the prayer immediately moves to the *Gerichtsdoxologie* which praises God's righteousness within the context of his deeds. The description reflects the same language and ideas as found in Tob 3:2:[479]

Pr Azar 4-5a (3:27-28a)	Tob 3:2
Ὅτι δίκαιος, εἶ ἐπὶ πᾶσιν, οἷς ἐποίησας ἡμῖν,	Δίκαιος εἶ, κύριε,
καὶ πάντα τὰ ἔργα σου ἀληθινά,	καὶ πάντα τὰ ἔργα σου δίκαια,
καὶ αἱ ὁδοί σου εὐθεῖαι	καὶ πᾶσαι αἱ ὁδοί σου ἐλεημοσύνη
	καὶ ἀλήθεια
	σὺ κρίνεις τὸν αἰῶνα
καὶ πᾶσαι αἱ κρίσεις σου ἀληθεία	
καὶ κρίματα ἀληθείας ἐποιησας...	

Except for reversing the order of the statements, the reference to God's punishment again in v. 8 [3:31] virtually repeats v. 5 [3:28]. The author believes that the punishment is just because the people have sinned. Consequently, Azariah confesses this sin in v. 6 [3:29]:

Ὅτι ἡμάρτομεν ἐν πᾶσι καὶ ἠνομήσαμεν ἀποστῆναι ἀπὸ σοῦ καὶ ἐξημάρτομεν ἐν πᾶσιν καὶ τῶν ἐντολῶν τοῦ νόμου σου οὐχ ὑπηκούσαμεν.

For we have sinned in everything and acted lawlessly to turn from you, and we erred in everything and we did not obey the commandments of your law.

This confession expands the typical threefold confession seen in previous texts into a fourfold confession, the phrase, "We did not obey the commandments of your law," representing the addition. Otherwise, the confession probably translates the words חטא, עוה, and רשע (cf. 1 Kgs 8:47; Ps 106:6; Jer 14:7; Dan 9:5).[480] The confession clearly implies that the nation's trial has come because they disobeyed the commandments.

Language from Deuteronomy continues in the verses that follow. In v. 6 [3:30], the petitioner explains how the people transgressed the law: they did not "preserve" (συντηρέω/שמר) or "do" (ποιέω/עשה) it. If we combine these words with the final confession in v. 5 [3:29], "and we did not obey" (ἀκούω/שמע), the prayer has incorporated three key terms from Deuteronomy,

---

[479]Cf. Neh 9:33 and Dan 9:14.
[480]C. Kuhl, *Die drei Männer im Feuer*, 136; C. A. Moore, *Daniel, Esther, and Jeremiah*, 57.

עשה, שמר, and שמע (Deut 4:1-2, 5-6; 6:3; 7:12; 28:13; 1 Kgs 11:38).[481] Moses frequently exhorts the people in Deuteronomy to obey so that life might "go well" for them (Deut 5:16, 26; 6:18; 12:25, 28; 22:7).[482] The Prayer's recognition that things are not "going well" with the nation because the nation has violated the covenant through its disobedience is a reversal of a deuteronomic blessing. The people no longer enjoy this blessing. In v. 9 [3:32], the suppliants remember Deuteronomy's warning that God would deliver the people to their enemies if they rebelled (Deut 28:48; 1 Kgs 8:37).[483] The wicked king in v. 9 is Antiochus, and the "lawless and hateful rebels" may refer to the Jews supporting Antiochus IV's program.[484] Thus, the opening verses intend to conjure up ideas from Deuteronomy, and immediately establish its ideology as the prayer's dominant world view.

The Abrahamic Covenant

Once the supplicant of a penitential prayer admits to sin, he must base his petitions on something other than his own good deeds. In the Prayer of Azariah, the heroes found their petitions upon the covenant with Abraham (v. 12 [3:35]). Reference to the Abrahamic covenant is not foreign to penitential contexts, as the examinations of the Qumran Scrolls and Third Isaiah show. On at least three other occasions, the Hebrew Bible evokes the Abrahamic covenant as a reason for God to forgive the people. First, in the golden calf incident in Exodus 32, when God tells Moses that he is going to destroy these "stiff—necked" people, Moses intercedes on behalf of the people by recalling the covenant with the patriarchs:

> Remember Abraham, Isaac and Israel, your servants, to whom you swore by your own self and said to them, "I will make your descendants as great as the stars of the heaven, and all this land which I said I will give to your descendants, and they will inherit it[485] forever" (Exod 32:13).

His argument persuades God, who changes his mind and refrains from destroying the people (v. 14). Second, Leviticus 26 informs Israel that God will, in part, restore the people because of the promise to the patriarchs. Of

---

[481]C. Kuhl, *Die drei Männer im Feuer*, 136; C. A. Moore, *Daniel, Esther, and Jeremiah*, 57.
[482]C. Kuhl, *Die drei Männer im Feuer*, 136.
[483]Cf. Bar 4:15.
[484]C. A. Moore, *Daniel, Esther, Jeremiah*, 57-58.
[485]Following the LXX and the Syriac texts.

course, confessing sins, humility, and restitution must also precede restoration (vv. 40-41). However, as God says: "Then I will remember my covenant with Jacob, and my covenant with Isaac, and I will remember my covenant with Abraham. And I will remember the land" (v. 42). That is, in remembering the covenant God will allow the people to regain possession of the land that he promised to Abraham and his descendants. Finally, Micah refers to the patriarchs in his discussion of Israel's sin, punishment, repentance, forgiveness, and restoration (Mic 7:8-20).[486] A voice belonging to the nation of Israel recognizes that punishment has come because of the people's sin (v. 9). Following another voice that calls for vindication from Israel's enemies as in the Exodus (vv. 14-17), the passage ends with an expression of confidence that God will be faithful to the promise made to the patriarchs:

> And you will demonstrate faithfulness to Jacob, and loyalty to Abraham,
> As you swore to our fathers in days of old (v. 20).

These three texts, Exodus 32, Leviticus 26, and Micah 7, show that Biblical authors incorporate the Abrahamic covenant into penitential contexts because the nation cannot ask for mercy based on its good deeds; it has sinned. So, the petitioner asks God to remember the Abrahamic covenant as motivation for forgiveness.

The Prayer of Azariah also recalls a specific aspect of the Abrahamic covenant in the following statement:

> As you spoke to them saying that you would multiply their seed as the stars of the heaven, and as the sand on the sea shore
>
> For we, O Lord, have become fewer than any nation.
> (vv. 13-14 [3:36-37]).

In several passages in Genesis, God tells Abraham that his descendants will increase until they are as numerous as the stars of the heavens and the sand of the sea (see Gen 15:5; 22:17; cf. 32:12; and 41:49). The prayer contrasts this promise to the nation's present miserable condition with a reference to a curse in Deuteronomy that God would reduce the people if they were disobedient: "You will be left few in number instead of as numerous as the stars of the heaven if you do not obey the voice of the Lord your God" (Deut 28:62).[487] Thus, the author deftly combines these two traditions, the promise to Abraham

---

[486]In many ways the passage resembles portions of Third Isaiah. See Chapter One.
[487]Cf. Deut 4:27.

and the covenantal curses, in order to supply the reason for the frustration of these promises.

The Rhetoric of Lament and the Themes of Shame and Reproach

Even after explicitly presenting the principles of deuteronomic ideology—that God punishes sinners but rewards the righteous—the prayer's petitionary section considers the injustice that these three men are enduring. It does this with a series of petitions in the form of negative commands:

> Do not completely abandon us.
>
> μὴ δὴ παραδῷς ἡμᾶς εἰς τέλος (v. 11 [3:34]);

> And do not annul your covenant.
>
> καὶ μὴ διασκεδάσῃς σου τὴν διαθήκην (v. 11 [3:34]);

> Do not remove your mercy from us.
>
> καὶ μὴ ἀποστήσῃς τὸ ἔλεός σου ἀφ' ἡμῶν (v. 12 [3:35]);

> Do not shame us.
>
> μὴ καταισχύνῃς ἡμᾶς (v. 19 [3:41]).

These negative imperatives, which call on God to manifest his merciful character and reputation and his faithfulness to the covenant, occur in several psalms that use the literary features of lament, e.g.:

> O Lord, do not withhold your mercy from me.
>
> אתה יהוה לא־תכלא רחמיך ממני (Ps 40:12[11]);[488]

---

[488] For the use of the imperfect as a strong command see Gesenius, 107 o.

Let me not be ashamed.

אל־אבושה (Ps 25:2; cf. Ps 31:18);[489]

Do not hide your face from me... Do not abandon me and do not forsake me.

אל־תסתר פניך ממני... אל־תטשני ואל־תעזבני (Ps 27:9);[490]

These negative commands have not been prevalent in many penitential prayers, as Chapter One notices, because strict adherence to deuteronomic ideology precludes lament. However, Lamentations and the penitential lament in Jeremiah 14 provide examples of coupling confession with lament. In Jeremiah 14, e.g., the people acknowledge their sin and then continue:

> Do not spurn us on account of your name,
> And do not despise the throne of your glory,
> Remember and do not break your covenant with us (v. 21).

The three men also convey their shame and reproach through the phrase "we cannot open our mouths" (v. 10 [3:33]). In other passages, the inability to speak depicts the silence and shame of the condemned:

> The nations shall see and be ashamed of all their might,
> And they will place their hands upon their mouths... (Mic 7:16).

The prayer hopes for the termination of this shame by wishing it upon the persecuters.

> Let those who mark out your servants for evil be ashamed, and let them be stripped of all sovereignty, and their strength be broken (Par Azar v. 21 [3:44]).[491]

This idea is reminiscent of the Biblical psalms in which psalmists ask for God to transfer the shame they bear onto the enemy (cf. Pss 25:3 and 40:15[14]). The designation of the three men as "servants" may also allude to

---

[489]For the use of the cohortative to express a strong wish in the negative, see Ibid., 108 c.

[490]See Ibid., 107 o.

[491]See G. W. E. Nickelsburg (*Resurrection, Immortality*, 60-62) for a fuller discussion of this reversal.

Deuteronomy 32, a text in which God set his wrath against the foreign power in order to vindicate his "servants" (see vv. 34-42).[492]

At this point in the context, the prayer introduces the theme of the arrogant foreign ruler, which will surface in all the remaining prayers in this Chapter. Within this theme, authors typically assert that God must not allow the foreign ruler to continue his severe punitive task with the assumption that he operates by his own volition and sovereignty. The foreign ruler's presumptuous deeds not only threaten the Jewish people, but also a fundamental tenet of their faith—God alone is sovereign king of the universe. Thus, the Prayer of Azariah petitions God to reveal to the wicked ruler that God alone is the true sovereign ruler of the universe (v. 22 [3:45]).

As the supplicant makes his appeal for deliverance from these enemies in v. 20 [3:43], he echoes the Exodus themes present in other prayers. However, the theme occurs in rather oblique language as the petitioner seeks for deliverance (ἐξελοῦ ἡμᾶς/והצילנו) in the form of God's "marvelous works" (τὰ θαυμάσια/נפלאותיך). The Song of Moses also describes the Exodus events as "wonders" (פלא)(Exod 15:11).[493]

The Central Sanctuary and the Loss of the Sacrificial System

Because the prayer most likely originates from the era of Antiochus IV's persecution, the author must deal with the loss of access to the Temple, the primary means for atonement in Judaism.[494] The prayer wastes little time in mentioning this loss. In v. 5 [3:28], the supplicant recognizes that the people's sins not only influence their fate, but the Temple's as well. However, by the time of this prayer, the penitential tradition is well equipped to handle this problem. From the exilic period onward, prayer has substituted as a means for expiation apart from the sacrificial system. Vv. 16-17 [3:39-40] rely upon this function of prayer. The petitioner asks that a "broken soul" and "humble spirit" may serve as a sacrifice, ideas and language that undoubtedly derive from Ps 51:17:[495]

---

[492]For a more detailed discussion on this theme in Deuteronomy 32, see the section below on 2 Maccabees 7.

[493]Cf. Neh 9:17 where the ancestors forgot the wonders that God performed.

[494]See J. J. Collins, *Daniel*, 200-201.

[495]C. Kuhl (*Die drei Männer im Feuer*, 154) notices that Isa 61:1; 66:2; and Bar 2:18 substitute ψυχή for πνεῦμα.

Pr Azar 16-17 [3:39]	Ps 51 [50]:16-17 [19]
ἀλλ᾽ ἐν ψυχῇ συντετριμμένῃ καὶ πνεύματι τεταπεινωμένῳ προδεχθείημεν ὡς ἐν ὁλοκαυτώμασι κριῶν καὶ ταυρων καὶ ὡς ἐν μυριάσιν ἀρνῶν πιόνων.	θυσία τῷ θεῷ πνεῦμα συντετριμμένον, καρδίαν συντετριμμένην καὶ τεταπεινωμένην ὁ θεὸς οὐκ ἐξουθενώσει.[496]

The terms "broken soul" and "humble spirit" probably have a meaning similar to the metaphors in Isa 66:2—they depict an oppressed person rather than simply inward contrition. They are, therefore, requesting that God accept their suffering in place of sacrifice. As a result, the visitation of evil upon the righteous will have at least some meaning. If God accepts this substitution, then he may also turn from his wrath and anger, and bring deliverance.[497] Their prayer, then, also functions as the turning point in the sin—punishment—deliverance cycle.

A Comparison to 2 Maccabees 7 and Testament Moses 9

Modern critics quickly draw attention to the inconsistencies between the Prayer of Azariah and the context of Daniel 3. Their questions center on why the author who inserted the prayer did not recognize the inappropriateness of placing a penitential prayer (especially vv. 5-8 [3:28-29]) in the mouths of those suffering for their piety and obedience to Torah. Moore, for example,

---

[496] Cf. 3 Macc 2:20.

[497] The text in v. 40 is corrupt. The reading in Rahlfs' LXX makes good sense: καὶ ἐξιλάσαι ὀπιθέν σου, "to make atonement" or "propitiate you." Kuhl does not accept this reading because it is only represented in codex 88 (C. Kuhl, *Die drei Männer im Feuer*, 146). Theodotian reads καὶ ἐκτελέσαι ὀπιθέν σου, literally, "to complete after you," which C. A. Moore (*Daniel, Esther, and Jeremiah*, 59) says appears to translate מלא אחריך. The RSV and NRSV follow this variant and translate the phrase, "and may we unreservedly follow you." Kuhl conjectures the following reading, "to bring an end to your wrath." He arrives at this by arguing that ἐκτελέσαι translates the Hebrew כלה. He then proposes that the author made a mistake and read אחריך instead of חרנך (Kuhl, *Die drei Männer im Feuer*, 146-147). While suggestive, Kuhl, of course, has no manuscript evidence for his position. J. J. Collins (*Daniel*, 202) accepts Koch's (*Deuterokanonische Zusätze zum Danielbuch* 2.55-59) hypothesis that ἐξιλάσαι was an attempt to render the Aramaic phrase לרעוא מן קדמך. This means that ὄπισθεν is a corruption of ἔμπροσθεν, and ἐκτελέσαι in Theodotian is a misreading of ἐξιλάσαι. Although one cannot have certainty in this problem, and every suggestion has its flaws, I follow the position of Moore and the NRSV.

holds that an interpreter cannot fail to perceive "the obvious inappropriateness of much of the prayer for its situation or context."[498]

As the discussion above argues, the author of the prayer acknowledges this problem by his incorporation of the theme of the arrogant foreign ruler and the tone and rhetoric of lament. Further, the Prayer of Azariah does not stand alone as an example of pious Jews who suffer because of their faithfulness. Both 2 Maccabees 7 and the *Testament of Moses* 9 relate stories about martyrdom that include the issues of piety and suffering because of the nation's sins. A comparison of the Prayer of Azariah with these two texts might provide an avenue for understanding this addition to Daniel.

In 2 Maccabees 7, a mother and her seven sons face torture and death due to their obedience to Torah, which the story epitomizes in their refusal to eat pork (2 Macc 7:1-2). As the first son dies, the mother and the brothers refer explicitly to the Song of Moses in order to encourage one another: "And he will relent concerning his servants" (2 Macc 7:6; cf. Deut 32:36). That is, the mother and her sons believe that God sees their martyrdom and will be unable to remain passive. He will bring quick retribution and vindication. While the family suffers greatly, the sons maintain that God has not abandoned his people (v. 16). Suffering has come as a result of sins—obviously not the sins of the mother and the sons for they refuse to disobey the Law—but because of the nation's sins. Both the sixth and seventh sons speak of the nation's sin before their death. The sixth says: "For we suffer these things because of ourselves, for we have sinned against our God" (v. 18). Certainly he speaks as a member of Israel as a whole; the nation as a whole is sinful. The seventh son affirms the same idea: "For we suffer because of our sins" (v. 32).[499] The son continues by explaining that God becomes angry with Israel in order to "chastise" (ἐπίπληξις) and "discipline" (παιδεία) it (v. 33). After a while, God will be "reconciled" (καταλλαγεόμαι) to his servants (v. 33). This explanation for suffering matches the narrator's words after Eleazar's death (6:12-17), in which he claims that God does not punish Israel in order to

---

[498] C. A. Moore, *Daniel, Esther, and Jeremiah*, 44, 60.

[499] M. de Jonge (*Christology in Context*, 181-183) holds that the death of the seven sons functions as a "death for others." He claims that 2 Maccabees 7 provides a context from which to understand the early church's notion that Jesus' death was a "death for others." Even though 4 Maccabees interprets the death of the sons as expiatory, I remain unconvinced that the author of 2 Maccabees 7 holds to this position. The seven sons die simply *because* Israel has sinned. For this notion, see S. Williams (*Jesus' Death as a Saving Event: The Background and Origin of a Concept*, 76-90). However, even though their deaths do not have a vicarious effect, this marks the turning point for Israel in its struggle against Antiochus IV. See J. Goldstein (*II Maccabees*, 315-316).

destroy it. Rather, he disciplines his people so that their sins do not reach their full measure and bring Israel to total destruction. Thus, discipline is evidence of God's mercy and the Jews' special relationship with him in comparison to the other nations. As the final son concludes his speech, he expresses his hope that his own death and his brothers' deaths will bring an end to God's "just anger" with Israel. Then God's mercy would return to the nation (vv. 37-38).[500] As for other nations, God refuses to discipline them so that their sin reaches its full measure and brings destruction on them.

In the next chapter of 2 Maccabees, Judas immediately meets success in turning back the Seleucids. According to the author, "God's wrath" has been turned to "mercy" (2 Macc 8:5). So, the death of the pious martyrs has a causal effect on the nation's situation. That is, their courage fulfills the preconditions of Deuteronomy 32 so God acts to vindicate his "servants," and in the process the nation experiences deliverance.

The *Testament of Moses*, which receives more detailed attention in Chapter Three, follows the basic outline of Deuteronomy 31-34,[501] and also includes the deuteronomic cycle of Deuteronomy 28-30—sin—punishment—turning point—salvation.[502] The narrative reaches a critical point in chapter 8 when God's fierce wrath settles on the people in the form of a wicked king who commits sundry atrocities. Of course, God's wrath comes as a result of the people's sinfulness.[503] While the righteous face torture and death, unfaithful Jews are "uncircumcising" themselves. With evil unleashed, the king and the rebellious Jews even offer a pig on the altar. In the midst of this crisis, the mysterious figure Taxo instructs his sons to fast in preparation for martyrdom. After the necessary preparation, they will go out into a cave and die there rather than transgress God's commandments.[504]

As Nickelsburg[505] and Goldstein[506] argue, the author believes that the actions just described would fulfill Deuteronomy 32. This text, the Song of Moses, depicts a great punishment resulting from Israel's sins. When God reduces the people to utter helplessness, God responds:

---

[500]Cf. J. Licht, ("Taxo, Or the Apocalyptic Doctrine of Vengeance," 95-103) who argues that God responds on behalf of his servants once the punishment has become excessive.

[501]G. W. E. Nickelsburg, *Jewish Literature*, 80-81.

[502]G. W. E. Nickelsburg, *Resurrection, Immortality*, 44; *Jewish Literature*, 81.

[503]See *Test Mos* 5 for a description of the people's sins.

[504]Cf. the story of the "Seekers of Justice and Vindication" in I Macc 2:29-38. I have borrowed the designation for this group from J. Goldstein, *II Maccabees*, 294.

[505]G. W. E. Nickelsburg, *Resurrection, Immortality*, 97.

[506]J. Goldstein, *II Maccabees*, 294-295.

> For the Lord will vindicate his people
> and have compassion on his servants,
> when he sees their power is gone,
> and there is none remaining, bond or free (Deut 32:36).

The Song closes with the same theme:

> Praise his people, O you nations;
> for he avenges the blood of his servants,
> and takes vengeance on his adversaries,
> and makes expiation for the land of his people (Deut 32:43).

Taxo alludes to Deut 32:43 in *Test Mos* 9:7: "For if we do this, and do die, our *blood will be avenged* before the Lord."[507] Because, as Taxo claims, he and his fathers never transgressed the commandments of God, he and his sons will become innocent sufferers and invoke God's vindication. According to Taxo, their deaths will lead to the eschaton and the arrival of God's kingdom.

Although 2 Maccabees 7[508] and *Testament of Moses* 9[509] share virtually no language with the Prayer of Azariah, the texts have a similar function. All three texts either originate in or explain the same time period, Antiochus' reign of terror. They also contain the idea that the innocent or pious suffer because of the nation's sin. Thus, the Prayer of Azariah, is not unique in its notion that the pious suffer because of the sins of the nation as a whole. Just as 2 Maccabees 7 and *Testament of Moses* 9 maintain that God responds to the suffering of the "servants," the Prayer of Azariah assumes in v. 10 [3:33](cf. v. 21 [3:44]) that God will act because his "*servants*" and "those who fear" him are "shamed." Because they hold this position, God cannot overlook their plight. Finally, like 2 Maccabees' declaration that Antiochus will one day be forced to confess that God is the only God (2 Macc 7:37), the Prayer of Azariah asks God to punish those who oppress the servants so that the oppressor might recognize that God is the sovereign ruler over the universe.

---

[507]Translation used is J. Priest in *OTP*, Vol 1.

[508]J. Goldstein *(II Maccabees*, 83) holds that Jason of Cyrene completed his version by 86 BCE. The abridger produced his work between 78/7 and 63 BCE.

[509]Although the *Testament of Moses* went through several revisions, its oldest layers describe the crisis of Antiochus. G. W. E. Nickelsburg (*Resurrection, Immortality*, 43-45) has shown that except for chapter 6, the work originates early in the Antiochian persecution. See also Licht "Taxo, Or the Apocalyptic Doctrine of Vengeance," 95-103. Priest (*OTP*, Vol 1, 920-921) claims that the book is a product of the first century CE with recognition that some material may have come from earlier periods.

Chapter Four   179

Summary

Like Tobit, 2 Maccabees 7, and the *Testament of Moses*, the Prayer of Azariah represents the confluence of two conflicting traditions. First, this penitential prayer displays the influence of deuteronomic ideology, which asserts that suffering comes as punishment for the nation's sin. Only repentance expressed in penitential prayer can reverse the situation. Second, the author inserts the prayer into the righteous sufferer motif since the righteous have become those who suffer most. The turning point in this genre comes when God acts to avenge his servants. Only this act can relieve the tension present in the prayer.

3 Maccabees 2:1-20[510]

The Arrogant Plot

3 Maccabees also depicts people praying in a moment of distress and also attests to the incorporation of the idea of persecution at the hand of an arrogant, powerful Gentile into the penitential tradition. The penitential moment in 3 Maccabees occurs as a result of Ptolemy Philopator's decision to enter the Jerusalem Temple after his victory at Raphia. In a response reminiscent of the story of Heliodorus in 2 Macc 3:14b-21, the whole city is greatly troubled. The people pray to God with the hope of averting the temple's profanation. As part of the appeal, the high priest, Simon,[511] offers a prayer with a penitential tone.

---

[510]Scholars still disagree on the date of 3 Maccabees. Some (e.g., Emmet, *APOT*, vol 1, 156-159; G. W. E. Nickelsburg, *Resurrection, Immortality*, 90; Anderson, "3 Maccabees," *OTP*, vol 2, 512) propose a date around 100 BCE. Those who accept this date hold that 3 Maccabees must ante-date Greek Esther since it probably borrows from 3 Maccabees. Greek Esther dates to about 77 BCE. The argument depends as well on 3 Maccabees relationship to 2 Maccabees, *Letter of Aristeas*, and Daniel.

The term *laographia* is important in the debate. M. Hadas (*The Third and Fourth Books of Maccabees*, JAL [New York: Harper, 1953] 3, 19-21) maintains that the term must refer to the "poll tax" which Augustus levied on Egypt when it became a province in 24 BCE. 3 Maccabees would then date to Augustus' reign. J. J. Collins (*Between Athens and Jerusalem*, 105-107), though, claims that the term *laographia* can only provide the *terminus a quo*. For him, 3 Maccabees must depict a time when Rome threatened the temple before 70 CE. Such a threat came during Caligula. Hadas' and Collins' positions suffer from their over dependence on the word *laographia*. Because the word appears in papyri from Ptolemaic Egypt, one cannot use it to conclude that 3 Maccabees could only come from the Roman period (Anderson, "3 Maccabees," *OTP*, vol 2, 511). The arguments for 100 BCE are more convincing.

[511]Probably Simon II.

Because Ptolemy's plot springs from his hubris, the prayer immediately establishes that true power and sovereignty belong only to God. Thus, Simon acclaims God as the absolute sovereign of the universe (v. 2). He is "Lord," "king," "despot," "monarch," and "almighty." In contrast, Ptolemy, whom the author describes with terms synonymous with arrogance,[512] only pretends to have power. By his decision to enter the sanctuary of the only God, he demonstrates his failure to recognize the true ruler of the universe. Such action deserves punishment. Thus, Simon recounts past cases in which God opposed the arrogant—the giants who died in the flood (v. 4), the people of Sodom (v. 5), and Pharaoh (v. 6)—as precedents for God punishing Ptolemy (v. 3).

These features also correspond to Eleazar's prayer in the midst of the crisis in 3 Macc 6:1-15, as the Alexandrian Jews face death as martyrs in the hippodrome. He extols God as the powerful ruler who consistently opposes arrogant human rulers who oppress his people. Comparable to Simon, Eleazar provides examples of arrogant rulers whom God humbled: Pharaoh and Sennacherib.[513] He adds to this God's deliverance of famous characters in desperate circumstances: the three youths in the fiery furnace, Daniel in the lions' den, and Jonah in the fish.[514] He concludes this recollection of God's past deeds by addressing God as the one who hates insolence (v. 9), and, therefore, should attend to the cries of his people who again suffer from an arrogant king.

3 Maccabees 2 draws its language for its protest against Ptolemy from Isaiah's oracles that condemn haughty foreign rulers. Isaiah promises that the king of Babylon eventually will cease from his insolence, and his pomp will go to Sheol with him in death (Isa 14:4-21). In another oracle against Babylon, Isaiah records God's judgment: "I will make the pride of the insolent cease, and I will bring low the pride of the powerful" (13:11). The ideas surface again in the oracle against the king of Assyria. Although the king of Assyria executes God's punishment upon Israel for its sin (10:5-6), the king fails to recognize that he is but an instrument of God, and has not been successful by his own might (cf vv. 13-14). In his arrogance, the Assyrian king says that he will do to Jerusalem what he has done to the idols of the other countries (vv. 10-11):

---

[512]Consistent with the language of the rest of 3 Maccabees, the words infrequently appear in the LXX.

[513]For an example of a list of those who fail to follow God's law and are punished, see CD 2-3.

[514]Cf. C. A. Moore, *Daniel, Esther, and Jeremiah*, 210-211.

> Has not my hand gone out to all the kingdoms of the idols? And are not their idols greater than those of Jerusalem and Samaria? Shall I not do to Jerusalem and her images as I did to Samaria and her idols.

God must punish the king of Assyria because he cannot vaunt over the one who gave him his power (vv. 15-16). Similarly, the author of 3 Maccabees draws from the king of Assyria's words to warn God how Ptolemy and his armies will boast if they enter the sanctuary. They will vaunt:

> We have trampled down the house of the sanctuary as the houses of abominations are trampled down" (3 Macc 2:18).

With this allusion to Isaiah, the author of 3 Maccabees informs God that the enemy will view him and his Temple as any idol and its Temple.[515] The prevention of Jerusalem's desolation will prevent both this misperception from developing and punish those who think this way.

Temple Ideology and Deuteronomic Traditions

Since the arrogant foreign ruler threatens the Temple, Simon's prayer pays special attention to its importance. Simon's location and posture while offering his prayer bring into relief the Temple's centrality. The author pictures Simon praying on his knees[516] with hands extended[517] while facing the Temple (2:1). As the prayer continues, the Temple figures prominently in the prayer's ideology. The Temple stands in the city which God chose after creating the earth, and is the place where God's name dwells (v. 14).[518] The "audacious" and "profane" king cannot continue to threaten such a holy place.

The author develops his Temple ideology from the deuteronomic traditions in Deuteronomy 4, 12, 30, and 1 Kings 8, all of which speak of the place where God makes his name dwell in order to validate the centralization of the cult.[519] Simon picks up other important concepts from these texts as well. For example, like Solomon, Simon emphasizes that God is not confined to the Temple, but his dwelling is in the highest heavens:

---

[515]Cf. also Jdt 9:9.
[516]Contrast Solomon who stands before the altar in 1 Kgs 8:22. Ezra kneels in Ezr 9:5. The priests in the Heliodorus story prostrate themselves before the altar (2 Macc 3:15).
[517]Cf. Solomon in 1 Kgs 8:22, Ezra in Ezr 9:5, and the women in 2 Macc 3:20.
[518]Cf. Judith's prayer in Jdt 9:14.
[519]See Chapter One.

1 Kgs 8:27	3 Macc 2:15
כי האמנם ישב אלהים על־הארץ הנה השמים ושמי השמים לא יכלכלוך אף כי־הבית הזה אשר בניתי	τὸ μὲν γὰρ κατοικητήριόν σου οὐρανὸς τοῦ οὐρανοῦ ἀνέφικτος ἀνθρώποις ἐστίν

Simon's statement in v. 9 that God really has no need of anything, including the Temple, is also reminiscent of Isa 66:1.[520] The "magnificent epiphany," to which v. 9 refers, probably recalls the descent of God's glory when Solomon dedicated the Temple (1 Kgs 8:11). As this collection of ideas shows, the author attempts to stress the Temple's sanctity while also protecting God's sovereignty, a key concept in the prayer.

Simon's prayer also echoes Solomon's request for God to hear the people's prayers when they direct them to the Jerusalem Temple. However, the author transforms Solomon's words from a request to a promise:

1 Kgs 8:29	3 Macc 2:10
להיות עינך פתחות אל־הבית הזה לילה ויום אל־המקום אשר אמרת יהיה שמי שם לשמע אל־התפלה אשר יתפלל עבדך אל־המקום הזה	ἐπηγγείλω διότι, ἐὰν γένηται ἡμῶν ἀποστροφὴ καὶ καταλάβῃ ἡμᾶς στενοχωρία καὶ ἐλθόντες εἰς τὸν τόπον τοῦτον δεηθῶμεν εἰσακούσῃ τῆς δεήσεως ἡμῶν.

The author undoubtedly inserts this tradition into the prayer with the hope that he can bind God to a promise, and, thus, secure the nation's future. With this prayer before the Temple, the author believes that the nation has met the requirements of 1 Kings 8 and that God will presently fulfill his word.

Confession of Sin

The discussion condemning Ptolemy's arrogance combines with the admission that the people's sin has brought punishment:

> But see now, O Holy King, we are subdued on account of our many and great sins, and we are subjected to our enemies, and we are disregarded in helplessness (v. 13).

In other words, Israel's sins have "subdued" them, not the ruler of Egypt. Near the conclusion of the prayer, Simon petitions God: "Wipe out our sins,

---

[520]See Chapter One for expositions of 1 Kings 8 and Isaiah 66.

and scatter our errors" (v. 19). While we do not see the simple confession found in other prayers ("I/We have sinned"), the author clearly connects the nation's distress to its sin, and asks for forgiveness.

Summary

Simon argues that despite Israel's sin, God cannot allow these insolent pagans to enter the Temple and believe that they have subdued Israel's God. Even if Israel is sinful, this does not justify profanation of the Temple and God's reputation. Eleazar's prayer in chapter 6 argues similarly, and basically summarizes Simon's contention:

> Even if our lives have become entangled in the ungodliness in our exile, rescue us from the hand of the enemy, then, O Lord, destroy us by the fate which you choose. But do not let the impious minded bless the vanities upon the destruction of the ones whom you love, by saying, "Not even their God could rescue them" (3 Macc 6:10-11).[521]

In this manner, the prayer also resembles 2 Maccabees 7,[522] which evinces the notion that Antiochus' arrogant torturing of the seven sons perhaps exceeds God's intentions.[523] The prayers in 3 Maccabees seek to avert the martyrdom that occurs in 2 Maccabees by encouraging God to keep the arrogant deeds of the pagans in check. Israel has sinned, but the these pagans want to bring damage to the Temple and God that is disproportional to Israel's sin.

Esther's Prayer in the Greek Additions to the LXX

Greek Esther, which probably originates in Egypt around 77 BCE,[524] depicts a court contest in which a persecuted innocent figure triumphs over an enemy.[525]

---

[521] Cf. Dan 3:15.

[522] J. Goldstein discusses this problem of arrogant pagan rulers punishing Israel beyond God's intentions in *II Maccabees*, 293.

[523] Ibid. See 2 Macc 7:16, 19, 27, 31, 34, 36.

[524] E. Bickerman, "The Colophon of the Greek Book of Esther," *JBL* 63 (1944) 339-62. C. A. Moore (*Daniel, Esther, and Jeremiah*, 161) finds 114 BCE to be a more likely date. The relationship between Greek Esther and 3 Maccabees suggests that 3 Maccabees influenced the translator/author of Greek Esther (see G. W. E. Nickelsburg, *Jewish Literature*, 174, 190 n 43).

[525] See G. W. E. Nickelsburg, *Resurrection, Immortality*, 50-51; W. L. Humphreys, "A Life-Style for Diaspora: A Study of the Tales of Esther and Daniel," *JBL* 92 (1973) 211-223.

Addition C of this Greek text contains Esther's penitential prayer that she delivers at a critical point in the story—the discovery of Haman's plot to kill the Jews. The Jews face this predicament because of Mordecai's refusal to bow to Haman, an act to which both his and Esther's prayers refer. According to Mordecai, such a display would slight God's glory. The addition also preserves Esther's piety by confirming that, like the heroes of Daniel, she abstains from eating the pagans' food and from drinking their wine of libation. Further, she finds her marriage to a Gentile detestable, an opinion that the Hebrew Bible does not divulge. In response to this news, and in preparation for Esther's appearance before the king, Mordecai and Esther pray.

Before praying, Esther humbles herself by removing her regal apparel, dressing in mourning garments, and putting ashes and dung on her head (vv. 2-3).[526] Like Simon in 3 Maccabees 2, Esther extols God as the only king (14:3; cf 3 Macc 2:2, 12). Mordecai's prayer emphasizes the same characteristic of God and recognizes his omnipotence and omniscience (13:9-12). In the context, recognition of these very attributes prevents Mordecai from paying homage to Haman. For Mordecai, bowing to Haman, he would be elevating a human's glory over God's glory (13:14). Esther's prayer also views the Persian plot against the Jews as a challenge to God's sovereignty and future recognition of it. If the Persians fulfill their covenant with their idols to bring the Jews' end (14:8),[527] then they will have silenced the voices of those who praise the true God.[528] As a result, the nations will lift their voices in praise of idols (εἰς ἀρετὰς ματαίων) and honor a mortal king (βασιλέα σάρκινον), and God would abdicate his rule to that which has no being (14:11). In this way, Esther's prayer echoes Simon's petition that God must deliver his people so that the Gentiles do not have occasion to praise their vain gods (3 Macc 6:11).

Esther also expresses concern about the threat against the altar and the Temple (14:9).[529] While these same issues emerge in Simon's supplication in 3 Maccabees 2, in the case of Esther, these ideas constitute an obvious anachronism. Still, the prayer impresses upon God that he cannot allow a pagan to trample his Temple like the temple of idols.

Like Simon's prayer, Esther's language reveals that her predicament results from a blending of arrogant, vain oppressors and Israel's sins. Accordingly, Esther confesses the nation's sin, which in typical deuteronomic fash-

---

[526] Cf. Jdt 9:1.

[527] The Greek literally reads: "They placed their hands on the hands of their idols" (ἀλλὰ ἔθηκαν τὰς χεῖρας αὐτῶν ἐπὶ τὰς χεῖρας τῶν εἰδώλων αὐτῶν).

[528] Cf. Bar 3:1-8.

[529] Cf. Jdt 9:8 where the Assyrians threaten the tabernacle and the altar.

ion, is primarily idolatry: "And now we have sinned before you" (14:6).[530] God has delivered the people over to their enemies[531] who have exiled Israel and reduced it to slavery.[532] The prayer's inclusion of the *Gerichtsdoxologie* formula recognizes that God is rightfully punishing the nation: "You are righteous, O Lord" (14:7). In contrast, Mordecai's prayer does not contain a confession nor does it incorporate deuteronomic themes.

Using deuteronomic expressions, Esther speaks of learning through family stories that God chose Israel from among the nations to be his special "inheritance" (נחלה) (v. 5), Deuteronomy's term for election (Deut 7:6; 14:2; 32:8-9; and 1 Kgs 8:53). In several texts, God makes the people his "possession" (סגלה) by the Exodus (Exod 19:4; Deut 4:20; 9:26-27, 29; and 1 Kgs 8:51). Based on this special relationship with Israel, Esther tries to persuade God to act.

As in other deuteronomic stories, Esther's prayer functions as the turning point in this tale. Following her prayer, Haman's plot is revealed, he is punished, and the Jews are vindicated. Once again, the tension between the pious sufferer and the deuteronomic scheme of history finds its relief in the triumph of the pious sufferer. Therefore, these penitential prayers make no attempt at offering a theoretical explanation for the righteous' suffering. Instead, it simply resolves it through the plot.

Summary

Esther's prayer is a response to a foreigner's plot to kill the Jews. Thus, like the other prayers in this Chapter, the petitioner is faced with excessive suffering. Esther confesses the Jews' sins and admits God's right to punish them, however she also informs God that if Haman succeeds in his plot, his arrogance will bring disrepute upon God's reputation. Claiming that Israel is God's "inheritance" from days of old, Esther petitions God to act. Her prayer influences God, and Haman's plot is revealed.

The Psalms of Solomon

The arrogant ruler theme figures prominently in the *Psalms of Solomon*. As in the previous prayers, the psalms combine this theme with deuteronomic ideas. Although the *Psalms of Solomon* are difficult to date individually, and may

---

[530] Deut 4:19 and 25.
[531] Cf. 1 Kgs 8:37.
[532] Cf. Ezr 9:9.

have gone through several redactions, a few psalms have a connection to Pompey's career. Psalms 1, 2, and 8 speak of his conquest of Jerusalem, while Psalm 2 celebrates his death in Egypt. The references to these events suggest a first century BCE date for at least some of the *Psalms of Solomon*.[533] While most scholars agree that they originate in Hebrew,[534] the group responsible for their composition remains undetermined. Formerly, scholars attributed them to the Pharisees,[535] a position that is now untenable.[536]

Psalms 1 and 2 agree that Pompey's desecration of the Temple is the result of Israel's "secret sins" that profaned the sanctuary (1:7-8 and 2:7). In 2:12-13 and 8:8-12, the author describes the deeds in contemporary polemical rhetoric for expressing disagreements with the Jewish leaders over halakhoth. Therefore, *Ps Sol* 2:15-18 asserts that Pompey's campaign is a demonstration of God's rightful punishment for the Jews' halakhic failures:

> I will acclaim you righteous, O Lord, in uprightness of heart,
>   for in your judgments, you are right, O Lord,
> For you reward sinners according to their works,
>   and according to their exceeding wicked sins.
> You have revealed their sins, in order that your judgments might be manifested...
>
> God is a righteous judge, and he is not a respecter of persons.

Such vocabulary for declaring God's righteousness, which sounds similar to Tob 3:2 and Pr Azar 4-5a, dominates the *Psalms of Solomon*.[537] For the psalmist(s), Israel must accept God's righteous punishments as discipline.[538]

---

[533]D. Flusser, "Psalms, Hymns and Prayers," 573; R. B. Wright, "The Psalms of Solomon," *OTP* 2, 641; G. W. E. Nickelsburg, *Jewish Literature*, 203; J. Trafton, *The Syriac Version of the Psalms of Solomon*, SCS 11 (Atlanta: Scholars, 1985) 2-3; R. R. Hann, *The Manuscript History of Psalms of Solomon*, SCS 13 (Chico: Scholars, 1982) 1.

[534]R. B. Wright, "The Psalms of Solomon," *OTP* II, 640.

[535]E.g., J. Schüpphaus, *Die Psalmen Salomos: ein Zeugnis Jerusalemer Theologie und Frommigkeit in der Mitte des Vorchristlichen Jahrhunderts* (Leiden: Brill, 1977) 158: "... so daß ihre Einstufung als die 'klassische Quelle für den Pharisäismus' gerechtfertigt erscheint."

[536]See Charlesworth's inserted paragraph in R. B. Wright, "The Psalms of Solomon," *OTP* 2, 642; E. P. Sanders, *Paul and Palestinian Judaism*, 388; J. O'Dell, "The Religious Background of the Psalms of Solomon," *RQ* 3 (1961-62) 241-257.

[537]Occurrences of words from the root δικ-. For Δίκαιος see *Ps Sol* 2:10, 18, 32, 34; 3:3, 4, 5, 7, 11; 4:8; 5:1; 8:8; 9:2, 7; 10:3, 5; 13:6, 7, 9, 11; 14:9; 15:3, 6, 7; 16:15; 17:32; for δικαιοσύνη see 1:2, 3; 2:15; 4:24; 5:17; 8:6, 24, 25, 26; 9:2, 3; 14:2; 17:19, 23, 26, 29, 37, 40; 18:7, 8; for δικαιόω see 2:15 3:5; 4:8; 8:7, 23, 26; 9:2; for δικαίωσις see 3:3 (from O. von Gebhart, *Die Psalmen Salomos*, 142-143).

[538]Cf. E. P. Sanders, *Paul and Palestinian Judaism*, 407.

While the author of Psalm 2 acknowledges God's right to discipline the people, as Psalm 2 continues, the author concludes that God's punishment of Jerusalem has been severe enough. Thus, he "entreats" God on behalf of the city (v. 22). He hopes that this will prevent the people's total annihilation (v. 23). As in 2 Maccabees 7, 3 Maccabees 2, the Prayer of Azariah, and Greek Esther, the author of *Psalms of Solomon* 2 decries the arrogance of God's punishing rod, the foreign ruler and hopes for his punishment (vv. 24-25).

Psalm 8 also describes Pompey's conquest as the result of the God's rightful punishment of the nation's sins (v. 23). However, in this passage, the psalmist also distinguishes between righteous and wicked Jews. The "pious ones" (ὅσιοι) are innocent lambs who acknowledge God's righteous discipline (παιδεία)(vv. 25-26). Because they recognize God's deeds, they believe that they can now appeal to God to "turn" to show mercy (v. 27). Comparable to Third Isaiah and Tobit 13, the author of Psalm 8 hopes that the declaration of God's righteousness and demonstration of his mercy will lead further to the gathering of Israel from the nations. Like Third Isaiah and the texts in Chapter Three, the wicked should anticipate judgment. Penitence has again become one of the actions that distinguishes between people in Second Temple Judaism.

The *Psalms of Solomon* also address the problem of individual sin and its accompanying punishment. Thus, the righteous confess:

> The righteous remember the Lord continuously,
>   with confession and justification, the Lord's judgments (3:3)

As in the psalms with a national or communal perspective, the righteous again view God's punishment as "discipline" (παιδεία)(v. 4; cf. *Psalms of Solomon* 13), and, therefore, they accept the punishment, seek correction (v. 6), and do not persist in sin (v. 7). In this instance, the righteous atone for their sins done in ignorance (ἄγνοια) through fasting and "humility of soul" (καὶ ταπεινώσει ψυχῆς αὐτοῦ)(v. 9). In contrast, the wicked continue in sin and despise discipline (vv. 9-11).

Besides fasting and humility, confession functions as a means to purify the righteous in *Ps Sol* 9:

> He will cleanse a soul in sin by confession, and by redeeming.[539]

---

[539] The word seems odd. The Syriac omits it (R. B. Wright, "The Psalms of Solomon," *OTP* II, 661 n. e). S. P. Brock ("The Psalms of Solomon," *AOT*, 668) translates the word "acknowledgement."

The next line echoes ideas of shame like that found in the penitential confession in Ezra 9:6:

Ps Sol 9:6	Ezra 9:6
ὅτι αἰσχύνη ἡμῖν καὶ τοῖς προσώποις ἡμῶν περὶ ἁπάντων	בשתי ונכלמתי להרים אלהי פני אליך

Psalm of Solomon 9 closes with a return to national interests. Like previous penitential texts, the author asks God to act based on Israel's election and the Abrahamic covenant (vv. 8-10).[540]

Summary

The authors of the *Psalms of Solomon* fashion their poetry under the influence of the penitential prayer tradition in order to address the problems of both national and individual sin. The group responsible for the psalms believes that the Roman conquest and occupation have come upon the nation because of God's just punishment for the people's sins. However, because the Romans have carried out the punishment in arrogance, they must now receive punishment. With this idea, the *Psalms of Solomon* resemble Deuteronomy 32, Isaiah 14, the Prayer of Azariah, and 2 Maccabees 7. In regards to the individual, the pious person can atone for sin by fasting, humility, and confession. These acts, and the pious person's attitude toward sin and discipline, separate the pious person from the wicked. Like the Qumran Scrolls, confession draws a sociological line between the righteous and the wicked.

Conclusion

Deuteronomic language and ideology are readily evident in the texts in this Chapter. The suppliants, praying in a moment of crisis which they understand to have arrived because of sin, acknowledge that the covenantal curses have descended upon them. Therefore, they often describe their predicament with allusions to passages like Deuteronomy 4, 28-30, and 1 Kings 8. All the prayers employ the *Gerichtsdoxologie*: God is righteous in his punishment. Obviously, the prayers preserve the idea that the deuteronomic cycle reaches its turning point when the nation or, in the case of Tobit and the three youths in the fire, individuals repent and pray a penitential prayer. Solomon's prayer in 1 Kings 8 solidly anchors this idea in the deuteronomic tradition. Simon's

---

[540]Cf. e.g., Pr Azar 12 [3:35].

prayer in 3 Maccabees 2, in fact, explicitly recalls Solomon's prayer, and even transforms Solomon's plea for God to respond when Israel prays from a conditional petition into a promise.

In tension with deuteronomic ideology several prayers incorporate the image of the pious sufferer. With this addition, the prayers' authors have correctly observed that those who strictly adhere to the Law frequently experience more intensive persecution. Such conditions seem unjust. Thus, in Tobit and the Prayer of Azariah stands rhetoric that is elsewhere associated with lament. As Chapter One explains, lament and deuteronomic ideologies are generally unable to cohabit the same text because lament pours forth from a perceived injustice while deuteronomic thought supposes a correlation between righteousness and blessing, sin and punishment. Despite the dissonance that the conflicting themes generate in these prayers, the authors do not resolve the tensions nor answer the related questions of theodicy through theoretical arguments. Instead, the stories' plots end the tensions as the prayers function as turning points in the narrative. God delivers the righteous, but never really explains why they suffer in the first place. Only a more careful analysis of all these texts could possibly determine if the authors seek a serious explanation for evil.

The other new feature in these prayers is the oppressive, arrogant ruler. While God has always temporarily employed him as a rod of discipline to punish the nation, he has become a special problem in these texts. Because of his inflated opinion of himself, he takes credit for the glory of Israel's defeat, insolently defames God, and inflicts Israel with excessive abuse. The authors undoubtedly introduce these ideas in order to coax God to protect his sovereignty. They hope that in the process of God punishing the foreign ruler, the Jews will experience salvation. The problem of the arrogant ruler certainly relates to the issue of theodicy, but the authors live with the tensions that the deuteronomic ideology creates rather than attempt a full explanation for evil.

The prayers suggest that penitential prayers pervade Jewish life. First, Tobit democratizes penitential prayer by situating the prayer within the daily life of a character. The *Psalms of Solomon* also attest to the importance of confession in the life of the individual. Confession, along with other actions, distinguishes the "holy ones" from the wicked. Second, if 3 Maccabees actually originates in Egypt, then this text testifies that penitential prayer has reached the Egyptian diaspora. Even though Simon's language is bombastic, he stands firmly within the deuteronomic traditions of the prayers we have examined. Thus, the literary evidence confirms that penitential prayer with its deuteronomic language and ideology has reached three key communities in Second Temple Judaism—the Babylonian, Palestinian, and the Alexandrian communities.

CONCLUSION

Jerusalem's fall to Babylon along with the people's subsequent exile creates a religious crisis in Israel. The survivors are left to answer the question: "Why did this happen?" Among those considering this question are the authors responsible for Deuteronomy and the deuteronomic history. These authors believe that God has made a covenant with his people, Israel. A key component of this covenant is a theory of causality that works as follows. When the nation is righteous, God gives peace and prosperity. However, if the people sin, God activates the covenantal curses and punishes the people. Therefore, the authors writing within the deuteronomic traditions know the cause of the disaster of 586 BCE. The people had sinned against God and he is punishing them. They have even committed the "quintessential sin"—idolatry. Thus, the nation's predicament has a simple and logical explanation.

Having determined why Israel is suffering, the authors also instruct the people how to bring an end to Israel's miserable situation. Deuteronomy 4 and 30 advise about this issue. In fact, these two passages remain the foundational texts for the penitential prayer tradition from the exile to the Qumran community. These two chapters teach Israel that only repentance brings deliverance. In the metaphors of Deuteronomy, the people must "search (שׁוב) their heart," "turn" (שׁוב) and "seek" (דרשׁ and בקשׁ) God. If the people do this with "all their heart and soul," God will recognize their sincere contrition and restore them to the land.

Of course, Babylon's victory leaves the Temple in ruins, brings the cessation of the cult, at least as the people practice it, and creates a group of exiles who, living in a foreign land, no longer have access to Jerusalem. When the Temple was standing and the cult functioning, the people knew how to repent—they offered sacrifices at the Temple. How could they perform Deuteronomy's repentance without these religious institutions? Interpreting the traditions in Deuteronomy 4 and 30, the deuteronomic historian constructs a narrative in which Solomon prays at the Temple's dedication (1 Kings 8). His prayer explains how the people properly repent even in exile: they should pray a penitential prayer. According to the theory contained within the prayer, even though the Temple is destroyed and many people are in exile, one can direct a prayer toward the Temple and God will "hear" in heaven. This prayer, therefore, transforms the traditions from Deuteronomy 4 and 30 into a theory for the use and practice of penitential prayer.

Penitential prayer, then, is in part a response to history. It arises from Israel's attempt to understand its painful experiences and desire to find its way out of misery. For authors in the deuteronomic traditions, one must analyze the historical situation in light of what it means to be in a covenant with God and be the recipients of either blessings or curses. Further, whenever the people feel as if the divine promises are not fulfilled, especially prophetic promises, they must ask themselves if they have sinned. Third Isaiah, for example, seeks to explain the failure of Second Isaiah's glorious prophecies. Even in the Second Temple period, the nation's persistent problems frequently lead to this notion that the people are suffering from the activation of the covenantal curses. This idea becomes expressed vividly in the metaphor that appears in Baruch and the Qumran Scrolls: "The curses cling to us!"

The post-exilic penitential prayers in Ezra-Nehemiah, therefore, stand within this tradition that stretches back into the exile to Deuteronomy 4 and 30 and 1 Kings 8. By this time in the Persian period, penitential prayer is a firmly established religious institution. Although penitential prayer is an institution, one must not conclude that the interpretive process has stopped and that the prayers have become fixed. As Ezra 9 reveals, prayer remains closely associated with reinterpreting tradition so that it addresses a new set of problems. Ezra offers his prayer because the people have violated the law prohibiting intermarriage. In prior texts, penitential prayers serve as a proper response to disaster and to the "quintessential sin"—idolatry. Ezra applies penitential prayer to a new category of sin.

How can one be reasonably certain, though, that the authors of these prayers are consciously reinterpreting biblical traditions and prayer traditions or simply unconsciously employing pious language that they have heard in liturgy and songs? That is, are these prayers the result of intentional thought and interpretation? The evidence from the prayers supports the position that these authors are engaged in an intentional, reflective enterprise and are not simply repeating pious language. Two types of evidence suggest this conclusion. First, on occasion, the authors of the prayers seem to be conscious of the contents of the prayer traditions. One finds significant sections of prayers that resemble earlier prayers. Second, the evidence from Second Temple Judaism contains texts in which Jews explicitly state that they are engaged in interpretation. Daniel 9 and Bar 1:15-3:8 are examples of authors searching for the meaning and application of texts. Further, *Jubilees* 1 and 23 depict the righteous repenting, confessing their sins, and searching (דרש) the scriptures. Likewise, the members of the Qumran community claim that they originated as a penitential movement that sought for the proper understanding of scripture. Entrance into this sect includes confession of sin. In its daily life, the sect prays, including penitential prayer as 4Q504 demonstrates, and reads scrip-

Conclusion

ture. Therefore, during the Second Temple period, interpretation sometimes stands within a penitential context. The reason for this, once again, lies within Deuteronomy 4 and 30, the foundational texts for this penitential tradition. Deuteronomy states that the people must "seek" (דרש) God. In the Second Temple period, the term דרש can mean "to inquire in a text." Consequently, some Jews in the Second Temple period, those responsible for *Jubilees* and the Qumran Scrolls among them, believe that in order to meet Deuteronomy's prescription for repentance, one must "seek," i.e., interpret the scriptures. Therefore, one can safely assume that penitential prayers arise from a context in which Jews are consciously interpreting authoritative traditions in order to understand how to live in the midst of complicated political, social, and religious upheaval.

The incorporation of new ideas into the penitential prayer traditions and changes in meaning of important terms and ideas frequently occur. In contrast to the emergence of new ideas, some important ideas disappear from the tradition. For example, "to search your heart," an important metaphor in Deut 30:1, disappears from the tradition. The phrase, which connotes cognitive reflection, is rare in the Hebrew Bible. Perhaps this explains why it does not acquire any further importance in the traditions. That is, this metaphor is obscure and simply is not popular. However, Jewish interpreters do not generally back away from obscure phrases or difficult texts. In fact, these kinds of texts frequently attract interpreters. Thus, the modern reader is at a loss for why this phrase drops out of the tradition.

Another peculiar feature about these prayers is the minimal influence that Levitical traditions had on them. Of course, Leviticus is acutely interested in sin and how to remove it. As the explanation of Ezra 9 details, the author of Ezra-Nehemiah draws from the *'asham* offering in Leviticus in order to construct the scene that contains Ezra's prayer. Several important Levitical terms like מעל and אשם occur in the context. These words, however, do not continue to occupy a key role in the tradition. Occasionally, a prayer will allude to the Day of Atonement ceremony in Leviticus 16 (e.g., 4Q504), but not even this text figures as important for the penitential prayer tradition as those from the deuteronomic traditions. 2 Chronicles shares the notion of "humbling one's self" with Leviticus, but this metaphor does not recur in penitential prayers. The reasons for the relative insignificance of Levitical themes is uncertain. Perhaps the penitential tradition simply developed among people who found deuteronomic ideology to be more valuable in their critique of the nation than the instructions about sin in Leviticus. Further, Levitical ideology may have been impractical for those writing the prayers. Leviticus is especially concerned with proper offerings for various sins. At times, however, the authors of penitential prayers are not in a situation in which sacrifice is an option.

Indeed, prayer becomes a way to deal with sin in the absence of sacrifice. Because of the authors' historical situations, Deuteronomy's emphasis on repentance and "seeking" God as a way to reverse Israel's problems is more practical and invites theories about how one properly repents. Therefore, deuteronomic themes may dominate the prayers simply because they contain more practical and usable material.

The introduction to this study states that penitential prayer becomes a religious institution for dealing with sin. For a religious act to be an institution, it must have wide acceptance. Do the texts from the exilic, post-exilic, and Second Temple eras establish penitential prayer as an institution? While the answer is "yes," this affirmation must also be qualified. Scholars of antiquity are accustomed to working with small amounts of evidence. Sometimes they try to prove more than the evidence allows. While one could not say that the number of extant penitential prayer texts is overwhelming, it is significant. As this study shows, we have several actual prayer texts, texts that discuss the function of prayer, and several texts that allude to penitential traditions. Further, the prayers appear in a sundry of literary genres—historical narratives, apocalypses, sectarian literature, and a letter. The prayers occur in literature that originates in Babylon, Palestine, and Egypt. As my interpretations of the prayers indicate, the authors of the prayers come from disparate circumstances. Therefore, the number of prayers and their appearance in a variety of historical, literary, and social settings suggest that penitential prayer is widely known and accepted.

Still one must proceed with caution. The common element among almost all these prayers is that they occur in a moment of grave crisis. Further, these prayers generally have a national rather than an individual perspective. Even Tobit's prayer in Tobit 3 may be a model for the nation in the exile. If the nation repents as Tobit did, its fortunes will reverse. Therefore, as they are represented in the literature, these prayers are not daily prayers offered by individuals. The only possible exceptions to this conclusion are the prayers among the sectarians at Qumran. The Scrolls reveal that the sectarians pray everyday, and indeed, 4Q504 seems to contain daily penitential prayers. If the prayers of 4Q504 originate among the ancestors of the Qumran sectarians, then these prayers may have been used daily before the establishment of the Qumran community. However, 4Q504 seems to be unique. Even though they are daily prayers, the Qumran community believes that the Jews are in crisis. The nation's sin has brought God's judgment and the Jews are living in the last days. Therefore, while penitential prayer is a daily activity, it is also part of life in the "age of wrath" that leads to the eschaton. Thus, because the setting for penitential prayer in the literature is a moment of national crisis, and sometimes of eschatological proportion, one cannot determine with certainty if the prayers described in this study are a daily part of the lives of individual Jews. In fact, examples of penitential prayers of individuals, Psalm 51 and the Prayer of Manasseh, may testify that the penitential prayers in this study are not used by individuals on a daily basis. Psalm 51 and the Prayer of Manasseh not do not contain the same kinds of traditions and language that one typically finds in the prayers in this study. Therefore, many Jews probably knew of the prayers we have examined, or prayers like them, or even prayed them, but they may have reserved them for days of crisis. These prayers, then, function as the community's response to the harshness of history.

BIBLIOGRAPHY

Achtemeier, E. *The Community and Message of Isaiah 56-66: A Theological Commentary.* Minneapolis: Augsburg, 1982.

Ackroyd, P. R. *The Chronicler in His Age.* JSOT Supp 101. Sheffield: JSOT, 1991.

_____. *Exile and Restoration: A Study of Hebrew Thought of the Sixth Centrury B.C.* Philadelphia: Westminster, 1968.

_____. "The Historical Literature," *The Hebrew Bible and its Modern Interpreters,* ed. D. A. Knight and G. M. Tucker, Philadelphia: Fortress, 1985 pp. 297-323.

Allegro, J. M. *Qumrân Cave 4 (4Q158-4Q186). DJD* V. Oxford: Clarendon, 1968.

Alt, A. "The Origins of Israelite Law," *Essays on the Old Testament and Religion.* R. A. Wilson, trans., Oxford: Blackwell, 1966, pp. 79-132.

Andersen, F. I. and D. N. Freedman. *Hosea: A New Translation with Introduction and Commentary.* New York: Doubleday and Co., 1980.

Anderson, G. W. ed. *Tradition and Interpretation.* Oxford: Clarendon, 1979.

Argall, R. A. *1 Enoch and Sirach: A Comparative Literary and Conceptual Analysis of the Themes of Revelation, Creation and Judgment.* Early Judaism and Its Literature. Atlanta: Scholars, 1995.

Baillet, M. *DJD VII. Qumrân Grotte 4 (4Q482-4Q520).* Oxford: Clarendon, 1982.

Balentine, S. E. "Enthroned on the Praises and Laments of Israel." *PSB Supp* 2 (1992) 20-35.

_____. *The Hidden God: The Hiding of the Face of God in the Old Testament.* Oxford: Oxford, 1983.

_____. *Prayer in the Bible: The Drama of Divine-Human Dialogue.* Philadephia: Fortress, 1993.

Baltzer, K. *The Covenant Formulary: In Old Testament, Jewish, and Early Christian Writings.* D. E. Green, trans. Philadelphia: Fortress, 1971.

Bauer, W. *A Greek-English Lexicon of the New Testament and Other Early Christian Literature.* 2nd ed. Revised by F. W. Gingrich and F. W. Danker. Chicago: University of Chicago, 1979.

Becker, J. *Das Heil Gottes: Heils- und Sündenbegriffe in den Qumrantexten und im Neuen Testament*. SUNT 3. Göttingen: Vandenhoeck & Ruprecht, 1964.

_____. *Untersuchungen zur Entstehungsgeschichte der Testamente der zwölf Patriarchen*. AGJU 7. Leiden: Brill, 1970.

Bickerman, E. "The Civic Prayer for Jerusalem," *Studies in Jewish and Christian History*, Vol 2, Leiden: Brill, 1980, pp. 266-288.

_____. *The Jews in the Greek Age*. Cambridge: Harvard University, 1988.

Blenkinsopp, J. *Ezra-Nehemiah: A Commentary*. Philadephia: Westminster, 1988.

_____. *A History of Prophecy in Israel*. Philadelphia: Westminster, 1983.

Boyce, R. N. *The Cry to God in the Old Testament*. SBLMS 103. Atlanta: Scholars, 1988.

Bracke, J. M. "*šûb šᵉbût*: A Reappraisal." *ZAW* 97 (1985) 233-244.

Braulik, G. "Spüren einer Neubearbeitung des deuteronomistischen Geschichtswerkes in 1 Kön 8,52-53. 59-60." *Bib* 52 (1971) 20-33.

Bright, J. *A History of Israel*. Philadelphia: Westminster, 1959.

_____. *Jeremiah*. AB 21. Garden City, NY: Doubleday, 1965.

Brooke, A. E., N. McLean, and H. St John Thackeray. *The Old Testament in Greek*. Vol 3. Cambridge: Cambridge University, 1940.

Brooke, G. J. *Exegesis at Qumran: 4QFlorilegium in its Jewish Context*. JSOT Sup 29. Sheffield: Sheffield Academic Press, 1985.

Brown, F. S. R., Driver, and C. A. Briggs. *Hebrew and English Lexicon of the Old Testament*. Oxford: Clarendon, 1979.

Brownlee, W. "The Background of Biblical Interpretation at Qumran," *Qumrân: Sa piété, sa théologie et son milieu*, ed. M. Delcor, Paris: Leuven University, 1978, pp. 183-193.

_____. *The Dead Sea Manual of Discipline*. New Haven: American Schools of Oriental Research, 1951.

Bruce, F. F. "The Book of Daniel and the Qumran Community," *Neotestamentica et Semitica: Studies in Honour of Matthew Black*, ed. E. E. Ellis and M. Wilcox, Edinburgh: T. & T. Clark, 1969, pp. 221-235.

Burke, D. G. *The Poetry of Baruch: A Reconstruction and Analysis of the Original Hebrew Text of Baruch 3:9-5:9*. SBLSCS 10. Chico: Scholars, 1982.

Burrows, M., ed. *The Dead Sea Scrolls of St. Mark's Monastery.* Vol 2. New Haven: American Schools of Oriental Research, 1951.

_____. *More Light on the Dead Sea Scrolls.* New York: Viking, 1958.

Calloway, P. R. *The History of the Qumran Community: An Investigation.* JSP Sup 3. Sheffield: Sheffield Academic Press, 1988.

Carroll, R. P. *When Prophecy Failed: Cognitive Dissonance in the Prophetic Traditions of the Old Testament.* New York: Seabury, 1979.

Charles, R. H. *The Apocrypha and Pseudepigrapha of the Old Testament.* 2 Vols. Oxford: Clarendon, 1913.

_____. *The Book of Enoch.* Oxford: Clarendon, 1912.

_____. *The Book of Jubilees.* Oxford: Clarendon, 1902.

_____. *The Ethiopic Verson of the Book of Enoch.* Oxford: Clarendon, 1906.

_____. *The Greek Versions of the Twelve Patriarchs.* Oxford: Clarendon, 1908.

Charlesworth, J. H. "Jewish Hymns, Odes, and Prayers (ca. 167 B.C.E.-135 C.E.)," *Early Judaism and its Modern Interpreters*, ed. R. A. Kraft and G. W. E. Nickelsburg, Philadelphia: Fortress, 1986, pp. 411-436.

_____. *Graphic Concordance to the Dead Sea Scrolls.* Tübingen: J. C. B. Mohr, 1991.

_____. *The Lord's Prayer and Other Prayer Texts from the Greco-Roman Era.* Valley Forge: Trinity, 1994.

_____, ed. *The Old Testament Pseudepigrapha.* 2 Vols. Garden City: Doubleday, 1983, 1985.

_____. *The Pseudepigrapha and Modern Research.* Missoula, MT: Scholars, 1976.

Chazon, E. G. "Is *Divrei ha-me'oroth* a Sectarian Prayer?" *The Dead Sea Scrolls: Forty Years of Research*, ed. D. Dimant and U. Rappaport, Leiden: Brill, 1992, pp. 3-17.

_____. "Prayers from Qumran." SBLSP 32 (1993) 758-772.

Clifford, R. J. "In Zion and David a New Beginning: An Interpretation of Psalm 78," *Traditions in Transformation: Turning Points in Biblical Faith: Festschrift for F. M. Cross*, ed. Halpern and J. D. Levenson, Winona Lake: Eisebrauns, 1981, pp. 121-141.

Collins, J. J. *The Apocalyptic Imagination: An Introduction to the Jewish Matrix of Christianity.* New York: Crossroad, 1987.

_____. *Between Athens and Jerusalem: Jewish Identity in the Hellenistic Diaspora.* New York: Crossroad, 1983.

_____. *Daniel. Hermeneia.* Minneapolis: Fortress, 1993.

_____. *Daniel with an Introduction to Apocalyptic Literature.* FOTL 20. Grand Rapids: Wm. B. Eerdmans, 1984.

_____. "Patterns of Eschatology at Qumran," *Traditions in Transformation: Turning Points in Biblical Faith: Festschrift for F. M. Cross,* eds. B. Halpern and J. D. Levenson. Winona Lake, IN: Eisenbrauns, 1981, pp. 351-375.

_____. "The Testamentary Literature in Recent Scholarship," *Early Judaism and its Modern Interpreters,* ed. R. A. Kraft and G. W. E. Nickelsburg, Philadelphia: Fortress, 1986, pp. 268-285.

_____. "Testaments," *Jewish Writings of the Second Temple Period, CRJNT* Section 2, ed. M. E. Stone, Philadelphia: Fortress, 1984, pp. 325-355.

Corvin, J. "Stylistic and Functional Study of the Prose Prayers in the Historical Narratives of the Old Testament" (Diss., Emory University, Atlanta, GA, 1972).

Crenshaw, J. L. *Old Testament Wisdom: An Introduction.* Atlanta: John Knox, 1981.

Cross, F. M. *Canaanite Myth and Hebrew Epic: Essays in the History of the Religion of Israel.* Cambridge: Harvard University, 1973.

Davies, P. R. *Behind the Essenes: History and Ideology in the Dead Sea Scrolls.* BJS 94. Atlanta: Scholars, 1987.

_____. *The Damascus Covenant: An Interpretation of the "Damascus Covenant".* JSOT Supp 25. Sheffield: Sheffield, 1983.

Deselaers, P. *Das Buch Tobit: Studien zu seiner Entstehung, Komposition und Theologie.* Göttingen: Vandenhoeck and Ruprecht, 1982.

Deutsch, C. "The Sirach 51 Acrostic Poem: Confession and Exhortation," *ZAW* 94 (1982) 400-409.

De Vries, S. J. *1 and 2 Chronicles.* FOTL 11. Grand Rapids: Eerdmans, 1989.

Di Lella, A. A. "The Deuteronomic Background of the Farewell Discourse in Tob 14:3-11." *CBQ* 41 (1979) 380-389.

_____. *The Hebrew Text of Sirach: A Text-Critical and Historical Study*. London: Mouton, 1966.

Dimant, D. "Qumran Sectarian Literature," *Jewish Writings of the Second Temple Period*, CRINT Section 2, ed. M. E. Stond, Philadephia: Fortress, 1984, pp. 483-550.

Dupont-Sommer, A. *The Essene Writings from Qumran*. G. Vermes, trans. Oxford: Basil Blackwell, 1961.

Eissfeldt, O. *The Old Testament: An Introduction*. P. R. Ackroyd, trans. New York: Harper and Row, 1965.

Elliger, K. "Der Prophet Tritojesaja." *ZAW* 49 (1931) 112-141.

Endres, J. C. *Biblical Interpretation in the Book of Jubilees*. CBQMS 18. Washington: Catholic Biblical Association of America, 1987.

Eskenazi, T. C. *In an Age of Prose: A Literary Approach to Ezra-Nehemiah*. SBLMS 36. Atlanta: Scholars, 1988.

Fishbane, M. *Biblical Interpretation in Ancient Israel*. Oxford: Clarendon, 1985.

_____. *Text and Texture: Close Readings of Selected Biblical Texts*. New York: Schocken, 1979.

Fitzmyer, J. A. *The Dead Sea Scrolls: Major Publications and Tools for Study*. Rev. ed. Atlanta: Scholars, 1990.

Flusser, D. "Psalms, Hymns and Prayers," *Jewish Writings of the Second Temple Period*, CRINT Section 2, ed. M. E. Stone, Philadephia: Fortress, 1984, pp. 551-577.

Gerstenberger, E. S. *Der bittende Mensch: Bittritual und Klagelied des Einzelnen im Alten Testament*. WMANT 51. Neukirchener Verlag, 1980.

Ginzberg, L. *An Unknown Jewish Sect*. New York: The Jewish Theological Seminary of America, 1970.

Goldingay, J. E. *Daniel*. WBC 30. Dallas: Word, 1989.

Goldstein, J. A. "The Apocryphal Book of I Baruch." *PAAJR* 46-47 (1979-1980) 179-199.

_____. *I Maccabees*. AB 41. New York: Doubleday, 1976.

_____. *II Maccabees*. AB 41 A. New York: Doubleday, 1983.

_____. "The Testament of Moses: Its Content, its Origin, and its Attestation in Josephus," *Studies in the Testament of Moses*, SCS 4. ed. G. W. E. Nickelsburg, Cambridge: SBL, 1973, pp. 44-52.

Hadas, M. *The Third and Fourth Book of Maccabees*. New York: Harper, 1953.

Hanhart, R. *Tobit. Septuaginta. Vetus Testamentum Graecum*. Vol. 5. Göttingen: Vandenhoeck & Ruprecht, 1983.

Hann, R. R. *The Manuscript History of the Psalms of Solomon*. SCS 13. Chico, Scholars, 1982.

Hanson, P. D. "Apocalyptic Literature," *The Hebrew Bible and its Modern Interpreters*, ed. D. A. Knight and G. M. Tucker, Philadelphia: Fortress, 1985, pp. 464-488.

_____. *The Dawn of Apocalyptic: The Historical and Sociological Roots of Jewish Apocalyptic Eschatology*. rev ed. Philadelphia: Fortress, 1979.

_____. *Old Testament Apocalyptic*. Nashville: Abingdon, 1987.

Harrelson, W. *Interpreting the Old Testament*. New York: Holt, Rinehart and Winston, 1964.

Harrington, D. J. *Wisdom Texts from Qumran*. London: Routledge, 1996.

Hartman, L. *Asking for a Meaning: A Study of 1 Enoch 1-5*. CBNTS 12. Lund: CWK Gleerup, 1979.

Hatch, E. and H. A. Redpath. *A Concordance to the Septuagint and other Greek Versions of the Old Testament (Including the Apocryphal Books)*. 2 Vols. Grand Rapids: Baker, reprint 1987.

Hellholm, D., ed. *Apocalypticism in the Mediterranean World and the Near East: Proceedings of the International Colloquim on Apocalypticism, Uppsala, August 12-17, 1979*. Tübingen: Mohr (Siebeck), 1983.

Hengel, M. *The Atonement: The Origin of the Doctrine in the New Testament*. Philadelphia: Fortress, 1981.

_____. *Judaism and Hellenism: Studies in their Encounter in Palestine during the Early Hellenistic Period*. J. Bowden, trans. 2 Vols. in 1. Philadelphia: Fortress, 1974.

Himmelfarb, M. *Ascent to Heaven in Jewish and Christian Apocalypses*. New York, Oxford University, 1993.

Holladay, W. L. *Isaiah: Scroll of Prophetic Heritage*. Grand Rapids: Eerdmans, 1978.

_____. *Jeremiah 1: A Commentary on the Book of the Prophet Jeremiah, Chapters 1-25. Hermeneia*. Philadelphia: Fortress, 1986.

Bibliography

_____. *Jeremiah 2: A Commentary on the Book of the Prophet Jeremiah, Chapters 26-52. Hermeneneia*. Philadelphia: Fortress, 1989.

Holm-Nielsen, S. *Hodayot: Psalms from Qumran*. Aarhus: Universitets forlaget, 1960.

Hopper, S. R. "The Book of Jeremiah: Exposition." *The Interpreter's Bible*. G. A. Buttrick, ed. New York: Abingdon, 1956.

Humphreys, W. L. "A Life-Style for Diaspora: A Study in the Tales of Esther and Daniel." *JBL* 92 (1973) 211-223.

Hyatt, J. P. "The Book of Jeremiah: Exegesis." *The Interpreter's Bible*. ed. G. A. Buttrick. New York: Abingdon, 1956.

Jastrow, M. *A Dictionary of the Targumim, the Talmud Babli and Yerushalmi, and the Midrashic Literature*. 2 Vols. in 1. New York: Judaica Press, 1989.

Jeremias, G. *Der Lehrer der Gerichtigkeit*. SUNT 2. Göttingen: Vandenhoeck & Ruprecht, 1963.

Johnson, L. T. "The New Testament's Anti-Jewish Slander and the Conventions of Ancient Polemic." *JBL* 108 (1989) 419-41.

Jones, B. W. "The Prayer in Daniel ix," *VT* 18 (1968) 488-493.

Jonge, M. de. *Christology in Context: The Earliest Christian Response to Jesus*. Philadephia: Westminster, 1988.

_____. "Jesus' Death for others and the Death of the Maccabean Martyrs," *Text and Testimony: Essays On New Testament and Apocryphal Literature in Honor of A. F. J. Klijn*, ed. T. Baarda, Kampen: J. H. Kok, 1988, pp. 142-151.

_____, ed. *Studies on the Testaments of the Twelve Patriarchs: Text and Interpretation*. SVTP 3. Leiden: Brill, 1975.

_____. *The Testaments of the Twelve Patriarchs: A Study of their Text, Composition and Origin*. 2nd ed. Assen: Van Gorcum, 1975.

_____, in cooperation with H. W. Hollander, H. J. de Jonge, Th. Kortweg. *The Testaments of the Twelve Patriarchs: A Critical Edition of the Greek Text*. PVTG 1.2. Leiden: Brill, 1978.

Kappler, W. and R. Hanhart, eds. *Maccabaeorum liber II. Septuaginta. Vetus Testamentum Graecum*. Vol. 5. Göttingen: Vandenhoeck & Ruprecht, 1976.

Kee, H. C. *Christian Origins in Sociological Perspective*. Philadelphia: Westminster, 1980.

_____. *Miracle in the Early Christian World: A Study in Sociohistorical Method.* New Haven: Yale, 1983.

Klein, R. *Israel in Exile: A Theological Interpretation.* Philadelphia: Fortress, 1979.

Klinzing, G. *Die Umdeutung des Kultus in der Qumrangemeinde und im Neuen Testament.* Göttingen: Vandenhoeck & Rupprecht, 1971.

Kneucker, J. J. *Das Buch Baruch.* Leipzig: Brochhaus, 1879.

Knibb, M. A. "Exile in the Damascus Document." *JSOT* 25 (1983) 99-117.

_____. *The Qumran Community.* Cambridge: Cambridge University, 1987.

Knight, D. A. and G. M. Tucker, eds. *The Hebrew Bible and its Modern Interpreters.* Philadelphia: Fortress, 1985.

Knight, G. A. F. *The New Israel: A Commentary on the Book of Isaiah 56-66.* Grand Rapids: Eerdmans, 1985.

Knohl, I. "Between Voice and Silence: The Relationship between Prayer and Cult." *JBL* 115 (1996) 17-30.

Koch, K. *The Prophets: The Babylonian and Persian Periods.* Vol. 2. Margaret Kohl, trans. Philadelphia: Fortress, 1984.

_____. "חטא." *TDOT*, 1980, 4.309-319.

_____. "Die mysteriösen Zahlen der judäischen Könige und die apokalyptischen Jahrwochen," *VT* 28 (1978) 433-441.

Kolenkow, A. B. "The Literary Genre 'Testament,'" *Early Judaism and its Modern Interpreters,* ed. R. A. Kraft and G. W. E. Nickelsburg, Philadelphia: Fortress, 1986, pp. 259-267.

Kraft, R. A. and G. W. E. Nickelsburg, ed. *Early Judaism and Its Modern Interpreters.* Philadelphia: Fortress, 1986.

Kraus, H. J. *Psalms 1-59: A Commentary.* H. C. Oswald, trans. Minneapolis: Augsburg, 1988.

_____. *Theology of the Psalms.* K. Crim, trans. Minneapolis: Augsburg, 1986.

Kuhl, C. *Die drei Männer im Feuer.* BZAW 55. Giessen: Töpelmann, 1930.

Kuhn, H.-W. *Enderwartung und gegenwärtiges Heil: Untersuchungen zu den Gemeindeliedern von Qumran.* SUNT 4. Göttingen: Vandenhoeck & Ruprecht, 1966.

Kuhn, K. G. *Konkordanz zu den Qumrantexten.* Göttingen: Vandenhoeck & Ruprecht, 1960.

Kuntz, J. K. *The Self-Revelation of God.* Philadelphia: Westminster, 1967.

Lacocque, A. *Daniel et son temps.* Genève: Labor et Fides, 1983.

_____. "The Liturgical Prayer in Daniel 9." *HUCA* 47 (1976) 119-142.

Lambdin, T. O. *Introduction to Classical Ethiopic (Ge'ez).* HSS 24 Cambridge: The President and Fellows of Harvard College, 1978.

Leaney, A. R. C. *The Rule of Qumran and Its Meaning.* Philadelphia: Westminster, 1966.

Lieberman, S. *Hellenism in Jewish Palestine: Studies in the Literary Transmission of Beliefs and Manners of Palestine in the I Century B. C. E. - IV Century C. E.* New York: Jewish Theological Seminary, 1950.

Levenson, J. D. "From Temple to Synagogue: 1 Kings 8," *Traditions in Transformation: Turning Points in Biblical Faith,* ed. B. Halpern and J. D. Levenson, Winona Lake: Eisenbrauns, 1986, pp. 143-166.

Levine, A. J. "Diaspora as Metaphor: Bodies and Boundaries in the Book of Tobit," *Diaspora Jews and Judaism: Essays in Honor of, and in Dialogue with, A. Thomas Kraabel,* ed. J. A. Overman and R. S. MacLennan, Atlanta: Scholars, 1992, pp. 105-117.

Levine, L. I. "The Second Temple Synagogue: the Formative Years," *The Synagogue in Late Antiquity,* ed. L. I. Levine, Philadephia: American Schools of Oriental Research, 1987, pp. 7-31.

Licht, J. "Taxo, or the Apocalyptic Doctrine of Vengeance." *JJS* 12 (1961) 95-103.

Liddell, H. G. and R. Scott. *A Greek-English Lexicon.* Abridged. Oxford: Clarendon, 1984.

Lipinski, E. *La liturgie pénitentielle dans la Bible.* LD 52. Paris: Cerf, 1969.

Liskowsky, G. *Konkordanz zum hebräischen Alten Testament.* 2nd ed. Stuttgart: Deutsche Bibelgesellschaft, 1981.

Lohse, E. *Die Texte aus Qumran.* Munich: Kösel-Verlag, 1971.

Long, B. O. *1 Kings with an Introduction to Historical Literature.* FOTL. Grand Rapids: Eerdmans, 1984.

Lundbom, J. R. *Jeremiah: A Study in Ancient Hebrew Rhetoric.* SBLDS 18. Missoula, MT: Scholars, 1975.

Mack, B. L. *Wisdom and the Hebrew Epic: Ben Sira's Hymn in Praise of the Fathers*. Chicago: University of Chicago, 1985.

Mansoor, M. *The Thanksgiving Hymns: Translated and Annotated with an Introduction*. STDJ 3. Leiden: Brill, 1961.

Martínez, F. G. *The Dead Sea Scrolls: The Qumran Text in English*. Leiden: Brill, 1994.

Mason, R. *Preaching the Tradition: Homily and Hermeneutics after the Exile*. Cambridge: Cambridge University, 1990.

Mayes, A. D. H. *The Old Testament in Sociological Perspective*. London: Marshall Pickering, 1989.

Mays, J. L. *Hosea: A Commentary*. Philadelphia: Westminster, 1969.

McCarthy, D. J. "Covenant and Law in Chronicles-Nehemiah." *CBQ* 44(1982) 25-44.

McKane, W. *A Critical and Exegetical Commentary on Jeremiah*. Vol 1. *ICC*. Edinburgh: T. and T. Clark, 1986.

McKenzie, J. L. *Second Isaiah*. AB 20. Garden City: Doubleday, 1986.

McKenzie, S. L. *The Chronicler's Use of the Deuteronomistic History*. HSM 33. Atlanta: Scholars, 1985.

Mendenhall, G. E. "Law and Covenant in Israel and the Ancient Near East." *BA* 17 (1954) 26-76.

Milgrom, J. *Cult and Conscience: The 'Asham and the Priestly Doctrine of Repentance*. Leiden: Brill, 1976.

_____. *Leviticus 1-16*. AB 3. New York: Doubleday, 1991.

_____. *Studies in Cultic Theology and Terminology*. Leiden: E. J. Brill, 1983.

Milik, J. T. "La patrie de Tobit," *RB* 73 (1966) 523-530.

Miller, P. *They Cried to the Lord: The Form and Theology of Biblical Prayer*. Minneapolis: Fortress, 1994.

_____. "Trouble and Woe: Interpreting Biblical Laments." *Int* (1983) 32-45.

Moore, C. A. *Daniel, Esther and Jeremiah: The Additions*. AB 44. Garden City: Doubleday, 1977.

_____. "Book of Tobit," *ABD*, 1993, 6.585-584.

Bibliography

_____. *Tobit*. AB 40A. New York: Doubleday, 1996.

_____. "Toward the Dating of the Book of Baruch." *CBQ* 26 (1974) 312-320.

Mowinckel, S. *The Psalms in Israel's Worship*. Vols. 1 and 2. D. R. AP-Thomas, trans. New York: Abingdon, 1962.

_____. *Psalmenstudien*. Band 2. P. Schippers: Amsterdam, 1966.

Muraoka, T. "Sir. 51:13-30: An Acrostic Hymn to Wisdom?" *JSJ* 10 (1979) 166-178.

Murphy, R. E. *Wisdom Literature: Job, Proverbs, Ruth, Canticles, Ecclesiastes and Esther*. FOTL 13. Grand Rapids: Eerdmans, 1981.

Murphy-O'Connor, J. "La genèse littéraire de la Règle de la Communauté." *RB* 76 (1969) 528-549.

_____. "A Literary Analysis of Damascus Document xix,33-xx,34." *RB* 79 (1972) 544-564.

_____. "The Essenes and their History." *RB* 83 (1974) 215-244.

_____. "The Judean Desert," *Early Judaism and its Modern Interpreters*, ed. R. A. Kraft and G. W. E. Nickelsburg, Philadelphia: Fortress, 1985, pp. 119-156.

Muilenburg, J. "The Book of Isaiah Chapters 40-66" in *The Interpreter's Bible*. G. A. Buttrick, ed. New York: Abingdon, 1956.

Myers, J. M. *Ezra-Nehemiah*. AB 14. Garden City: Doubleday, 1965.

_____. *1 Chronicles*. AB 12. Garden City: Doubleday, 1965.

_____. *I and II Esdras*. AB 42. New York: Doubleday, 1974.

Nelson, M. D. *The Syriac Version of the Wisdom of Ben Sira Compared to the Greek and Hebrew Materials*. SBLDS 107. Atlanta: Scholars, 1988.

Nickelsburg, G. W. E. "The Apocalyptic Message of *1 Enoch* 92-105." *CBQ* 39 (1977) 309-328.

_____. "The Bible Rewritten and Expanded," *Jewish Writings of the Second Temple Period*, CRINT Section 2, ed. M. E. Stone, Philadelphia: Fortress, 1984, pp. 89-156.

_____. "The Books of Enoch in Recent Research." *RSR* 7 (1981) 210-217.

_____. "Enoch 92-104: A Study of the Greek and Ethiopic Texts," *Armenian and Biblical Studies*, ed. M. E. Stone, Jerusalem: St. James, 1976, pp. 90-156.

_____. "The Epistle of Enoch and the Qumran Literature." *JJS* (1982) 333-348.

_____. "Eschatology (Early Jewish)," *ABD*, 1994, 2.579-594.

_____. "*1 Enoch* and Qumran Origins: The State of the Question and Some Prospects for Answers." *SBLSP* (1986) 341-360.

_____. *Jewish Literature between the Bible and the Mishnah: A Historical and Literary Introduction.* Philadelphia: Fortress, 1981.

_____. "The Qumranic Radicalizing and Anthropologizing of an Eschatological Tradition (1QH 4:29-40)," *Ernten, was man sät: Festschrift für Klaus Koch.* ed. D. R. Daniels, U. Gleßmer, M. Rösel, Neukirchen: Neukirchener Verlag, 1991 pp. 423-435.

_____. *Resurrection, Immortality, and Eternal Life in Intertestamental Judaism.* HTS 26. Cambridge: Harvard, 1972.

_____. "Riches, the Rich, and God's Judgment in *1 Enoch* 92-105 and the Gospel According to Luke." *NTS* 25 (1979) 324-344.

_____. "Social Aspects of Palestinian Apocalypticism," *Apocalypticism in the Mediterranean World and Near East: Proceedings of the International Colloquium on Apocalypticism, Uppsala, August 12-17, 1979*, ed. D. Hellholm, Tübingen: Mohr (Siebeck), 1983, pp. 641-654.

_____. "Stories of Biblical and Early Post-Biblical Times," *Jewish Writings of the Second Temple Period*, CRINT Section 2, ed. M. E. Stone, Philadelphia: Fortress, 1984, pp. 33-87.

_____. "Tobit and Enoch: Distant Cousins With a Recognizable Resemblance." *SBLSP* (1988) 54-68.

Nickelsburg, G. W. E. and M. E. Stone. *Faith and Piety in Early Judaism: Texts and Documents.* Philadelphia: Fortress, 1983.

Nitzan, B. *Qumran Prayer and Religious Poetry.* Studies on the Texts of the Desert of Judah 12. J. Chipman, trans. Leiden: Brill, 1994.

Noth, M. *The Chronicler's History.* JSOT Sup 50. H. G. M. Williamson, trans. Sheffield: JSOT, 1987.

_____. *The Deuteronomistic History.* JSOT Sup 15. J. Doull, trans. Sheffield: University of Sheffeild, 1981.

Oesterley, W. O. E. *The Books of the Apocrypha: Their Origin, Teaching and Contents.* New York: Fleming H. Revell, 1914.

Petersen, D. L. *Late Israelite Prophecy: Studies in Deutero-Prophetic Literature and in Chronicles*. SBLMS 23. Missoula, MT: Scholars, 1977.

Pfeiffer, R. H. *History of New Testament Times With an Introduction to the Apocrypha*. New York: Harper and Brothers, 1949.

Plöger, O. "Reden und Gebete im deuteronomistischen und chronistischen Geschichtswerk," *Aus der Spätzeit des Alten Testament: Festschrift für Günther Dehn*, ed. W. Schneemelcher, Neukirchen: Kreis Moers, 1957, pp. 35-49.

_____. *Theocracy and Eschatology*. S. Rudman, trans. Richmond: John Knox, 1968.

_____. "Siebzig Jahre." *Festschrift für Friedrich Baumgärtel*. ed. L. Rost, Erlangen: Universitätsbund Erlangen, 1959, pp. 124-130.

Polan, G. J. *In the Ways of Justice Toward Salvation: A Rhetorical Analysis of Isaiah 56-59*. New York: Peter Lang, 1986.

Porteous, N. W. *Daniel: A Commentary*. OTL. Philadelphia: Westminster, 1965.

Pouilly, J. *La Règle de la Communauté de Qumrân: Son évolution littéraire*. RB 17. Paris: J. Gabalda, 1976.

Quell, G., G. Bertram, G. Stählin, and W. Grundmann. "ἁμαρτάνω, ἁμάρτημα, and ἁμαρτία" *TDNT*, 1978, 1.267-316.

Rad, G. von. *Deuteronomy: A Commentary*. Dorthea Barton, trans. Philadelphia: Westminster, 1966.

_____. *The Message of the Prophets*. D. G. M. Stalker, trans. New York: Harper and Row, 1967.

_____. *Old Testament Theology*. 2 vols. D. M. G. Stalker, trans. New York: Harper and Row, 1962, 1965.

_____. *The Problem of the Hexateuch and other Essays*. E. W. T. Dicken, trans. New York: McGraw-Hill, 1966.

_____. *Wisdom in Israel*. New York: Abingdon, 1972.

Rahlfs, A., ed. *Septuaginta*. 2 vols. in 1. Stuttgart: Württembergische Bibelanstalt, 1935.

Raitt, T. M. *A Theology of Exile: Judgment/Deliverance in Jeremiah and Ezekiel*. Philadelphia: Fortress, 1977.

Reif, S. C. *Judaism and Hebrew Prayer: New Perspectives on Jewish Liturgical History*. Cambridge: Cambridge University, 1993.

Reventlow, H. G. *Gebet im Alten Testament*. Stuttgart: Kohlhammer, 1986.

Rudolph, W. *Chronikbucher*. Tübingen: J. C. B. Mohr (Paul Siebeck), 1955.

_____. *Esra und Nehemiah*. Tübingen: J. C. B. Mohr (Paul Siebeck), 1949.

Sanders, J. A. *DJDJ IV: The Psalm Scroll of Qumran Cave 11*. Oxford: Clarendon, 1965.

Sanders, J. T. *Ben Sira and Demotic Wisdom*. Chico: Scholars Press, 1983.

Schiffman, L. H. "The Dead Sea Scrolls and the Early History of Jewish Liturgy," *The Synagogue in Late Antiquity*, ed. L. I. Levine, Philadephia: American Schools of Oriental Research, 1987, pp. 33-48.

Schüpphaus, J. *Die Psalmen Salomos: Ein Zeugnis Jerusalemer Theologie und Frömmigkeit in der Mitte des vorchristlichen Jahrhunderts*. Leiden: Brill, 1977.

Schechter, S and C. Taylor. *The Wisdom of Ben Sira: Portions of the Book Ecclesiasticus Hebrew Text, Edited from Manuscripts in the Cairo Genizah Collection*. Amsterdam: APA-Philo Press, 1979.

Skehan, P. W. and A. A. Di Lella. *The Wisdom of Ben Sira*. AB 39. New York: Doubleday, 1987.

Smart, J. D. *History and Theology in Second Isaiah: A Commentary on Isaiah 35, 40-66*. Philadelphia: Westminster, 1965.

Soll, W. "Misfortune and Exile in Tobit: The Juncture of a Fairy Tale Source and Deuteronomic Theology." *CBQ* 51 (1989) 209-31.

Steck, O. H. *Das apokryphe Baruchbuch: Studien zu Rezeption und Konzentration kanonischer Überlieferung*. Göttigen: Vandenhoeck & Ruprecht, 1993.

_____. *Israel und das gewaltsame Geschick der Propheten: Untersuchungen zur Überlieferung des deuteronomistischen Geschichtsbildes im Alten Testament, Spätjudentum und Urchistentum*. WMANT 23. Neukirchen-Vluyn: Neukirchen, 1967.

_____. "Das Problem theologischer Strömungen in nachexilischer Zeit." *EvT* 28 (1968) 445-458.

Stone, M. E. "Apocalyptic Literature," *Jewish Writings of the Second Temple Period*, *CRINT* Section 2, ed. M. E. Stone, Philadelphia: Fortress, 1984, pp. 383-441.

_____, ed. *Jewish Writings of the Second Temple Period: Apocrypha, Pseudepigrapha, Qumran Sectarian Writings, Philo, Josephus*. CRINT Section 2. Philadelphia: Fortress, 1984.

_____, and D. Satran, eds. *Emerging Judiaism: Studies on the Fourth and Third Centuries B. C. E.* Minneapolis: Fortress, 1989.

Stuhlman, L. *The Prose Sermons of the Book of Jeremiah: A Redescription of the Correspondences with the Deuteronomic Literature in Light of Recent Text-critical Research.* SBLMS 83. Atlanta: Scholars, 1986.

Suter, D. W. *Tradition and Composition in the Parables of Enoch.* SBLDS 47. Missoula, MT: Scholars, 1979.

Talmon, S. "The Emergence of Institutionalized Prayer in Israel in the Light of the Qumran Literature," *Qumrân: Sa piété, sa théologie son milieu*, ed. M. Delcor, Paris: Leuven University, 1978, pp. 265-284.

_____. *The World of Qumran.* Paris: Leuven University, 1978.

_____. *The World of Qumran from Within.* Jerusalem: Brill, 1989.

Thackeray, H. St. J. *The Septuagint and Jewish Worship: A Study in Origins.* London: Oxford University, 1923.

Thompson, J.A. *The Book of Jeremiah.* Grand Rapids: Eerdmans, 1980.

Tiller, P. A. *A Commentary on the Animal Apocalypse of 1 Enoch.* Early Judaism and its Literature. Atlanta: Scholars, 1993.

Torrey, C. C. *Ezra Studies.* New York: KTAV, 1970.

Tov, E. *The Book of Baruch.* Missoula, MT: Scholars, 1975.

_____. "The Relations between the Greek Versions of Baruch and Daniel," *Armenian and Biblical Studies*, ed. M. Stone, Jerusalem: Armenian Patriarchate, 1976, pp. 27-34.

_____. *The Septuagint Translation of Jeremiah and Baruch: A Discussion of an Early Revision of the LXX of Jeremiah 29-52 and Baruch 1:1-3:8.* HSM 8. Missoula, MT: Scholars, 1976.

Towner, W. S. *Daniel. Interpretation.* Atlanta: John Knox, 1984.

_____. "Retributional Theology in the Apocalyptic Setting." *USQR* 26 (1971) 203-214.

Trafton, J. L. *The Syriac Version of the Psalms of Solomon: A Critical Evaluation.* SCS 11. Atlanta: Scholars, 1985.

Tromp, J. *The Assumption of Moses: A Critical Edition with Commentary.* Leiden: Brill, 1993.

Unterman, J. *From Repentance to Redemption: Jeremiah's Thought in Transition.* JSOTSup 54. Sheffield: Sheffield, 1987.

VanderKam, J. C. *The Book of Jubilees: A Critical Text.* Scriptores Aethiopici 87. Lovanii: Adeibus E. Peeters, 1989.

_____, trans. *The Book of Jubilees.* Scriptores Aethiopici 88. Lovanii: Adeibus E. Peeters, 1989.

_____. *The Dead Sea Scrolls Today.* Grand Rapids: Eerdmans, 1994.

_____. *Enoch and the Growth of an Apocalyptic Tradition.* CBQMS 16. Washington, D. C.: Catholic Biblical Association, 1984.

_____. "Studies in the Apocalypse of Weeks (*1 Enoch* 93:1-10; 91:11-17)." *CBQ* 46 (1984) 511-523.

_____. *Textual and Historical Studies in the Book of Jubilees.* Missoula, MT: Scholars, 1977.

Volz, P. *Jesaia II. Kommentar zum Alten Testament.* Band IX. Leipzig: A. Deichertsche Verlagsbuchhandlung D. Werner Scholl, 1932.

von der Osten Sacken, P. *Gott und Belial: Traditionsgeschichtiche Untersuchungen zum Dualismus in den Texten aus Qumran.* Göttingen: Vandenhoeck and Ruprecht, 1969.

Wacholder, B. Z. *The Dawn of Qumran: The Sectarian Torah and the Teacher of Righteousness.* Cincinnati: Hebrew Union College Press, 1983.

Watts, J. D. W. *Isaiah 34-66.* WBC 25. Waco: Word, 1987.

Weinfeld, M. *Deuteronomy and the Deuteronomistic School.* Oxford: Oxford University Press, 1972.

_____. *Deuteronomy 1-11.* AB 5. Garden City: New York, 1991.

_____. "Prayer and Liturgical Practice in the Qumran Sect," *The Dead Sea Scrolls: Forty Years of Research,* ed. D. Dimant and U. Rappaport, Leiden: Brill, 1992, pp. 241-258.

Wernberg-Møller, P. *The Manual of Discipline.* Leiden: Brill, 1957.

Westermann, C. *Basic Forms of Prophetic Speech.* H. C. White, trans. Philadelphia: Westminster, 1968.

_____. *Isaiah 40-66: A Commentary.* OTL. D. M. G. Stalker, trans. Philadelphia: Westminster, 1969.

_____. *The Psalms: Structure, Content, and Message.* R. D. Gerhke, trans. Minneapolis: Augsburg, 1980.

_____. "Struktur und Geschichte der Klage im Alten Testament." *ZAW* 66 (1954) 44-80.

White, S. A. "A Comparison of the 'A' and 'B' Manuscripts of the Damascus Document." *RQ* 12 (1987) 237-253.

Whybray, R. N. *Isaiah 40-66. The New Century Bible Commentary.* Grand Rapids: Eerdmans, 1981.

Williamson, H. G. M. *Ezra and Nehemiah.* Sheffield: JSOT, 1987.

_____. *Ezra, Nehemiah.* WBC Vol. 16. Waco: Word, 1985.

Williams, S. K. *Jesus Death as Saving Event: The Background and Origin of a Concept.* HDR Num 2. Missoula, MT: Scholars, 1975.

Wilson, R. R. *Prophecy and Society in Ancient Israel.* Philadelphia: Fortress, 1980.

_____. *Sociological Approaches to the Old Testament.* Philadelphia: Fortress, 1984.

Wolff, H. W. *Hosea. Hermeneia.* G. Stansell, trans. Philadelphia: Fortress, 1974.

_____. "Das Kerygma des deuteronomistischen Geschichtswerks." *ZAW* 73 (1961) 171-186.

_____. *Joel and Amos.* W. Janzen, S. D. MacBride, Jr., and C. A. Muenchow, trans. Philadelphia: Fortress Press.

Yadin, Y. *The Message of the Scrolls.* New York: Simon and Schuster, 1957.

Zeitlin, S. *The Zadokite Fragments. JQRMS* 1. Philadelphia: Dropsie College, 1952.

Zimmerli, W. "Zur Sprache Tritojesajas," *Gottes Offenbarung,* Munich: Chr. Kaiser, 1963, pp. 217-233.

Zimmerman, F. *The Book of Tobit. Jewish Apocryphal Literature.* New York: Harper and Bros., 1958.

INDEX OF ANCIENT SOURCES

Genesis
1 110
4:6 .... 162 n. 443
15:5 171
22:17 171
25:22 .... 111 n. 282
32:12 171
41:49 171

Exodus
4:22 .... 150 n. 420
6:7 .... 102 n 260
7:5 .... 102 n. 260
7:17 .... 102 n. 260
8:10 .... 102 n. 260
8:22 .... 102 n. 260
9:14 .... 102 n. 260
9:29 .... 102 n. 260
10:2 .... 102 n. 260
11:7 .... 102 n. 260
12 110
14:4 .... 102 n. 260
14:8 .... 102 n. 260
15:1-18 .... 40 n. 95
15:11 174
16:6 .... 102 n. 260
16:12 .... 102 n. 260
18:15 .... 111 n. 282
19:5 150
19:4 185
29:46 .... 102 n. 260
32 .... 170, 171
32:13 .... 120 n. 318, 170
32:14 170
33:3 ....97 n. 248
33:5 ....97 n. 248
34:9 ....97 n. 248
34:11-17 46

Leviticus
5 .... 48, 49, 52
5:5 48
5:6 48
5:14 .... 156 n. 436
5:15 55
5:21 .... 55, 156 n. 436
10:18 .... 111 n. 282
13:2 23
13:18 23
13:24 23
13:29 23
13:38 23
13:47 23
16 .... 47, 49, 193
16:21 .... 23, 137, 137 n. 379
18 .... 46, 53
18:10-11 ....
26 .... 47, 49, 50, 77, 121, 156,
    170, 171
26:18 .... 149 n. 416
26:21 .... 156 n. 435
26:23 ... 153 n. 428, 156 n. 435
26:24 ... 149 n. 416, 156 n. 435
26:27 .... 156 n. 435
26:28 .... 149 n. 416
26:29 96
26:39-40 49
26:40 .... 55, 111
26:40-41 . 49, 156, 156 n. 436,
    171
26:41 .... 156 n. 435
26:42 171
26:42-45 98
26:44-45 .... 153, 154

Numbers
5:6 .... 55, 156 n. 436

5:7 .... 49 n. 124
5:12 .... 156 n. 436
5:22 148
5:27 .... 156 n. 436
6:24 138
6:25 .... 80 n. 209
14 149
14:19 149
21:18 133

Deuteronomy
1:26 149
1:43 149
2:27 .... 70 n. 190
4..1, 7, 12, 13, 14, 15, 16, 17, 18, 19, 21, 21 n. 39, 23, 25, 28, 29, 30, 47, 62, 63, 74, 97, 105, 110, 112, 113, 115, 120, 135, 137, 164, 181, 188, 191, 192, 193
4:1-2 170
4:5-6 170
4:7 20
4:9 .... 70 n. 190
4:15 13
4:19 .... 13, 185 n. 530
4:20 .... 20, 21, 185
4:25 .... 13, 185 n. 530
4:27 13, 15, 55, 101, 105, 164, 166, 171 n. 487
4:28 13
4:29..15, 20, 29, 32, 111, 113, 135
4:29-30 .... 14, 29, 112, 158
4:30 ..61, 61 n. 171, 111, 125 n. 338, 155
4:31 17
4:39 .... 19 n. 37, 20
5:16 170
5:26 170
5:29 .... 70 n. 190
5:31 54
5:32 ...... 70 n. 190, 150 n. 418
6:1 54
6:3 170
6:18 170

7 53
7:1-3 46
7:6 .... 150, 185
7:8 .... 149 n. 415, 152
7:9 .... 54, 57, 69
7:11 54
7:12 170
7:13 .... 149 n. 415
7:16 .... 149 n. 415
7:19 39
7:21 .... 54, 69
8:5 .... 151 n. 421
8:19 .... 13 n. 21
9:6 .... 97 n. 248
9:7 .... 92, 92 n. 238
9:8 149
9:13 .... 57, 97 n. 248
9:12 .... 70 n. 190
9:26-27 185
9:29 .... 149, 185
10:16 57
11:16 .... 70 n. 190
11:28 .... 70 n. 190
12 ....26, 27, 27 n. 59, 55, 181
12:5 .... 26, 55 n. 149
12:11 .... 26 n. 57, 55 n. 149
12:14 .... 26 n. 57
12:21 .... 26 n. 57, 55 n. 149
12:25 170
12:26 .... 55 n. 149
12:28 170
14:2 185
15:12 ff. .... 22 n. 44
17:2 ff. .... 22 n. 44
17:8 ff. .... 22 n. 44
17:11 .... 150 n. 418, 70 n. 190
17:20 .... 70, 150 n. 418
18:6-8 .... 22 n. 44
21:15-17 .... 22 n. 44
21:18-22 .... 22 n. 44
22:7 170
22:13-19 .... 22 n. 44
22:22-24 .... 22 n. 44
22:28-29 .... 22 n. 44
23 53
24:1-4 .... 22 n. 44

23:4-9 46
25:1-3 .... 22 n. 44
25:5-10 .... 22 n. 44
26:15 .... 103 n. 261
26:17 54
28 ...... 17, 21, 33, 53, 77, 107
28-29 15
28-30 1, 15 19, 21, 23, 49, 52, 121, 135, 177, 188
28:13 170
28:14 .... 70 n. 190, 150
28:15 120
28:16-68 120
28:20 .... 105 n. 268
28:21 94
28:22 .... 22, 52, 105 n. 268
28:23-24 22
28:25 .... 22, 96 n. 247
28:27-28 149
28:29 ...... 39, 128, 164 n. 453
28:30-33 39
28:31 .... 22, 164 n. 453
28:37 .... 81, 96, 164
28:41 .... 52 n. 454
28:42 22
28:47-52 52
28:48 .... 22, 52, 170 n. 422
28:49-50 106
28:53 .... 22, 96
28:55 22
28:57 22
28:59 .... 151 n. 422
28:60 94
28:62 .... 101, 171
28:65 103
28:68 22
29:17-26 15
29:22 20
29:24 15
29:24-28 25
29:25-26 15
29:28 .... 17, 130 n. 355
29:27 15
30 ... 7, 12, 16, 17, 18, 21, 25, 28, 30, 47, 62, 63, 74, 97, 105, 110, 113, 115, 181, 192, 193
30:1 15 n. 26, 16, 19, 19 n. 36, 76, 97, 98, 154, 156, 193
30:1-2 15
30:1-4 29
30:1-5 98
30:2 .15, 15 n. 26, 20, 55, 111, 120, 155
30:3 . 15, 16, 17, 105, 164, 166
30:3-4 .... 30, 166
30:3-5 17
30:3-10 120
30:4 .... 55, 76
30:5 .... 17, 98
30:10 20
30:15 52
30:18 .... 105 n. 268
30:20 98
31-34 177
31:16 153
31:20 153
31:21 .... 155 n. 433
31:24-26 120
31:29 .... 70 n. 190, 152
32 . 39 n. 89, 42, 57, 123, 153, n. 425, 174 n. 492, 177, 188
32:4 163
32:8-9 185
32:12 153
32:16-17 106
32:17-20 .... 42 n. 100
32:30-31 .... 42 n. 100
32:32 .... 42 n. 100
32:34-42 174
32:36 .... 175, 177
32:40 .... 42 n. 100
32:42 .... 42 n. 100, 164 n. 454
32:43 177
32:51 .... 55 n. 148
32:56-57 .... 42 n. 100
33:26-29 .... 40 n. 95

Joshua
1:8 .... 144, 145

Judges
5:4-5........ 40 n. 95, 45 n. 105

1 Samuel
14:27 51

2 Samuel
7 28

1 Kings
2:4 .... 164 n. 455
3:6 .... 164 n. 455
8. 2, 3, 7, 12, 13 n. 23, 18, 19, 19 n. 35, 21, 21 n. 39, 22, 23, 24, 25, 26, 27, 27 n. 59, 28, 29, 34, 43, 45, 47, 50, 54, 55, 56, 60, 62, 64, 73, 97, 152, 181, 182, 182 n. 520, 188, 191, 192
8:11 182
8:16 152
8:22 27, 50, 122 n. 324, 181 n. 516, 181 n. 517
8:22-53 1
8:22-61 ....
8:23 .... 20, 69
8:26 .... 55 n. 149
8:27 .... 26, 34, 103 n. 261, 182
8:27-30 24
8:28 .... 24, 26 n. 54, 54
8:29 .. 24, 26, 26 n. 54, 79, 182
8:30 .. 25, 26, 26 n. 54, 78, 103 n. 263
8:31 22
8:32 .... 22, 25, 103 n. 263
8:33 ... 22, 26 n. 54, 105 n. 272
8:34 22, 25, 26, 78, 103 n. 263, 125 n. 334
8:35 .. 22, 26 n. 54, 105 n. 272, 151 n. 422
8:36 22, 25, 26, 78, 103 n. 263
8:37 21, 22, 42, 93 n. 241, 151 n. 422, 185 n. 531
8:37-39 22
8:37-40 22
8:38 .... 26 n. 54
8:39 ..... 25, 26, 79, 103 n. 263
8:41 .... 20, 149 n. 416
8:41-43 19
8:41-44 22
8:42 .... 26 n. 54
8:43 25, 26, 103 n. 263, 149 n. 417
8:44 .... 22, 26 n. 54
8:44-45 19
8:45 .. 22, 25, 26, 26 n. 54, 78, 103 n. 263
8:46 .... 22, 28, 151 n. 422
8:47 19, 15 n. 26, 19 n. 36, 23, 26 n. 54, 40, 69, 70, 97, 98, 101, 137, 155, 169
8:48 .... 19, 26 n. 54, 28, 98
8:48-49 30
8:49 .. 22, 25, 26, 26 n. 54, 78, 102 n. 258, 103 n. 263
8:50 102
8:50-51 60
8:51 ... 20, 21, 70 n. 191, 70 n. 192, 185
8:52 .. 20, 26 n. 54, 54, 79, 103 n. 263
8:53 .... 21, 70, 185 n. 192
8:61 ..... 125 n. 333, 128 n. 347
8:62-64 27
9:5 .... n. 324
9:6-9 47
9:7 .... 81, 164
10:1-11 152
11:4 ..... 125 n. 333, 128 n. 347
11:38 170
15:3 ..... 125 n. 333, 128 n. 347
15:14 .... 125 n. 333

2 Kings
17 .... 61 n. 173
17:7-18 47

Index of Ancient Sources 219

17:13 .... 61, 71 n. 193
17:13-14 .... n. 155,
17:23 ......61 n. 173, 71 n. 193
20:3....................128 n. 347
21:15 .... 92 n. 238
22:5........................... 111
22:7........................... 111
22:8........................... 111
23:26-27 47

1 Chronicles
2:7 .... 55 n. 148
5:25.................... 55 n. 148
10:13 .... 55 n. 148
12:39 ....128 n. 347
28:9.....125 n. 334, 128 n. 347
29:9....................128 n. 347
29:19 ....128 n. 347

2 Chronicles
6....................................60
6:13....................................60
6:18....................103 n. 261
6:19....................102 n. 258
6:24....................105 n. 272
6:26....................105 n. 272
6:32....................149 n. 416
6:37.......... 101, 19 n. 36, 137
6:40.............................61
6:41-42............................60
7:13-15............................60
7:14........................ 60, 61
12:2....................... 55 n. 148
12:6-7.............................60
12:7...............................77
12:14 ....112 n. 284
14:3....................112 n. 284
15:17 ....128 n. 347
16:9....................128 n. 347
17:3....................112 n. 284
19:9....................128 n. 347
20:20 61
24:19 .... 11 n. 280
25:2....................128 n. 347

26:16 .... 55 n. 148
26:18 .... 55 n. 148
28:19 .... 55 n. 148
28:22 .... 55 n. 148
29:6..................... 55 n. 148
28:8....................... n. 246
29:8.................... 96 n. 247
30:7..................... 55 n. 148
30:22 .... 48 n. 118
32:26 60
33:10-13 61
33:12 61
33:18-20 61
34:13-18 61
34:21 112
34:25 77
34:27 ....50, 61
36 61
36:11-14 61
36:12 61
36:13 61
36:14 .... 55 n. 148
36:15-16 .... 57 n. 155, 61
36:16 61

Ezra
9. 5, 6, 7, 11, 46, 48, 52, 52 n.
  141, 56, 57, 63, 64, 68, 73,
  74, 113, 122, 142 n. 390,
  192 , 193
9-10................. 5, 30, 159
9:1 .... 46 n. 107
9:2 ....47, 55
9:3 .... 57 n. 153, 164 n. 454
9:3-5....................... 50, 68
9:4 . 36, 47, 53, 55, 164 n. 454
9:5 122 n. 324, 164 n. 454, 181
  n. 516, 181 n. 517
9:5-15 1
9:6 .... 50, 188
9:6-7......................50, 51
9:7 ..47, 51, 52, 75, 91, 231 n.
  231
9:8 .... 51, 52, 89
9:8-9........................51, 58

9:9 .... 51, 52, 185 n. 532
9:10 71
9:10-11 .... 45, 72
9:10-12 45
9:11 .... 57 n. 155
9:13 51
9:15 .. 52, 75, 89 n. 231, 163 n. 446
9:36 .... 89 n. 231
10 17
10:2 .... 47, 55 n. 148
10:3 .... 36, 53
10:6 .... 47, 55
10:9 53
10:10 .... 47, 55 n. 148
10:11 .... 47, 57
10:19 47

Nehemiah
1 .... 11 n. 56
1:2 .... 68, 164 n. 454
1:3 56, 164, n. 457, 164 n. 454
1:4 .... 50, 53, 57 n. 153
1:4-11 .... 1, 53, 53 n. 145
1:5 .... 49, 69 n. 129
1:5-6 53
1:6 .... 54, 78, 163 n. 450
1:7 53
1:7-9 54
1:8 .... 54, 55, 156 n. 436
1:8-9 .... 53, 56
1:9 55
1:10 55, 100, 70 n. 192, 102 n. 258
1:10-11 53
1:11 .... 53 n. 145, 54, 79
8-10 63
8:1-12 56
8:6 148
8:18 56
9 .. 3, 6, 11, 56, 58, 63, 64, 76, 92 n. 239, 136, 149, 153 n. 425
9-10 .... 57, 159
9:2 .... 50, 57, 68, 71

9:3 90
9:4 .... 58, 156 n. 436
9:5 57
9:6-37 1
9:8 .... 77, 163 n. 446
9:9 .... 57, 61 n. 171
9:9-10 100
9:9-11 .... 70 n. 191
9:9-25 .... 70 n. 192
9:10 100
9:16 57
9:17 ..... 153 n. 429, 174 n. 493
9:19 .... 57, 153 n. 429
9:23-25 58
9:25 .... 153 n. 424
9:26 57
9:26-31 57
9:27 57
9:28 57
9:29 57
9:30 57
9:31 .... 57, 153 n. 429
9:32 .... 54, 58, 69, 70, 76, 100
9:33 58, 163 n. 446, 169 n. 479
9:36-37 58
9:37 .... 58, 61 n. 171
10:28-39 57

Job
3 165
7:11 105

Psalms
1:2 144
1:6 .... 105 n. 267
2:12 .... 105 n. 267
4:2 25
5:3 .... 79 n. 207
5:9 .... 39 n. 89
6:10 25
7:14-16 .... 39 n. 89
9:4 .... 105 n. 267
9:7 105
9:14 24

Index of Ancient Sources

9:19 (Q) .... 105 n. 267
10:5-11 .... 39 n. 89
10:17 .... 79 n. 207
13:1-3 .... 165 n. 461
13:4 51
14:4 .... 39 n. 89
17:1 .... 24, 25, 79 n. 20
17:6 .... 79 n. 206
17:8-12 .... 39 n. 89
18:7-8 .... 45 n. 105
24:8 .... 40 n. 95
25:2 173
25:3 173
25:16 24
25:18 24
27:9 173
28:6 .... 168 n. 478
29:10 105
30:9 103
31:3 79
31:7 24
31:18 173
31:22 .... 168 n. 478
32:5 .... 48 n. 117
33:11 91
35:11-12 .... 39 n. 89
35:20-21 .... 39 n. 89
36:1-4 .... 39 n. 89
37:20 .... 105 n. 267
38:10 51
40:12 172
40:15 173
41:6 .... 162 n. 443
42:5 .... 162 n. 443
44 .... 41, 43 n. 102
44:1-3 42
44:1-8 42
44:17-19 .... 43 n. 102
44:23 .... 43 n. 102
44:23-24 .... 43 n. 102
44:26 .... 43 n. 102
45:11 .... 79 n. 206
51 .... 1, 146, 195
51:3 .... 156 n. 434
51:4 .... 156 n. 434
51:15-17 104

51:16-17 175
51:17 174
52:5 .... 128 n. 345
53:1-4 .... 39 n. 89
55:3 .... 79 n. 207
61:2 .... 24, 79 n. 207
61:3 105
66:19 .... 79 n. 207
68 .... 40 n. 95
68:3 .... 105 n. 267
69:7 .... 165 n. 461
69:9 .... 165 n. 461
69:10 .... 165 n. 461
69:17 24
69:19 .... 165 n. 461
69:20 .... 165 n. 461
71:2 .... 79 n. 206
71:16 41
71:20 .... 52 n. 140
72:19 148
74 ..... 41, 43 n. 102, 48 n. 103
74:4-8 43
74:5-6 .... 43 n. 102
74:7 .... 43 n. 102
74:11 .... 43 n. 102
74:22 .... 43 n. 102
78 .... 41, 42, 136
78:1 .... 79 n. 206
78:1-55 42
79 .... 41, 43, 149
79:5 43
79:8-9 43
79:12 .... 165 n. 461
80:20 .... 80 n. 209
80:4 .... 80 n. 209
80:8 .... 80 n. 209
81:13 91
84:53 .... 168 n. 478
85:6 .... 52 n. 140
86:1 .... 79 n. 206
86:6 .... 79 n. 207
86:11 .... 164 n. 456
86:16 24
88:3 .... 24, 79 n. 206
88:50 .... 165 n. 461
89:52 148

99:4 25
102:3 .... 79 n. 206
102:11 105
102:18 24
105 .... 41, 136
105:12-42 42
106 .... 41, 42, 136
106:6 ...... 42, 111 n. 279, 169
106:7-12 42
106:48 .... 168 n. 478
116:2 .... 79 n. 206
119:32 24
119:39 .... 165 n. 461
119:84 25
124:6 .... 168 n. 478
132:8-10 60
135:21 .... 168 n. 478
136 .... 41, 43
136:10-22 42
140:13 25
142:4 105
142:7 .... 24, 79 n. 207
146:7 25

Proverbs
11:11 .... 105 n. 267
15:8 146
28:13 .... 48 n. 117
34:18 35

Isaiah
1:15 38
10:5-6 180
10:10-11 180
10:13-14 180
10:15-16 181
11 33
13 .... 121 n. 316
13:11 180
14 188
14:4-21 180
30 129
30:9 ....
30:10 .... 129 n. 368

30:13 129
37:17 79
38:3 .... 128 n. 347
40:1-2 31
40:3 134
40:15 150
40:17 150
42:9 33
42:16 39
43:7 .... 148 n. 417
43:18-19 33
43:25 .... 156 n. 434
44:3 155
44:18-19 16
44:19 16
46:8 16
48:6 33
49:26 .... 102 n. 259
50:2 38
51:4-5 39
53 .... 73 n. 198
53:5 .... 74 n. 201
53:7 .... 74 n. 201
53:11 .... 73 n. 198
55 32
55:6-7 .... 32, 112
56:2-8 34
56:7 .... 34, 37
57 .... 33, 44
57:15 .... 33, 35, 36, 105
57:18 .... 33, 165 n. 465
57:21 34
58:8 39
58:10 39
59 .... 41, 44
59:1 38
59:1-3 37
59:9 39
59:1-20 .... 37, 41
59:2 38
59:3 38
59:4 40
59:4-8 .... 37, 39
59:9-10 39
59:9-13 41
59:9-15 39

59:10 128
59:10-15 37
59:11 39
59:12 .... 128 n. 345
59:12-13 39
59:13 40
59:15 41
59:15-20 .... 37, 40, 45
59:20 .... 34, 39, 40, 45
60:1 39
60:15-16 .... 153 n. 427
60:19-20 39
61:1 .... 174 n. 495
62:8-9 39
63 .... 70 n. 191
63:1-6 44
63:5 .... 44 n. 261
63:7 .... 41, 43, 137 n. 380
63:7-14 .... 41, 70 n. 192
63:7-64:12 .... 41, 42, 43, 43 n.
   102, 44, 45, 136, 149
63:8-9 41
63:9 .... 38, 42 n. 87
63:10 42
63:10-14 44
63:11 41
63:12 41
63:13-14 41
63:14 100
63:15 .... 42, 44
63:15-64:5 41
63:16 .... 35, 43
63:18 43
63:19 .... 149 n. 417
64:1-3 44
64:2 .... 38 n. 87
64:4-7 41
64:5-7 42
64:6 .... 38 n. 87, 42
64:7 42
64:8 43
64:8-12 41
64:9 42
64:10-11 43
64:12 43
65 .... 32, 33

65:1-2 .... 32, 38, 112
65:8-9 33
65:10 33
65:11 33
65:13-15 33
65:15 33
65:17-25 33
65:21 39
66 .... 182 n. 520
66:1 .... 31, 34, 36, 182
66:234, 35, 36, 53 n. 144, 104,
   174 n. 495
66:3 45
66:5 35
66:6-16 34
66:18-19 153

Jeremiah
1:11-14 77
1:12 77
2:26 .... 50, 76
2:26-29 .... 13 n. 22
2:27 .... 14 n. 25
2:30 .... 57 n. 155
3:17 91
3:25 50
7:16 24
7:20 77
7:24 .... 91 n. 236
7:25 .... 61, 71 n. 193, 92
7:25-26 .... 61, 71
7:34 93
8:1-2 93
9:3-9 .... 39 n. 89
11:4 21
11:8 .... 91 n. 237
11:14 24
12:2 .... 127 n. 342
14 .... 33, 43, 173
14:1 44
14:7 23, 40, 40 n. 90, 40 n. 93,
   137, 169
14:8 .... 61 n. 171
14:9 .... 149 n. 417
14:10 .... 39 n. 89
14:12 .... 24, 93 n. 241

14:16 ....151 n. 422
14:19 ....33, 165 n. 465
14:20 42 n. 101, 44 n. 104, 71,
   111 n. 279, 128 n. 345
14:21 173
16:9................................93
16:12 91
18:12 91
19:9................................96
19:18 .... 96 n. 247
23:40 ....164 n. 451
24:6..................... 98 n. 250
24:7................................98
24:9-10................ 81 n. 451
24:10 .... 93 n. 241
25:4..................... 71 n. 193
25:9..................... 96 n. 247
25:11 .... 66, 68
25:12 .... 66, 68
25:18 .... 96 n. 247
26:4................................71
26:4-5 ....71, 93
26:5................................61
27:9................................93
27:11-12 .... 93, 89 n. 233
29 .... 29, 30, 45, 72, 107
29:10 .... 66, 68
29:10-14 ....29, 74
29:12 ....29, 30
29:12-14 32
29:13 .... 29, 111
29:14 30
29:18 ... 81, 96, 97, 164 n. 451
29:19 .... 98 n. 193
30:3..................... 98 n. 250
30:19 .... 98 n. 250
31:9..................... 150 n. 420
31:33 ....98 n. 251, 150
32:21 100
32:32 76
32:36 .... 93 n. 241
32:38 99
32:38-40 98
32:40 99
33:10-11 93
35:15 61

38:2..................... 93 n. 241
42:3....................101 n. 257
42:18 77
44:4................ 61, 71 n. 193
44:6................................77
51:37 .... 96 n. 247

Lamentations
3:21..............................16
3:40-43 43
5:7................................44
5:19 105
5:20-22 44

Ezekiel
4:6 ....128 n. 346
4:5 127
18:31 ....156 n. 434
29:6.....................102 n. 259
29:9.....................102 n. 259
29:16 ....102 n. 259
29:21 ....102 n. 259
30:8.....................102 n. 259
30:18 .... n. 259
30:19 ....102 n. 259
30:21 .... n. 259
30:25 ....102 n. 259
30:26 ....102 n. 259
32:36 .... n. 241
33:10 ....105 n. 269
38:2........................ n. 241
42:3........................ n. 257
44:4........................ n. 193
51:37 .... n. 247

Daniel
1:3-4.................... 83 n. 217
1:4 .... 73, 73 n. 194
1:17-21 .... 83 n. 217
2:12....................162 n. 443
2:49..................... 83 n. 217
3:8-12 168
3:13-15 168

Index of Ancient Sources

3:16-18 168
3:19-20 168
3:15 .... 183 n. 521
3:23 168
3:24 168
3:30 .... 83 n. 217
5:29-30 .... 83 n. 217
7-12 74
7:25 74
8 .... 74 n. 200
9 ..3, 6, 30, 67, 69, 72, 74, 77,
   78, 80, 81, 82, 85, 87, 92 n.
   204, 93, 95, 96, 107, 113,
   118 n. 304, 122, 123 n. 326,
   127, 134 n. 373, 138, 156 n.
   439, 192
9:1-4 .... 67, 68
9:1-27 65
9:2 .... 74, 80
9:3 85
9:3-19 .... 1, 7
9:4 .... 68, 69
9:4-19 .... 67, 68
9:5 .... 70, 137, 169
9:6 .... 71, 76
9:7 .... 75, 76, 89 n. 231, 91
9:7-8 75
9:8 75
9:10 .... 71, 93
9:11 ..70, 77, 92 n. 240, 153 n.
   427
9:12 .... 77, 80
9:12-13 95
9:12-14 77
9:13 .... 73, 74, 77, 121
9:13-14 91
9:14 .... 77, 169 n. 479
9:15 .... 70, 100, 101
9:16 .71, 80, 81, 89 n. 231, 96,
   101, 149, 153 n. 427, 156 n.
   438
9:16-19 80
9:17 ..... 78, 80, 80 n. 209, 102
9:18 .... 79, 80, 81, 103 n. 263,
   149 n. 417

9:19 ..79, 80 n. 209, 81, 149 n.
   417
9:21 68
9:22 74
9:20-27 67
9:23 .... 73 n. 194, 74
9:25 .... 73 n. 194, 74
10-11 .... 74 n. 200
11 73
11:31 74
11:32 74
11:33 .... 73, 73 n. 194
11:35 .73 n. 194, 73 n. 198, 74
12 73
12:3 ...73, 73 n. 194, 73 n. 198
12:10 .... 73 n. 194

Hosea
5:15 .... 61 n. 171
5:15-6:1 14
6:1 61
6:1-2 ..17 n. 29, 33, 165 n. 465
6:2 52
11:1 .... 150 n. 420
11:1-7 .... 151 n. 421

Joel
1:8 .... 57 n. 153
1:13 .... 57 n. 153
1:14 .... 57 n. 153
2 .... 21 n. 40
2:12-13 50
2:13 .... 50, 63

Amos
4 .... 21 n. 40

Jonah
3:5-8 50

Micah

6:16 .... 96 n. 247
7 171
7:8-20 171
7:9 171
7:14-17 171
7:16 173
7:20 171

Zephaniah
   3:1-3 76

Haggai
   1:9-11 36

Zechariah
   12:6 .... 150 n. 418

Malachi
   1:7 116
   1:10 116

Tobit
   1:3 .... 163, 164 n. 454
   1:9 .... 164 n. 454
   1:10 .... 164 n. 454
   1:3-20 168
   1:15-20 168
   1:19 168
   2:1-10 162
   2:2 .... 164 n. 454
   2:11-14 162
   2:14 165
   3 .... 8, 166, 194
   3:1 .... 162, 164, 165
   3:1-6 .... 1, 162
   3:2 .... 163, 169, 186
   3:2-3 163
   3:3 .... 163, 166
   3:3-4 163
   3:4 .... 156 n. 440, 164, 166
   3:5 163

3:6 .... 165, 164 n. 458, 166
3:7 165
3:8-9 165
3:10 .... 165 n. 462
3:13 .... 165 n. 462
3:14 .... 168 n. 478
3:15 ..... 164 n. 454, 165 n. 462
4:3-4 .... n. 445
7:3 .... 164 n. 454
8:4-9 167
8:5 168
8:15 .... 168 n. 478
8:15-17 167
11:15 166
11:14-15 167
12:8 167
13 .... 166, 187
13:1 167
13:2 166
13:3 166
13:5 166
13:5-6 167
13:6 166
13:9-17 166
14:4 .... 164 n. 454, 166
14:5 .... 125 n. 334, 166
14:11 167
14:15 .... 164 n. 454

Judith
   9:1 .... 184 n. 526
   9:2 .... 168 n. 478
   9:8 .... 184 n. 529
   9:9 .... 181 n. 515
   9:14 .... 181 n. 518

Additions to Esther
   13:9-12 184
   13:14 184
   14:2-3 184
   14:2 68
   14:3 184
   14:5 185
   14:6 185

Index of Ancient Sources

14:7 185
14:8 184
14:9 184
14:11 184

Wisdom of Solomon
5:3 .... 121 n. 316
5:4 .... 165 n. 461

Sirach
16:11 .... 97 n. 248
24:30-34 84
38:24, 34-39:11 82
38:32 82
38:34 82
39 85
39:1 .... 82, 83
39:2 83
39:2-3 83
39:5 84
36:6 .... 84, 85
36:17 .... 150 n. 420
38:32-33 82
39:7 84
51:1-12 85
51:12 85
51:13-30 ..... 83, 83 n. 214, 84
51:19 85
51:22 85

Baruch
1:1-14 .... 88, 89
1:1-3:8 88
1:5 89
1:11-12 102
1:12 .... 89, 106
1:13 .... 89, 91
1:14 90
1:15 .... 89 n. 231, 91
1:15-16 76
1:15-18 91
1:15-2:10 88
1:15-2:35 104

1:15-3:8 .1, 3, 6, 7, 65, 88, 90, 106, 107, 113, 192
1:18 .... 105 n. 271
1:19 .... 92, 95 n. 243
1:19-22 91
1:20 .. 89 n. 231, 91, 94, 105 n. 271, 130 n. 352, 151
1:20-21 151
1:21 93
2:1-2 95
2:1-5 95
2:3-5 96
2:4 .... 97, 105 n. 271
2:5 95
2:6 91
2:6-10 91
2:10 .... 105 n. 271
2:11 .. 70 n. 191, 89 n. 231, 91, 100, 156 n. 439
2:11-16 99
2:11:-18 88
2:12 .... 100, 101, 137
2:12-13 101
2:13 101
2:13-16 101
2:14 102
2:15 102
2:16 .... 89 n. 231, 103
2:16-18 .... 103, 104
2:17 103
2:17-18 103
2:18 .... 103, 174 n. 495
2:19-26 88
2:20 151
2:21-24 .... 89 n. 233
2:22 93
2:23 93
2:24 93
2:24-25 93
2:25 .... 93, 151 n. 422
2:26 ..... 89 n. 231, 91, 94, 107
2:27-35 .... 88, 97
2:30 .... 97, 98
2:31 98
2:32 98
2:33 98

2:34 .... 98, 121
2:35 ....98, 99, 149
3:1 104
3:1-8 . 88, 104, 104 n. 264, 184 n. 528
3:2 104
3:3 105
3:4 .... 94, 105, 352 n. 352
3:5 105
3:6-7 105
3:7 105
3:8 105, 105 n. 271, 156 n. 440
3:12 .... 153 n. 426
3:10 106
3:14 .... 89, 106
4:1 106
4:5-16 106
4:7 106
4:15 .... 106, 170 n. 483
4:21-5:9 97
4:36-5:9 106

Prayer of Azariah
3 168
4-5 .... 169 186
5 .... 169, 174
5-8 175
6 169
8 169
9 170
10 .... 173, 178
11 172
12 .... 170, 172, 188 n. 540
12-13 121
13-14 171
14 .... 101 n. 257
16-17 174
19 172
20 174
21 .... 173, 178
22 174
29 168
31 .... 103 n. 261

1 Maccabees
2:29-38 ....177 n. 504
6:10 ....121 n. 316
7:37 ....37 n. 82

2 Maccabees
3:14-21 179
3:15 ......122 n. 324, 181 n. 516
3:20 ....181 n. 517
6:12-17 176
7 ......8, 123, 174 n. 492, 175, 176, 176 n. 499, 178, 179, 183, 187, 188
7:1-2 176
7:6 176
7:16 .... 176, 183 n. 523
7:18 176
7:19 ....183 n. 523
7:27 ....183 n. 523
7:31 ....183 n. 523
7:32 176
7:33 176
7:34 ....183 n. 523
7:36 ....183 n. 523
7:37 178
7:37-38 177
8:5 177

3 Maccabees
2 .... 180, 184, 187, 189
2:1 .... 122 n. 324, 181
2:1-10 .... 1, 8
2:1-20 179
2:2 .... 180, 184
2:3 180
2:4 180
2:5 180
2:6 180
2:9 .... 180, 182
2:9-10 .... 80 n. 208
2:10 182
2:12 184
2:13 182
2:14 181

Index of Ancient Sources

2:14-18 .... 80 n. 208
2:15 182
2:18 181
2:19 183
2:20 .... 175 n. 496
6 183
6:1-15 180
6:10-11 183
6:11 184

Community Rule (1QS)
1.1 .... 141 n. 388
1.1-2 .... 136, 158
1.6-7 136
1.16-2.18 .... 6, 135, 136
1.18-20 136
1.21-22 136
1.22-24 136
1.24-25 .... 111 n. 279
1.25-26 145
1.24-26 137
1.26 137
2 139
2.1 137
2.1-4 139
2.3 138
3.14 .... 156 n. 437
3.23 .... 156 n. 437
4.12 .... 156 n. 437
5.8-9 150
6.6 111
6.6-8 144
8 .... 134, 138
8.1-10 146
8.11 134
8.11-12 134
8.12 134
8.12-16 134
8.15 134
8.16 134
9 .... 134, 138, 145, 146
9.4-5 146
9.18-20 134
9.19-20 134
9.20 .... 134 n. 373

9.21 .... 134 n. 373
9.25-26 ....
9.26 .... 146 n. 402
10 145
10-11 90 n. 235, 138, 139, 142, 143
10.6 .... n. 402
10.11 139
10.12-13 139
10.14 .... 146 n. 402
11 139
11.3 139
11.5-9 139
11.9-10 139
11.20-22 139

Damascus Document (CD)
1 .... 127, 130, 131, 133
1.1-7.9 .... 145 n. 401
1.4 .... 127, 130
1.7 127
1.8-9 .... 128, 111 n. 278
1.10 .... 112, 125 n. 333, 128
1.11 128
1.11-12 128
1.13 129
1.14 .... 129 n. 133
1.15-16 129
1.16 .... 129, 133
1.17 130
1.17-18 .... 127, 130
1.18 .... 129, 133
1.19 129
1.20-21 130
2 130
2-3 .... 180 n. 513
2.1 129
2.4 130
2.4-5 .... 131 n. 358
2.5 132
2.12 .... 131 n. 360
2.17-3.12 130
3 .... 131, 133
3.1 .... 153 n. 428
3.11 127

3.11-12 130
3.12-13 130
3.13-16 130
3.16 131
3.17-18 131
3.18 131
4.2 132
5.20 133
5.20-6.11 131
5.21 133
5.6-11 .... 116 n. 298
6 133
6:1-2 133
6:4 131
6:5 132
6.6 133
6.7 111
6.9-11 133
7.18 111
8 153
8-9 .... 145 n. 401
8.16 132
11.20-21 146
19-20 .... 145 n. 401
19.29 132
19.33-34 132
19.34 .... 153 n. 426
20.17 132
20.28-31 137
20.29-30 .... 137 n. 379
20.26-32 145
20.26-34 .... 145 n. 401
20.27-30 145

Hodayot (1QH)
4.8 .... 156 n. 437
4.20 140
4.21-22 140
4.25 140
5.2 140
5.2-3 140
5.6 140
5.19-21 140
5.23 140
5.25 140

5.25-26 140
6.9-13 140
6.15-16 140
6.25 140
7.2 140
7.17 140
7.16 140
7.25 140
8.15 .... 156 n. 437
9.21-25 140
9.18 .... 156 n. 437
9.26-27 140
9.31-38 140
9.32 .... 156 n. 437
9:33 .... 156 n. 437
10.7 .... 156 n. 437
11.19-23 140
11.19-28 140
12 142
12.27-29 140
12.29-30 140
12.29-31 142
12.31 140
12.33-34 142
12.36 .... 156 n. 437
12.37 .... 140, 142
13.28 .... 156 n. 437
15.26 140
15.28-32 140
15.32-33 140
16.27 .... 156 n. 437
17.12 .... 156 n. 437
17.6 .... 156 n. 437
17.10 .... 156 n. 437
17.25 .... 156 n. 437
18.19 .... 156 n. 437
19 141
19.3 140
19.4 140
19.7-8 140
19.8 .... 156 n. 437
19.10-12 140
19.11 141
19.12-14 140
19.16-17 140
19.17-18 140

19.20-21	140
19.22	156 n. 437
19.24	140
19.28	140
19.31	140
20.9	156 n. 437
20.24-27	140
20.29	140
20.31	140
21	141
21.5	140
21.6-8	140
21.6-14	141
21.10	140
21.16	140
21.29	141
22.4	140
22.7	140
22.8	140
22.13	140
22.14	140
22.15	140
23.11-13	140

The War Scroll (1QM)
12-13 .... 136 n. 378

4QFlorilegium
1.11 111

Commentary on Nahum (4QpNah)
2 129
7 129

Commentary on Habakkuk (1QpHab)
1.4-2.10 .... 129 n. 350

Words of the Heavenly Lights (4Q504)
1 148
1.8-10 148

2	149, 150
2.7	149, 156 n. 439
2.7-8	149
2.7-10	149
2.7-9	149
2.8	149
2.11	149 n. 427
2.10	149
2.12	149
2.12-13	150
2.13-14	150
2.14	149
2.14-15	149
2.16	149
3	150, 153
3.8-9	151
3.9-10	150
3.9-11	151 n. 427
3.10-11	153 n. 427
3.10-13	130 n. 352, 151
3.15	152
3.20	152
4	152, 153
4.2-6	152
4.4-5	152
4.7	152
5	153
5.15-21	155
5.9-13	148
5.6-11	153, 154
5.11-13	154
5.17	153
5.16	155
5.17	155 n. 433
6	156
6.2	156 n. 434
6.2-3	156
6.3-4	156
6.5-6	156
6.12-14	157
7	157
7.2	148, 157

1 Enoch
1-5 118

5................................. 118	1:10............................ 110
5:4................................ 119	1:11-12........................ 110
5:6 .... 119, 119 n. 308, 138	1:12............................ 112
5:7................................ 119	1:13............................ 110
5:7-9....................... 119, 138	1:14............................ 112
5:8................................ 119	1:15............................ 110
5:9................................ 119	1:15-16........................ 111
10:3....................... 118 n. 305	1:16............................ 111
13:4-7 .... 142 n. 390	1:16-18........................ 110
48:8-10................. 142 n. 390	1:19-20........................ 111
62:1-12................. 142 n. 390	1:22 .... 111, 125 n. 336, 128
63:1.............................. 111	1:22-25........................ 110
63:5................... 121 n. 316	1:23-25........................ 111
85-90 115	23 . 4, 8, 105 n. 270, 109, 113, 115, 192
89:32-33 116	
89:73 116	23:16-21 113
90:6.............................. 116	23:19 .... 113, 114
90:20-27 117	23:21 .... 113, 114, 116, 129
90:28-29 117	23:21-23 .... 113 n. 287
90:30............................ 117	23:22 114
92-105.................. 177 n. 300	23:22-25 113
93:1-10, 91:11-17 117	23:24 114
91:10 119	23:26 .... 111, 113, 114, 116
91:11 117	23:27-31 113
91:18 129	23:30 .... 113, 165 n. 465
93:2.............................. 118	
93:5.............................. 118	Psalms of Solomon
93:10............................ 118	1............................... 186
98:14............................ 118	1:2 .... 186 n.537
98:15............................ 118	1:3 .... 186 n.537
99:2.............................. 118	1:7-8........................... 186
99:10............................ 129	2........................ 186, 187
99:11-16 118	2:7 186
104:9............................ 118	2:10.................... 186 n. 537
104:10.......................... 118	2:12-13......................... 186
105:1 119	2:15.................... 186 n. 537
	2:15............................ 186
4 Ezra	2:18.................... 186 n. 537
8:31-36...................... 122	2:22............................ 187
	2:23............................ 187
	2:24-25........................ 187
Jubilees	2:32................... 186 n.537
14, 8, 109, 110, 112, 113, 115, 130, 192	2:34.................... 186 n. 537
	3:3 .... 186 n. 537, 187
1:7-9........................... 110	3:4 .... 186 n. 537, 187

3:5 ....186 n. 537
3:6 187
3:7 .... 186 n. 537, 187
3:9 187
3:9-11 187
3:11 ....186 n. 537
4:8 ....186 n. 537
4:24 ....186 n. 537
5:1 ....186 n. 537
5:17 ....186 n. 537
8 .... 186, 187
8:6 ....186 n. 537
8:7 ....186 n. 537
8:8 ....186 n. 537
8:8-12 186
8:23 ....187 n. 537
8:24 ....186 n. 537
8:25 ....186 n. 537
8:25-26 187
8:26 ....186 n. 537
8:27 187
9 .... 187, 188
9:2 ....186 n. 537
9:3 ....186 n. 537
9:6 188
9:7 ....186 n. 537
9:8-10 188
10:3 ....186 n. 537
10:5 ....186 n. 537
13 187
13:6 ....186 n. 537
13:7 ....186 n. 537
13:9 ....186 n. 537
13:11 ....186 n. 537
14:2 ....186 n. 537
14:9 ....186 n. 537
15:3 ....186 n. 537
15:6 ....186 n. 537
15:7 ....186 n. 537
16:15 ....186 n. 537
17:19 ....186 n. 537
17:23 ....186 n. 537
17:26 ....186 n. 537
17:29 ....186 n. 537
17:32 ....186 n. 537
17:37 ....186 n. 537

17:40 ....186 n. 537
18:7 ....186 n. 537
18:8 ....186 n. 537

Testament of Asher
7:2 125
7:7 ....121 n. 318
7:5-7 125

Testament of Benjamin
9:1 125

Testament of Dan
5:4-9 125
5:9 125

Testament of Gad
8:2 125

Testament of Issachar
6 125
6:3 125

Testament of Judah
18:1 124
23 125
23:5 .... 125, 128 n. 348

Testament of Levi
15:5 ....121 n. 318
10 124
14 124
16 124

Testament of Moses
2 120
2:7-9 ....121 n. 317
3-4 120

3:1-4 120
3:5 121
3:5-4:4 120
3:10 .... 122, 128 n. 345
3:10-14 121
4:1 122
4:2 120
4:5-8 .... 109, 120
5 ..... 109, 120, 122, 177 n. 503
7 .... 109, 122
8 .... 120, 17
9 .... 120, 175, 176, 178
9:2 122
10 .... 120, 122, 123
9:7 178

Testament of Naphtali
    4:1-3 125
    4:3 125
    4:4-5 125

Testament of Zebulun
    9:5-7 125
    9:7 125

INDEX OF AUTHORS

Achtemeier, E., 31 n. 71, 37 n. 83, 37 n. 85, 41 n. 96
Ackroyd, P. R., 17 n. 31, 25 n. 51, 27 n. 60, 27 n. 61, 27 n. 62, 28 n. 64, 28 n. 66, 59 n. 160
Allegro, J. M., 146 n. 404
Alt, A., 5, 5 n. 12
Argall, R. A., 82 n. 210, 119 n. 309
Aschermann, H., 124 n. 399
Baillet, M., 147, 147 n. 408, 147 n. 409, 147 n. 410, 156 n. 434, 157 n. 441
Balentine, S. E., 38 n. 88, 56 n. 150, 65 n. 176
Baltzer, K., 2 n. 5, 5, 5 n. 14, 6 n. 19, 115 n. 289, 125 n. 330, 125 n. 335, 135 n. 375
Baumgarten, J. M., 132 n. 364
Becker, J., 139 n. 385
Bickerman, E., 26 n. 53, 27 n. 58, 83 n. 216, 166 n. 469, 167 n. 470, 183 n. 524
Blenkinsopp, J., 36 n. 79, 37 n. 83, 37 n. 85, 46 n. 108, 51 n. 137, 51 n. 138, 53 n. 144, 58 n. 158
Bracke, J. M., 17 n. 30
Braulik, G., 19 n. 36, 21, 21 n. 39, 26 n. 56, 27 n. 59, 28 n. 63
Brock, S. P., 187 n. 539
Bruce, F. F., 127 n. 341
Burke, D. G., 87 n. 224
Burrows, M., 134 n. 369
Caroll, R. P., 51 n. 135
Charles, R. H., 111 n. 277, 111 n. 278, 111 n. 280, 115 n. 290, 117 n. 300, 121 n. 308, 121 n. 314, 122 n. 321, 124 n. 330, 124 n. 329

Charlesworth, J. H., 1 n. 4, 186 n. 536
Chazon, E. G., 1 n. 3, 144 n. 396, 147 n. 409, 148 n. 413
Clifford, R. J., 42 n. 100
Collins, J. J., 66 n. 178, 73 n. 195, 73 n. 198, 74 n. 200, 82 n. 211, 114 n. 288, 117 n. 299, 118 n. 304, 118 n. 306, 132 n. 364, 133 n. 367, 147 n. 411, 167 n. 474, 174 n. 494, 175 n. 497, 179 n. 510
Corvin, J., 3, 3 n. 6
Crenshaw, J. L., 82 n. 210
Cross, F. M., 27 n. 62, 40 n. 95
Deselaers, P., 163 n. 448, 165 n. 463
Deutsch, C., 85 n. 220
De Vries, S. J., 22 n. 41, 59 n. 159, 59 n. 160, 60 n. 166, 60 n. 165, 60 n. 169, 62 n. 174
Di Lella, A. A., 83 n. 213, 83 n. 214, 83 n. 215, 163 n. 448, 164 n. 452, 167, 167 n. 472, 167 n. 473
Dimant, D., 128 n. 344, 129 n. 353, 143 n. 392
Doan, R., 168 n. 474
Dupont-Sommer, A., 131 n. 359, 131 n. 360, 132 n. 365, 133 n. 366, 134 n. 372, 144 n. 397
Eissfeldt, O., 67 n. 183
Eskenazi, T., 46 n. 106, 53 n. 145, 57 n. 152, 59, 59 n. 160, 58 n. 161, 60 n. 170
Fishbane, M., 46 n. 108, 131 n. 356
Fitzmyer, J., 162 n. 442
Flusser, D., 167 n. 470, 186 n. 533

Gebhart, O. von, 186 n. 537
Ginzberg, H. L., 73 n. 198, 127 n. 342, 131 n. 360
Goldstein, H., 35 n. 78
Goldstein, J., 36 n. 81, 65 n. 175, 67 n. 183, 67 n. 184, 67 n. 187, 68 n. 188, 87 n. 224, 87 n. 225, 88 n. 226, 88 n. 228, 88 n. 229, 94 n. 242, 95 n. 243, 122 n. 323, 151 n. 423, 176 n. 499, 177, 177 n. 504, 177 n. 506, 179 n. 508, 183 n. 522
Greenberg, M., 22, 22 n. 47
Gunkel, H., 4, 6, 6 n. 18
Hadas, M., 179 n. 510
Hann, R. R., 186 n. 533
Hanson, P. D., 31 n. 71, 34 n. 76, 36 n. 80, 37 n. 83, 37 n. 84, 37 n. 86, 40 n. 95, 41 n. 96, 41 n. 99
Harrington, D., 84 n. 219, 85 n. 220
Hartman, L., 118 n. 307, 188 n. 308, 119 n. 308
Hengel, M., 83 n. 213, 115 n. 291
Heinemann, J., 1 n. 4
Holladay, W. L., 17 n. 31, 29 n. 67, 29 n. 69, 40 n. 90, 50 n. 134
Hollander, H. W., 124 n. 328, 124 n. 330, 125 n. 332, 125 n. 337, 125 n. 338
Holm-Nielsen, S., 143 n. 393
Humphreys, W. L., 183 n. 525
Johnson, L. T., 39 n. 89
Jonge, M. de, 124, 124 n. 328, 124 n. 331, 125 n. 332, 126 n. 333, 126 n. 338, 127 n. 339, 176 n. 499
Kee, H. C., 124 n. 329
Kiley. M., 1 n. 3
Kister, M. 113 n. 287
Kneucker, J. J., 88, 88 n. 240, 98 n. 249, 101 n. 252, 105 n. 265
Knibb, M., 113 n. 285, 117 n. 300, 130 n. 354, 132, 132 n. 364, 134 n. 370, 134 n. 371, 138 n. 382, 144 n. 398, 145 n. 399, 146 n. 405, 146 n. 406
Knohl, I., 26 n. 53
Koch, K., 31 n. 71, 31 n. 72, 175 n. 497
Kraft, R. A., 143 n. 391, 145 n. 401
Kuhl, C., 168 n. 474, 169 n. 480, 169 n. 481, 169 n. 482, 174 n. 495, 175 n. 497
Kuhn, H.-W., 143 n. 393
Kuntz, J. K., 45 n. 105
Lacocque, A., 67 n. 183, 77 n. 203, 85 n. 222
Leaney, A. R. C., 134 n. 370, 136 n. 378, 146 n. 405
Lehmann, M. R., 147 n. 409
Levenson, J. D., 19 n. 35, 19 n. 37, 21 n. 38, 26 n. 54, 27 n. 58
Levine, A-J., 162 n. 445, 167 n. 472
Licht, J., 123 n. 326, 177 n. 500, 178 n. 509
Lipinski, E., 5 , 6, 50 n. 132
Lohse, E., 132 n. 365
Long, B. O., 19 n. 34, 22 n. 41, 22 n. 42, 43, 23 n. 45
Mack, B. L., 82 n. 210, 83 n. 213, 83 n. 218
Mason, R., 60 n. 167
McKenzie, J. L., 35 n. 78, 37 n. 83
McKenzie, S. L., 60 n. 168
Mendenhall, G. E., 5, 5 n. 13
Milgrom, J., 27 n. 58, 48, 49
Milik, J. T., 162 n. 442, 166 n. 469
Miller, P., 16 n. 28, 23 n. 47, 24 n. 49, 25 n. 50, 39 n. 89, 47 n. 112, 52 n. 142
Montgomery, 70 n. 190, 77 n. 204
Moore, C. A., 66 n. 180, 87 n. 223, 87 n. 224, 90 n. 235, 92 n. 240, 96 n. 244, 101 n. 254, 104 n. 264, 162 n. 442, 165 n. 464, 166 n. 466, 166 n. 467,

Index of Authors

167 n. 470, 167 n. 471, 167 n. 473, 168 n. 474, 169 n. 480, 169 n. 481, 169 n. 484, 175, 175 n. 497, 176 n. 498, 180 n. 514, 183 n. 524
Mowinckel, S., 4, 5, 5 n. 10
Muraoka, T., 85 n. 220
Murphy, R. E., 82 n. 210
Murphy-O'Connor, J., 131 n. 357, 132, 132 n. 361, 132 n. 363, 135 n. 374, 137 n. 379, 143 n. 391, 143 n. 393, 145 n. 401
Muilenberg, J., 37 n. 83, 37 n. 86, 40 n. 91, 40 n. 92, 40 n. 94, 41 n. 98
Myers, J. M., 57 n. 154
Nelson, M. D., 83 n. 214
Nickelsburg, G. W. E., 2 n. 5, 33 n. 74, 37 n. 82, 50 n. 133, 73 n. 141, 74 n. 198, 74 n. 199, 75 n. 202, 83 n. 212, 83 n. 213, 87 n. 224, 91 n. 237, 106 n. 273, 110 n. 276, 113 n. 286, 115 n. 292, 116 n. 295, 116 n. 298, 117, 117 n. 299, 117 n. 300, 117 n. 301, 117 n. 302, 118 n. 303, 120 n. 310, 120 n. 311, 120 n. 312, 121 n. 313, 121 n. 349, 134 n. 370, 138 n. 382, 141 n. 387, 142 n. 390, 143 n. 391, 145 n. 391, 146 n. 405, 147 n. 411, 147 n. 412, 147 n. 442, 162 n. 444, 163, 163 n. 449, 165 n. 462, 166, 166 n. 466, 167 n. 470, 167 n. 471, 168, 168 n. 476, 173 n. 491, 177, 177 n. 501, 177 n. 502, 177 n. 505, 178 n. 509, 179 n. 510, 183 n. 524, 183 n. 525, 186 n. 533
Nitzan, B., 3 n. 7, 4 n. 8, 90 n. 235, 136, 136 n. 376, 137 n. 381, 138 n. 382, 138 n. 383, 141 n. 386, 143 n. 394, 144 n. 396, 146 n. 403, 147, 147 n. 409, 147 n. 412, 149 n. 414, 150 n. 419

Noth, M., 5, 13 n. 23, 17 n. 31, 27 n. 60, 28 n. 63
O'Dell, J., 186 n. 536
Oesterley, W. O. E., 67 n. 186
Petersen, D. L., 31 n. 71, 31 n. 72
Pfeiffer, R. H., 67 n. 183, 87 n. 223, 87 n. 224, 88 n. 228
Polan, G. J., 37 n. 82, 37 n. 83, 37 n. 86
Priest, J., 9, 120 n. 310, 121 n. 315, 121 n. 316, 121 n. 317, 122 n. 321, 178 n. 507, 178 n. 509
Rad, G. von, 5, 5 n. 11, 17 n. 31, 22 n. 44, 25 n. 51, 29 n. 68, 52, 82 n. 210
Reventlow, H. G., 2 n. 5, 3, 3 n. 6, 13 n. 23, 18 n. 33, 28 n. 63
Sanders, E. P., 139 n. 384, 142 n. 389, 186 n. 536, 186 n. 538
Sanders, J. A., 83 n. 214, 85 n. 220
Sanders, J. T., 83 n. 213
Schechter, S., 83 n. 214
Schiffman, L. H., 147 n. 409
Schüpphaus, J., 186 n. 535
Scott, J. M., 2 n. 5
Skehan, P. W., 83 n. 213, 83 n. 215, 83 n. 217, 85 n. 221
Soll, W., 167 n. 473.
Steck, O. H., 2 n. 5, 5, 47 n. 100, 52 n. 143, 61 n. 173, 67 n. 186, 87 n. 224, 89 n. 230, 111 n. 280, 111 n. 281, 115 n. 289, 124 n. 331, 124 n. 329
Suter, D. S., 116 n. 298
Sweet, J. P. M., 121 n. 314
Talmon, S., 4 n. 8, 122 n. 341, 128 n. 343, 128 n. 346, 132 n. 364, 137 n. 379, 141 n. 388
Terrien, S., 38 n. 88
Thompson, J. A., 40 n. 93
Tiller, P. A., 114 n. 288, 115 n. 292, 116 n. 293, 116 n. 294, 116 n. 296
Tov, E., 66 n. 179, 90 n. 234, 92 n. 240, 101 n. 253, 101 n. 255

Towner, W. S., 65 n. 176
Trafton, J. L., 186 n. 533
Tromp, J., 120 n. 310, 120 n. 311, 121 n. 314, 121 n. 318, 122 n. 322, 122 n. 325, 123 n. 327
Unterman, J., 14 n. 24, 21 n. 40, 28 n. 63, 29 n. 67
VanderKam, J. C., 84 n. 219, 110 n. 275, 117 n. 300, 118 n. 303
Vermes, G., 132 n. 365, 146 n. 402
Wacholder, B. Z., 127 n. 341
Wambacq, B. B., 67 n. 183, 67 n. 186
Weinfeld, M., 13 n. 23, 14 n. 24, 15 n. 27, 17 n. 29, 17 n. 31, 18 n. 32, 26 n. 56, 27 n. 58, 28 n. 65, 29 n. 68, 49 n. 128, 52 n. 140, 61 n. 171, 155 n. 432
Wernberg-Møller, P., 138 n. 382
Westerman, C., 25 n. 50, 31 n. 71, 33 n. 75, 37 n. 83, 37 n. 84, 37 n. 85, 41 n. 97
White, S. A., 127 n. 341
Wilson, R. R., 5 n. 9
Williams, S. K., 176 n. 499
Williamson, H. G. M., 47 n. 111, 51 n. 136, 51 n. 138, 51 n. 139, 56 n. 151, 58 n. 156, 56 n. 157, 59 n. 164, 59 n. 165
Wintermute, O. S., 111 n. 277
Wolff, H. W., 13 n. 23
Wright, R. B., 186 n. 533, 186 n. 534, 186 n. 536, 187 n. 539,
Zeitlin, S., 127 n. 341
Zimmerli, W., 31 n. 72
Zimmerman, F., 163 n. 447
Zoebel, H. -J., 54 n. 146

www.ingramcontent.com/pod-product-compliance
Lightning Source LLC
Chambersburg PA
CBHW021807220426
43662CB00006B/218